CHATGPT
API BIBLE

CUANTUM

MASTERING PYTHON PROGRAMMING
FOR CONVERSATIONAL AI

ChatGPT API Bible: Mastering Python Programming for Conversational AI

First Edition

Copyright © 2023 Cuantum Technologies

First edition: May 2023

Published by Cuantum Technologies LLC.

Dallas, TX.

ISBN 9798393907020

"Artificial Intelligence, deep learning, machine learning — whatever you're doing if you don't understand it — learn it. Because otherwise, you're going to be a dinosaur within 3 years."

- Mark Cuban, entrepreneur, and investor

CUANTUM
TECHNOLOGIES

Who we are

Welcome to this book created by Cuantum Technologies. We are a team of passionate developers who are committed to creating software that delivers creative experiences and solves real-world problems. Our focus is on building high-quality web applications that provide a seamless user experience and meet the needs of our clients.

At our company, we believe that programming is not just about writing code. It's about solving problems and creating solutions that make a difference in people's lives. We are constantly exploring new technologies and techniques to stay at the forefront of the industry, and we are excited to share our knowledge and experience with you through this book.

Our approach to software development is centered around collaboration and creativity. We work closely with our clients to understand their needs and create solutions that are tailored to their specific requirements. We believe that software should be intuitive, easy to use, and visually appealing, and we strive to create applications that meet these criteria.

This book aims to provide a practical and hands-on approach to starting with **Mastering ChatGPT for Developers and Enthusiasts**. Whether you are a beginner without programming experience or an experienced programmer looking to expand your skills, this book is designed to help you develop your skills and build a **solid foundation in ChatGPT API**.

Our Philosophy:

At the heart of Cuantum, we believe that the best way to create software is through collaboration and creativity. We value the input of our clients, and we work closely with them to create solutions that meet their needs. We also believe that software should be intuitive, easy to use, and visually appealing, and we strive to create applications that meet these criteria.

We also believe that programming is a skill that can be learned and developed over time. We encourage our developers to explore new technologies and techniques, and we provide them with the tools and resources they need to stay at the forefront of the industry. We also believe that programming should be fun and rewarding, and we strive to create a work environment that fosters creativity and innovation.

Our Expertise:

At our software company, we specialize in building web applications that deliver creative experiences and solve real-world problems. Our developers have expertise in a wide range of programming languages and frameworks, including Python, AI, ChatGPT, Django, React, Three.js, and Vue.js, among others. We are constantly exploring new technologies and techniques to stay at the forefront of the industry, and we pride ourselves on our ability to create solutions that meet our clients' needs.

We also have extensive experience in data analysis and visualization, machine learning, and artificial intelligence. We believe that these technologies have the potential to transform the way we live and work, and we are excited to be at the forefront of this revolution.

In conclusion, our company is dedicated to creating web software that fosters creative experiences and solves real-world problems. We prioritize collaboration and creativity, and we strive to develop solutions that are intuitive, user-friendly, and visually appealing. We are passionate about programming and eager to share our knowledge and experience with you through this book. Whether you are a novice or an experienced programmer, we hope that you find this book to be a valuable resource in your journey towards becoming proficient in **ChatGPT and its API**.

Code Blocks Resource

To further facilitate your learning experience, we have made all the code blocks used in this book easily accessible online. By following the link provided below, you will be able to access a comprehensive database of all the code snippets used in this book. This will allow you to not only copy and paste the code, but also review and analyze it at your leisure. We hope that this additional resource will enhance your understanding of the book's concepts and provide you with a seamless learning experience.

https://books.cuantum.tech/chatgpt-api/code/

Premium Customer Support

At Cuantum Technologies, we are committed to providing the best quality service to our customers and readers. If you need to send us a message or require support related to this book, please send an email to **books@cuantum.tech**. One of our customer success team members will respond to you within one business day.

TABLE OF CONTENTS

Introduction

Welcome to "**ChatGPT API Bible: Mastering Python Programming for Conversational AI**"! In this comprehensive guide, we will dive deep into the world of conversational AI, focusing on the powerful ChatGPT API by OpenAI. As the demand for intelligent conversational agents and virtual assistants grows, the ChatGPT API has become a go-to solution for developers looking to build state-of-the-art conversational applications.

This book, brought to you by **Cuantum Technologies**, is specifically designed to equip you with the knowledge and skills required to harness the full potential of the ChatGPT API using Python programming. Whether you are a beginner or an experienced developer, this book will serve as your ultimate guide to mastering conversational AI and implementing it in various industries and use cases.

To ensure a thorough understanding of the subject matter, we have structured the book into several chapters, each tackling a specific aspect of the ChatGPT API and its applications.

Chapter 1 provides an introduction to ChatGPT and the broader field of conversational AI. We will discuss the history, evolution, and key concepts of conversational AI, along with an overview of the OpenAI platform and the ChatGPT model.

In Chapter 2, we will dive into the ChatGPT API, exploring its capabilities, features, and pricing. We will also discuss the API documentation, API key management, and the necessary Python libraries and tools required for a smooth development experience.

Chapter 3 focuses on getting started with the ChatGPT API in Python. We will cover the basics of setting up the development environment, authenticating with the API, and making API requests. This chapter will lay the foundation for more advanced topics and practical examples in the subsequent chapters.

Chapter 4 dives into advanced API usage, covering topics such as conversation management, fine-grained control, and managing tokens. We will also discuss best practices and strategies for optimizing API usage and ensuring efficient system performance.

Chapter 5 delves into model fine-tuning and adaptation. You will learn how to customize and train the ChatGPT model to better suit your specific use cases and domains. We will cover

techniques like data preprocessing, model training, and evaluation, as well as discuss tips and tricks for effective model fine-tuning.

In Chapter 6, we will explore the adaptation of ChatGPT for specific industries. We will discuss various applications across healthcare, legal, customer support, content generation, finance, e-commerce, education, and gaming, along with practical examples and code snippets for each industry.

Chapter 7 discusses the critical aspects of ensuring responsible AI usage. We will cover topics such as mitigating biases in AI, privacy and security considerations, ethical guidelines and best practices, user consent and transparency, AI governance and accountability, and fairness, accessibility, and inclusivity.

Chapter 8 focuses on scaling and deploying ChatGPT solutions. We will cover integration with web applications, building chatbots and virtual assistants, infrastructure and cost optimization, performance monitoring and analytics, and ensuring reliability and high availability.

In Chapter 9, we will discuss staying up-to-date with ChatGPT developments, touching upon the OpenAI community and resources, AI research and improvements, and industry trends and future directions.

Finally, Chapter 10 serves as the conclusion of this book, summarizing the key takeaways and providing guidance on expanding your ChatGPT knowledge and pursuing further opportunities in AI.

Throughout this book, you will find practical examples, code snippets, and tips that will aid you in your journey to master the ChatGPT API and Python programming for conversational AI. Our goal is to provide you with a comprehensive, accessible, and engaging resource that will empower you to create innovative and impactful AI-driven solutions.

Once you have completed this book, we encourage you to explore our other offerings at Cuantum Technologies. Our diverse range of books, available at **https://books.cuantum.tech**, covers a wide array of topics in technology, programming, and AI. By continuing to expand your knowledge and skills, you will be better equipped to stay ahead in the rapidly evolving world of AI and technology.

We hope that "**ChatGPT API Bible: Mastering Python Programming for Conversational AI**" serves as an invaluable resource in your journey towards becoming an expert in the ChatGPT API and conversational AI. As you progress through the book, remember that the possibilities for applying conversational AI are virtually limitless, and with the right knowledge and skills, you have the power to create truly innovative solutions that can transform industries and improve lives.

Thank you for choosing this book, and we look forward to supporting you in your learning journey. See you soon at **https://books.cuantum.tech** for more exciting and informative resources!

Chapter 1 - Introduction to ChatGPT

1.1. Overview of ChatGPT

Welcome to "**ChatGPT API Bible: Mastering Python Programming for Conversational AI,**" brought to you by Cuantum Technologies. As a leading software company, we are committed to providing our readers with cutting-edge information and practical guidance to help you understand, implement, and optimize the powerful capabilities of ChatGPT.

In this first chapter, we will introduce you to ChatGPT, a state-of-the-art language model built on the Generative Pre-trained Transformer (GPT) architecture. ChatGPT is a revolutionary language model that is changing the way we interact with chatbots. The GPT family of models has a rich history of development, and we will explore this history in detail. We will also dive deep into the foundations of ChatGPT, examining the technical details that make this model so powerful.

But before we delve too deeply into the technical aspects of ChatGPT, we must first consider the broader context of chatbot technologies. Chatbots have a long and storied history, and they have been deployed in a wide range of applications, from customer service to entertainment. By understanding the evolution of chatbot technologies, we can better appreciate the significance of ChatGPT and the ways in which it represents a major milestone in the field.

So join us as we embark on this exciting journey into the world of ChatGPT. Whether you are a seasoned developer or simply an enthusiastic learner, we are confident that you will find this guide to be a valuable resource in your quest to master this powerful technology.

1.1.1. Evolution of Chatbot Technologies

The journey of chatbot technologies began in the 1960s, marking a significant milestone in the field of artificial intelligence. This breakthrough was made possible by the development of the first chatbot, ELIZA, created by Joseph Weizenbaum at MIT. ELIZA was a simple rule-based

system that mimicked human conversation by using pattern-matching techniques. Despite its limitations, ELIZA demonstrated the potential for computers to engage in conversation with humans, paving the way for further advancements in the field.

Over the years, chatbots evolved, incorporating more advanced technologies like keyword matching, decision trees, and machine learning algorithms. A notable example from the 1990s is ALICE (Artificial Linguistic Internet Computer Entity), which used heuristic pattern matching for more natural-sounding responses. These improvements enabled chatbots to interact more effectively with users, leading to more extensive applications in various industries.

However, it wasn't until the advent of deep learning and natural language processing techniques that chatbots made significant progress in language understanding and generation. These technologies have enabled chatbots to understand and generate more complex and nuanced language, leading to more human-like interactions. In recent years, we have witnessed the development of powerful models like Google's BERT, OpenAI's GPT series, and Facebook's Blender, which have revolutionized the way chatbots interact and understand human language.

The GPT series, in particular, has made significant advancements, starting with GPT, followed by GPT-2, GPT-3, and now the latest and most advanced GPT-4 architecture, which forms the basis of ChatGPT. These advancements have greatly expanded the capabilities of chatbots, allowing them to perform more sophisticated tasks and interact with users in more natural ways. As the field of artificial intelligence continues to evolve, we can expect chatbot technologies to become even more advanced and ubiquitous in our daily lives.

As chatbot technologies continue to evolve, they have the potential to revolutionize the way we interact with technology and expand the possibilities for AI-driven language understanding and generation. The ongoing efforts by the AI research community, including OpenAI, to overcome these obstacles and push the boundaries of what is possible with AI-driven language models, are paving the way for exciting new developments in the field.

Chatbots are rapidly becoming an essential tool for businesses and individuals seeking to streamline their workflow, increase productivity, and provide personalized support to their customers and audiences. With the continuing advancements in AI-driven language understanding and generation, the potential for chatbots to transform the way we communicate and interact with technology is virtually limitless.

1.1.2. Generative Pre-trained Transformers (GPT)

The Generative Pre-trained Transformer (GPT) is a family of language models developed by OpenAI, a research organization dedicated to advancing artificial intelligence technology. These models are based on the Transformer architecture, which was first introduced in the paper

"Attention is All You Need" by Vaswani et al. in 2017. The Transformer architecture has since become highly regarded in the field of natural language processing due to its superior performance in comparison to traditional recurrent neural network (RNN) and convolutional neural network (CNN) based models.

The GPT models follow a two-step process to achieve their impressive results. First, in the pre-training phase, the model is trained on an enormous dataset to learn general language understanding and generation capabilities. For example, the latest iteration of the GPT family, GPT-3, was trained on the WebText dataset, which contains a diverse array of Internet text sources. This pre-training phase allows GPT models to learn the underlying patterns and structures of language, making them better equipped to tackle more specific tasks.

After pre-training, the model enters the fine-tuning phase, where it is fine-tuned on a smaller dataset for a specific task or domain. This phase allows the GPT model to further refine its capabilities for a particular use case. The two-step process enables the GPT models to achieve state-of-the-art performance in various natural language processing tasks, such as machine translation, question-answering, and sentiment analysis.

ChatGPT, a variant of the GPT family, is built on the GPT-4 architecture, which benefits from several enhancements compared to its predecessors. These enhancements include improved attention mechanisms, larger model sizes, and more advanced training techniques. As a result, ChatGPT is capable of generating highly coherent and contextually relevant responses, making it an ideal solution for developers and enthusiasts seeking to leverage AI-driven language understanding and generation in their applications.

One notable example of ChatGPT's capabilities is its use in customer service applications. Companies can deploy ChatGPT to handle common customer inquiries in an efficient and accurate manner, significantly reducing response times and improving overall customer satisfaction. In addition, ChatGPT has the potential to revolutionize the way we interact with technology, enabling more natural and human-like conversations with our devices.

In the following sections of this chapter, we will delve deeper into the GPT-4 architecture, exploring its underlying mechanisms and how it has evolved from previous iterations. We will also examine real-world applications of ChatGPT, including its use in customer service and other domains. Finally, we will examine the role of OpenAI in the development of this groundbreaking technology and its implications for the future of natural language processing and artificial intelligence.

1.2. Applications and Use Cases

In this section, we will delve into the multifaceted applications and use cases of ChatGPT, showcasing its adaptability and potential to revolutionize numerous industries and domains. As a cutting-edge AI language model, ChatGPT empowers developers and enthusiasts to create advanced, human-like conversational agents capable of understanding complex inputs and generating contextually relevant responses.

From enhancing customer service experiences to streamlining content generation, enabling seamless language translation to providing personalized tutoring and education, ChatGPT has proven to be an invaluable asset in various applications. We will examine these use cases in detail, focusing on the benefits, challenges, and opportunities that arise when integrating ChatGPT into different scenarios.

Moreover, as we discuss these diverse applications, we will present real-world examples of ChatGPT deployments, shedding light on how businesses and individuals are leveraging its capabilities to drive innovation and improve productivity. Additionally, we will explore some groundbreaking approaches and novel ideas that are redefining the possibilities of AI-driven language understanding and generation.

By gaining a comprehensive understanding of ChatGPT's applications and use cases, you will be better equipped to identify opportunities for its integration into your projects or business processes, ultimately harnessing the power of AI to enhance communication, automate tasks, and develop innovative solutions.

1.2.1. Real-world Examples of ChatGPT

ChatGPT has become a highly versatile and adaptable tool that has been applied across a wide range of industries and applications. It has proven to be a valuable asset in various real-world scenarios, some of which are listed below:

Customer Service

As previously mentioned, ChatGPT provides a revolutionary approach to customer service that is sure to enhance the way companies handle customer inquiries. By using ChatGPT, companies can provide their customers with not only quick and accurate responses to common questions and issues but also personalized assistance that is tailored to their individual needs.With this technology, companies can not only save time and resources but also improve the overall customer experience by building stronger relationships with their customers. In addition, ChatGPT is capable of handling a wide range of customer inquiries, from simple requests to

more complex issues, making it the ideal solution for businesses looking to improve their customer service capabilities.

Overall, ChatGPT is a game-changing technology that has the potential to transform the way companies interact with their customers, creating a more satisfying and rewarding experience for both parties.

Content Generation

ChatGPT's capabilities extend beyond customer service and can be used to benefit content creators in numerous ways. One of the most significant advantages of leveraging ChatGPT in content creation is the ability to produce high-quality content quickly and efficiently. With the use of this tool, content creators can draft articles, write marketing copy, create social media content, and develop engaging narratives with ease.

This feature of ChatGPT not only saves valuable time and effort but also ensures that the created content is of high quality and meets the desired objectives. By utilizing this tool, content creators can focus on other essential tasks such as research, editing, and publishing, without worrying about generating the content itself.

Moreover, ChatGPT can be used to generate content in a variety of styles, tones, and formats. Whether it is a blog post, white paper, product description, or email newsletter, ChatGPT can cater to the specific needs and preferences of content creators. The tool can be customized to align with the brand voice and style, making it an ideal solution for businesses and individuals looking to streamline their content creation process.

Another significant advantage of ChatGPT's content generation feature is that it can help content creators overcome writer's block. Writer's block can be a significant obstacle for content creators, leading to delays in the content creation process. With ChatGPT, content creators can overcome this challenge by generating new ideas and creative directions. This feature ensures that content creators have a steady stream of ideas to work with, making it easier to produce high-quality content consistently.

Additionally, ChatGPT's content generation feature can help content creators stay up-to-date with the latest trends and topics. The tool can be used to analyze social media trends, news articles, and other relevant sources to generate content that is relevant and timely. This ensures that the created content is not only high quality but also relevant to the target audience, increasing engagement and driving traffic to the content.

ChatGPT's content generation feature is a valuable asset for content creators looking to streamline their workflow, increase productivity, and produce high-quality content consistently.

The tool's versatility, customization options, and ability to generate ideas make it an ideal solution for businesses and individuals seeking to optimize their content creation process. With ChatGPT, content creators can focus on what they do best - creating engaging and informative content that resonates with their audience.

Language Translation

ChatGPT's language understanding capabilities make it an ideal tool for efficient and accurate translation between multiple languages. This can be particularly useful in industries that require frequent translation of documents and communications. For example, businesses that operate globally, multinational corporations, and organizations with a diverse workforce often need to communicate with people who speak different languages. In such cases, ChatGPT's language translation feature can help to bridge the language barrier, enabling seamless communication and collaboration. Moreover, the tool's accuracy and efficiency can save time and resources, which can be especially beneficial for companies with a high volume of translation needs. Additionally, ChatGPT's language translation feature can have applications in various other fields, such as education, healthcare, and international diplomacy. Overall, ChatGPT's language translation feature can be a valuable asset for anyone who needs to communicate across language barriers.

In the education field, ChatGPT's language translation feature can help students and educators communicate effectively in multilingual classrooms. For instance, students who are not fluent in the language of instruction can use the tool to understand lectures, assignments, and class materials. Similarly, educators can use ChatGPT to communicate with students who speak different languages, enhancing the learning experience for all students. In healthcare, ChatGPT's language translation feature can help medical professionals communicate with patients who speak different languages, improving patient outcomes and satisfaction. The tool can also help patients understand medical information, instructions, and prescriptions, reducing the risk of errors and misunderstandings.

Moreover, ChatGPT's language translation feature can facilitate international diplomacy by enabling seamless communication between officials who speak different languages. In global politics, this can be crucial for building relationships, negotiating agreements, and resolving conflicts. The tool's accuracy and efficiency can help to overcome language barriers, promoting understanding and cooperation between nations.

However, it is important to note that ChatGPT's language translation feature, like any machine translation tool, may not always be perfect. It can sometimes produce inaccurate translations, especially for complex or idiomatic expressions. Therefore, it is essential to review and verify the translations before sharing them with others, especially in situations where accuracy is critical.

ChatGPT's language translation feature is a powerful tool that can enable seamless communication across language barriers in various fields. Its accuracy and efficiency can save time and resources, enhance learning and healthcare outcomes, and facilitate international diplomacy. However, it is crucial to acknowledge its limitations and use it responsibly to ensure accurate and effective communication.

Tutoring and Education

ChatGPT's versatility makes it a valuable asset in the field of education. It can be employed as a virtual tutor to assist students with homework, explain complex concepts, and provide personalized learning experiences. In fact, personalized learning experiences are critical for all students, especially those with learning disabilities or those who need additional support. With ChatGPT, educators can focus on building a strong foundation for their students by providing personalized instruction based on their individual learning needs. This technology can enhance the quality of education and make it more accessible to learners across the world, especially in underprivileged areas where access to quality education is limited.

Moreover, ChatGPT's virtual tutoring capabilities can be particularly useful for students who may not have access to traditional tutoring services due to financial or geographic limitations. By leveraging ChatGPT, students can receive personalized support regardless of their location or financial situation. This can be especially beneficial for students in rural areas or developing countries, where access to quality education and educational resources is limited.

In addition, ChatGPT's virtual tutoring capabilities can also benefit adult learners who are seeking to develop new skills or further their education. With the rise of online learning platforms, ChatGPT can provide personalized support and guidance to adult learners who may be struggling with specific topics or concepts. This can be especially valuable for individuals who are juggling work, family, and other responsibilities, making it difficult to attend traditional classroom settings.

Furthermore, ChatGPT can also be used to provide language tutoring and translation services, making it an invaluable tool for individuals seeking to learn a new language or communicate with people from different cultures. With ChatGPT's language understanding and translation capabilities, individuals can receive personalized language instruction and communicate with people from different countries and backgrounds, promoting cross-cultural understanding and collaboration.

Overall, ChatGPT's virtual tutoring capabilities have the potential to revolutionize the way we approach education and learning. By providing personalized support and guidance to learners across the world, ChatGPT can enhance the quality of education and make it more accessible

and equitable for all. As this technology continues to evolve, it will be interesting to see how it will transform the field of education and enable learners to achieve their full potential.

1.2.2. Innovative Approaches and Impact

As ChatGPT continues to gain popularity, developers and enthusiasts are coming up with innovative ways to harness its capabilities, creating a significant impact across various domains. Some of these innovative approaches include:

Mental health support

Developers have been exploring the use of ChatGPT in mental health applications, where the AI can provide empathetic and supportive conversation for individuals seeking emotional support. In addition to its potential use in therapy sessions, ChatGPT can be employed in mental health hotlines and crisis centers where trained professionals may not always be available. Given the current shortage of mental health professionals, the use of ChatGPT can help fill the gap and provide people with readily available support. Moreover, the use of AI in mental health can also help reduce the stigma surrounding mental illness and encourage more people to seek help.

Furthermore, the use of ChatGPT in mental health support has the potential to provide a safe and non-judgmental space for individuals to express their feelings and concerns. People who are struggling with mental health issues may feel hesitant or embarrassed to open up to others, fearing judgment or stigma. However, ChatGPT can be a helpful tool in breaking down these barriers, as it can provide a non-judgmental and empathetic response to the individual's needs.

Additionally, ChatGPT can be customized to address specific mental health concerns, such as depression, anxiety, or trauma. The AI can be trained on relevant data and information to provide more accurate and tailored responses to the individual's needs. This can help improve the effectiveness of mental health support and ensure that people receive the appropriate care and attention they need.

It is worth noting, however, that the use of ChatGPT in mental health support should not replace professional counseling or therapy. While the AI can provide valuable support, it cannot replace the human connection and expertise that mental health professionals offer. Therefore, it is essential to use ChatGPT as a complement to traditional mental health care, rather than a replacement.

The use of ChatGPT in mental health support has the potential to improve access to care, reduce stigma, and provide a safe and supportive space for individuals to express their feelings and concerns. While it should not replace professional therapy, it can serve as a helpful tool in supplementing mental health care and providing people with the support they need. As with

any AI application, it is crucial to approach its use in mental health with caution and responsibility, ensuring that the individual's privacy and well-being are prioritized.

Voice assistants

One of the most significant technological advancements in recent years is the integration of chatbots like ChatGPT into voice assistants like Alexa, Siri, and Google Assistant. This integration allows users to interact with voice assistants in a more natural and human-like way, leading to more accurate and relevant responses. By leveraging the power of machine learning and deep learning algorithms, chatbots can understand user intent and provide personalized recommendations and solutions.

The integration of chatbots into voice assistants has the potential to revolutionize the way we interact with technology. Instead of having to navigate complex menus or search for information manually, users can simply ask a question or give a command, and the chatbot will handle the rest. This makes the user experience more intuitive, seamless, and user-friendly.

Voice assistants like Alexa, Siri, and Google Assistant have already become an integral part of our daily lives, from setting reminders and playing music to controlling smart home devices and answering general knowledge questions. With the integration of chatbots, these voice assistants can become even more powerful and versatile. For example, users can ask for personalized recommendations for products or services based on their preferences and previous behavior, or receive customized news summaries based on their interests and reading habits.

Moreover, the integration of chatbots into voice assistants can benefit businesses by enabling more efficient and effective customer service. Chatbots can handle routine queries and direct customers to the appropriate resources, freeing up human agents to focus on more complex issues. This can lead to faster response times, increased customer satisfaction, and reduced costs for businesses.

As this technology continues to evolve, we can expect to see more and more sophisticated chatbots that are able to handle even more complex tasks and provide even more value to users. For example, chatbots could be used to provide personalized health advice and guidance, or assist with financial planning and investment decisions. The possibilities are endless, and the integration of chatbots into voice assistants is only the beginning.

The integration of chatbots into voice assistants like Alexa, Siri, and Google Assistant is a significant technological advancement that has the potential to transform the way we interact with technology. By leveraging the power of machine learning and deep learning algorithms, chatbots can provide more accurate, relevant, and personalized responses to user queries, leading to a more intuitive, seamless, and user-friendly experience. As this technology continues

to evolve, we can expect to see even more sophisticated chatbots that are able to handle increasingly complex tasks and provide even more value to users and businesses alike.

Creative writing

ChatGPT has been used to assist writers in overcoming writer's block and generating new ideas, helping them to craft more engaging and imaginative stories.

With the advent of technology, writing has become more accessible than ever before. In fact, the proliferation of writing tools and apps has made it possible for anyone to become a writer. However, for aspiring writers, the process of writing can be daunting. They often struggle with generating new ideas and find themselves stuck in a rut, unable to break free from the constraints of their own writing. This is where ChatGPT comes in.

ChatGPT is an AI-powered writing assistant that helps writers overcome writer's block and generate new ideas for their stories. By using a combination of natural language processing and machine learning algorithms, ChatGPT is able to analyze a writer's work and provide them with personalized suggestions and prompts that are tailored to their specific needs. Whether it's coming up with a new character, plot twist, or setting, ChatGPT can help writers take their writing to the next level.

In addition to providing writers with new ideas, ChatGPT also helps them to craft more engaging and imaginative stories. By analyzing the language and structure of a writer's work, ChatGPT can identify areas where the story may be lacking or where it could be improved. It can suggest new ways of approaching a scene or provide feedback on the pacing and flow of the story. With ChatGPT's help, writers can take their stories from good to great.

Overall, ChatGPT is a powerful tool that has revolutionized the way writers approach their craft. By providing personalized suggestions and feedback, it has helped countless writers to overcome their creative blocks and take their writing to new heights.

The examples presented in this document underscore the potential of ChatGPT to revolutionize our interaction with technology. ChatGPT's innovative approaches serve as a testament to the vast potential of AI-driven language understanding and generation. As we continue to explore the possibilities of ChatGPT, we can only begin to imagine the ways in which this technology will transform the future of communication and language processing.

The use of ChatGPT in various industries including healthcare, education, and entertainment, among others, has already started to shape how we interact with chatbots and virtual assistants, and the potential applications of this technology is vast and far-reaching. With ChatGPT, the

possibilities are endless, and we are excited to see how this technology continues to evolve and shape the future of communication and language processing.

1.3. Understanding the GPT-4 Architecture

In this section, we will take a deep dive into the GPT-4 architecture, the foundation upon which ChatGPT is built. As a state-of-the-art AI language model, GPT-4 has enabled the development of advanced conversational agents that excel in various natural language understanding and generation tasks.

We will begin by examining the key concepts and components that make the GPT-4 architecture stand out, such as Transformer models and the attention mechanisms that underpin their success. By understanding these essential elements, you will gain valuable insights into how GPT-4 processes and interprets language, as well as the factors contributing to its remarkable performance.

Furthermore, we will discuss the various techniques and innovations that have been employed in the design and training of GPT-4, including large-scale pre-training, fine-tuning for specific tasks, layer normalization, and positional encoding. This will provide you with a comprehensive understanding of the GPT-4 architecture, equipping you with the knowledge to effectively utilize and optimize ChatGPT for your specific needs.

As we navigate through this exploration of GPT-4's architecture, you will also learn about the progression of GPT models, from the initial GPT release to the current GPT-4 version, and appreciate the significance of each iteration in advancing the field of AI-driven language understanding and generation.

1.3.1. Transformer Models and Attention Mechanisms

The success of ChatGPT can be largely attributed to the innovative Transformer architecture that it employs. The Transformer framework has revolutionized the field of natural language processing by introducing the concept of self-attention, which allows models to weigh the importance of different words in a sentence when generating responses or understanding context.

More specifically, the self-attention mechanism employed by ChatGPT computes a score for each word in relation to every other word in the sentence, enabling the model to identify the most contextually relevant words and generate more coherent and accurate responses. This approach has proven to be more efficient and effective than traditional RNN and CNN-based

models for a wide range of natural language tasks, including but not limited to language translation, text summarization, and sentiment analysis.

Furthermore, the implementation of the self-attention mechanism has allowed ChatGPT to achieve superior results when compared to other natural language processing models in various benchmarks and competitions. This has led to the continued growth and expansion of ChatGPT's capabilities, which has further solidified its position as a leading technology in the field of natural language processing.

However, it is essential to acknowledge that the use of AI-driven language models like ChatGPT also comes with limitations and challenges. One of the key limitations is the model's dependence on the quality and quantity of training data, which can contribute to biases and inaccuracies in language understanding and generation. To mitigate these issues, developers must continuously fine-tune the model and implement content filters and moderation systems to minimize biases.

Moreover, the deployment of AI-driven language models like ChatGPT also raises ethical concerns and potential risks. For instance, the model's ability to generate language indistinguishable from human-written text can create issues of misinformation and fake news. Hence, it is crucial to approach the use of AI-driven language models with caution and responsibility, ensuring that the individual's privacy and well-being are prioritized.

In conclusion, ChatGPT's innovative Transformer architecture and self-attention mechanism have revolutionized the field of natural language processing, enabling the model to achieve superior results in various benchmarks and competitions. The model's versatility and applicability in various fields, including healthcare, education, and mental health support, have also contributed to its success. However, it is essential to acknowledge the limitations and challenges of AI-driven language models and approach their use with caution and responsibility. By doing so, we can continue to harness the vast potential of ChatGPT and other AI-driven language models to benefit individuals and society as a whole.

1.3.2. Key Components of GPT-4 Architecture

The GPT-4 architecture incorporates several key components that contribute to its superior performance, including:

Large-scale pre-training

GPT-4's ability to learn from vast amounts of text data during pre-training is a critical factor in its impressive performance and a key advantage over other language models. The pre-training

process enables the model to capture a wide variety of linguistic patterns, structures, and knowledge, making it capable of handling diverse natural language processing tasks.

During pre-training, GPT-4 processes large volumes of text data, including books, articles, and other sources of written language. The model then uses this data to learn and analyze the patterns and structures within the text, allowing it to predict the next word in a given sequence with remarkable accuracy. By doing so, the model can develop a deep understanding of language and its complexities, enabling it to perform a wide range of tasks, such as language generation, summarization, and translation.

One of the significant benefits of pre-training is that it allows the model to learn from a diverse range of text data, which can include multiple languages, genres, and writing styles. This means that GPT-4 can handle tasks beyond just the English language. The model can also learn from text data in other languages, making it an ideal tool for multilingual natural language processing tasks.

Additionally, pre-training provides GPT-4 with a robust foundation upon which it can build specific language models for different tasks. By fine-tuning the model with specific datasets and tasks, the model can optimize its performance and achieve state-of-the-art results in a wide range of natural language processing applications. This fine-tuning process allows GPT-4 to adapt its pre-trained knowledge to specific tasks, such as sentiment analysis or summarization, optimizing its performance in diverse applications.

Overall, GPT-4's large-scale pre-training is a significant advantage, enabling the model to learn from vast amounts of text data and develop a deep understanding of language and its complexities. The model's ability to learn from diverse text data and adapt to specific tasks through fine-tuning makes it a versatile and powerful tool for natural language processing applications. As the amount of text data in the world continues to grow, GPT-4's pre-training capabilities will be increasingly valuable in handling complex natural language processing tasks.

Fine-tuning for specific tasks

One of the key advantages of GPT-4 is its ability to undergo fine-tuning for specific tasks. This is made possible by the model's pre-trained knowledge, which serves as a foundation for adaptation to new contexts and tasks. Fine-tuning involves adjusting the weights and biases of the pre-trained model based on new data and specific task requirements. This process is essential for achieving optimal performance in natural language processing applications, such as sentiment analysis, summarization, and chatbot development.

The fine-tuning process allows GPT-4 to apply its pre-trained knowledge to specific tasks, thereby improving its accuracy and effectiveness. This involves training the model on a relatively

small amount of task-specific data, which is used to adjust the model's parameters to better fit the specific task requirements. By fine-tuning GPT-4, we can optimize the model's performance for a wide range of natural language processing tasks, making it a versatile and powerful tool for language understanding and generation.

Fine-tuning also enables GPT-4 to learn from new data and adapt to evolving language patterns, ensuring that it remains relevant and effective in a constantly changing language landscape. This is particularly important as language is constantly evolving, and new words, phrases, and expressions are being introduced all the time. By fine-tuning the model, we can ensure that it is up-to-date and capable of processing and generating natural language that is relevant and accurate.

In addition to improving its accuracy and effectiveness, fine-tuning also enables GPT-4 to generalize to new tasks and domains, making it a valuable tool for a wide range of natural language processing applications. This versatility is particularly important in industries such as healthcare and finance, where natural language processing is used for a variety of tasks, such as medical diagnosis, financial analysis, and fraud detection.

Overall, the fine-tuning process is a critical step in the development of language models such as GPT-4. By adapting the model's pre-trained knowledge to specific tasks, we can optimize its performance, improve its accuracy and effectiveness, and ensure that it remains relevant and adaptable in a constantly changing language landscape. As such, fine-tuning is a key component of GPT-4's success and its ability to revolutionize the field of natural language processing.

Layer normalization and positional encoding

Layer normalization and positional encoding are two important techniques that have been widely used in the development of machine learning models, especially in natural language processing tasks.

Layer normalization is a technique used to ensure that the activations of each layer in the model are normalized and do not vary significantly across different inputs. This is important because it helps to stabilize the model during training and prevents it from being overly sensitive to variations in the input data. By normalizing each layer's activations, the model can learn meaningful representations of the input text that are consistent and reliable across different inputs.

On the other hand, positional encoding is used to provide the model with information about the sequence of the input text. Specifically, it encodes the position of each token in the sequence, thereby allowing the model to understand the order of the input. This is important because natural language is inherently sequential, and the order of the words in a sentence can

significantly affect its meaning. By incorporating positional encoding into the model, we can ensure that it is able to understand and process the sequential nature of the input text.

Together, these two techniques are crucial in the development of a machine-learning model that can accurately process and understand sequential data. By combining layer normalization and positional encoding, we can ensure that the model is stable during training and can effectively process the sequential nature of the input text.

It's important to note that these techniques are not only used in natural language processing tasks but also in other domains such as computer vision. For example, positional encoding has been used in the development of state-of-the-art image recognition models to encode the spatial information of the input image. This highlights the versatility of these techniques and their potential to be used in various machine-learning applications beyond natural language processing.

Layer normalization and positional encoding are two important techniques that are widely used in the development of machine learning models. These techniques are crucial in the development of models that can accurately process and understand sequential data, such as natural language text. By incorporating these techniques into machine learning models, we can ensure that they are stable during training and can effectively process the sequential nature of the input data.

1.4. OpenAI and the Development of ChatGPT

In this section, we will explore the role of OpenAI, the pioneering research organization responsible for the development of ChatGPT. As a leader in the AI research community, OpenAI is committed to advancing artificial intelligence and ensuring that it benefits all of humanity.

We will begin by examining OpenAI's mission, goals, and guiding principles, which have shaped the organization's approach to AI research and development. This will provide you with a clear understanding of the driving forces behind OpenAI's pursuit of cutting-edge AI models and technologies, such as ChatGPT.

As we delve deeper into the development of ChatGPT, we will discuss the progression of GPT models, starting with the initial GPT release and culminating in the current GPT-4 architecture. By tracing the evolution of these models, you will gain valuable insights into the advancements and innovations that have led to the creation of ChatGPT and its impressive language understanding and generation capabilities.

Furthermore, we will touch upon the challenges and limitations that come with the development of AI models like ChatGPT, including the need to address model constraints, inherent biases, and ethical concerns. By acknowledging and understanding these challenges, you will be better prepared to responsibly utilize ChatGPT and contribute to the ongoing development and refinement of AI-driven language models.

This exploration of OpenAI and the development of ChatGPT will equip you with a comprehensive understanding of the organization's goals, the evolution of GPT models, and the challenges that lie ahead in the pursuit of ever-more advanced AI-driven language understanding and generation technologies.

1.4.1. OpenAI's Mission and Goals

OpenAI is an organization that is at the forefront of AI research and development, with a focus on creating advanced AI models and technologies that can benefit society as a whole. The organization's mission is to ensure that artificial general intelligence is safe, reliable, and accessible to everyone. To achieve this mission, OpenAI is working tirelessly to develop cutting-edge AI models like ChatGPT that can facilitate seamless communication between humans and machines.

ChatGPT is one of OpenAI's most impressive AI-driven language models. It is an AI-powered writing assistant that has revolutionized the way writers approach their craft. By using a combination of natural language processing and machine learning algorithms, ChatGPT is able to analyze a writer's work and provide them with personalized suggestions and prompts that are tailored to their specific needs. Whether it's coming up with a new character, plot twist, or setting, ChatGPT can help writers take their writing to the next level.

But ChatGPT is more than just a writing assistant. The model is built on the foundation of the GPT-4 architecture, which is a state-of-the-art AI language model that enables the development of advanced conversational agents that excel in various natural language understanding and generation tasks. The GPT-4 architecture incorporates several key components that contribute to its superior performance, including large-scale pre-training, fine-tuning for specific tasks, layer normalization, and positional encoding.

One of the key advantages of ChatGPT is its ability to undergo fine-tuning for specific tasks. This is made possible by the model's pre-trained knowledge, which serves as a foundation for adaptation to new contexts and tasks. Fine-tuning involves adjusting the weights and biases of the pre-trained model based on new data and specific task requirements. This process is essential for achieving optimal performance in natural language processing applications, such as sentiment analysis, summarization, and chatbot development.

However, as with any AI model, ChatGPT is not without its limitations and challenges. One of the key challenges is the model's dependence on the quality and quantity of training data, which can contribute to biases and inaccuracies in language understanding and generation. To mitigate these issues, developers must continuously fine-tune the model and implement content filters and moderation systems to minimize biases.

Moreover, the deployment of AI-driven language models like ChatGPT also raises ethical concerns and potential risks. For instance, the model's ability to generate language indistinguishable from human-written text can create issues of misinformation and fake news. Hence, it is crucial to approach the use of AI-driven language models with caution and responsibility, ensuring that the individual's privacy and well-being are prioritized.

To address these challenges and limitations, OpenAI and the broader AI research community are actively working to improve the capabilities of AI-driven language models like ChatGPT. Future versions of ChatGPT may benefit from techniques like reinforcement learning from human feedback, adversarial training, and more diverse training data, leading to even more powerful, accurate, and unbiased AI-driven language understanding and generation.

In conclusion, OpenAI's mission to develop advanced AI models that benefit society is a worthy objective that is being achieved through innovative technologies like ChatGPT. While there are limitations and challenges associated with AI-driven language models, the ongoing efforts by the AI research community to address these issues and improve the capabilities of these models offer hope for a future where AI is safe, reliable, and accessible to all.

1.4.2. The Progression of GPT Models

Since its initial release, OpenAI's GPT series has undergone significant evolution. These changes include improvements in model size, training data, and architectural refinements, resulting in increasingly powerful language models. For example, GPT-2 introduced the concept of unsupervised learning, which allowed the model to generate coherent text without the need for explicit examples. This new approach to machine learning was a significant step forward, as it greatly expanded the model's potential applications.

In addition to its advancements in unsupervised learning, the GPT series has also made strides in supervised learning. GPT-3, for instance, was designed to be more versatile and capable of handling a wider range of tasks. This was achieved through the use of larger training data sets, which allowed the model to learn from a broader range of examples. As a result, GPT-3 has been able to perform tasks such as language translation and summarization with remarkable accuracy.

The development of GPT-4 and ChatGPT represents the latest milestones in this progression. These models build upon the successes of their predecessors, offering users unprecedented levels of natural language understanding and generation. GPT-4, for instance, promises to be even more advanced than GPT-3, with a focus on improving the model's reasoning and decision-making abilities. This will allow the model to perform more complex tasks, such as analyzing large data sets and making predictions based on that data.

Meanwhile, ChatGPT is designed specifically for conversational applications, allowing users to interact with the model in a more natural way. This is achieved through a combination of advanced natural language processing techniques and a deep understanding of human conversation patterns. As a result, ChatGPT is able to carry on complex and nuanced conversations with users, providing a more human-like experience.

Overall, OpenAI's GPT series continues to push the boundaries of natural language processing and generation. With each new release, the models become more sophisticated and capable, offering exciting possibilities for the future of AI-powered language technology. As these models continue to evolve, they will undoubtedly play an increasingly important role in our daily lives, helping us to communicate more effectively and making our interactions with machines more seamless and intuitive.

1.5. Limitations and Challenges of ChatGPT

In this section, we will delve into the limitations and challenges of ChatGPT, acknowledging the areas in which the model falls short and the hurdles that must be overcome to realize its full potential. As with any AI model, ChatGPT is not without its imperfections, and understanding these shortcomings is crucial to responsibly harnessing its capabilities and developing more advanced language models in the future.

We will begin by discussing the model constraints and inherent biases that can arise from ChatGPT's training data and architecture. By acknowledging these limitations, you will gain a deeper appreciation of the challenges associated with training and fine-tuning AI-driven language models, as well as the steps necessary to mitigate these issues and ensure more accurate, reliable, and unbiased performance.

Furthermore, we will explore the ethical concerns and potential risks that accompany the deployment of ChatGPT, highlighting the importance of responsible AI development and usage. By addressing these concerns, you will be better equipped to make informed decisions when integrating ChatGPT into your projects or business processes, ensuring that AI-driven language understanding and generation is leveraged ethically and effectively.

As we examine the limitations and challenges of ChatGPT, we will also touch upon the ongoing efforts by the AI research community, including OpenAI, to overcome these obstacles and push the boundaries of what is possible with AI-driven language models. By understanding the challenges and the steps being taken to address them, you will be better prepared to contribute to the advancement of AI and the development of even more powerful, accurate, and unbiased language understanding and generation technologies.

1.5.1. Model Constraints and Inherent Biases

Despite its impressive capabilities, ChatGPT has some limitations that must be considered. As an AI model, it is only as good as the data it has been trained on. Therefore, it is essential to ensure that the data used in training the model is diverse and representative of different groups and perspectives to avoid biases. In addition, ChatGPT can inherit biases present in the training data, which can sometimes result in unintended and potentially offensive responses. Hence, developers must implement content filters and moderation systems to minimize these biases and ensure that ChatGPT provides accurate and appropriate responses.

Furthermore, developers need to continuously fine-tune the ChatGPT model to keep up with the ever-changing nature of language and the evolution of cultural norms. This process involves updating the model with new data and retraining it to improve its accuracy and effectiveness. Additionally, developers must regularly evaluate the model's performance and identify any biases or errors that need to be corrected. This ongoing effort is crucial to maintaining ChatGPT's effectiveness and ensuring that it remains a valuable tool for communication and problem-solving.

1.5.2. Overcoming Limitations and Future Directions

The AI research community, including OpenAI, is actively working to improve the limitations of ChatGPT and other AI models. For instance, researchers are exploring the use of reinforcement learning from human feedback, which could enable ChatGPT to learn from its own mistakes and become more accurate over time. Similarly, adversarial training is another technique being investigated to help ChatGPT better understand and generate language. Additionally, researchers are also seeking to diversify the training data used to train ChatGPT, which could help ensure that the model is capable of understanding and generating language in a more unbiased way.

Moving forward, as we proceed through this book, we will delve into the practical aspects of utilizing ChatGPT. This will include API integration, advanced API features, fine-tuning for specific tasks and industries, and addressing the model's limitations. By exploring these topics in greater depth, we hope to provide you with a more complete understanding of how to effectively leverage the power of ChatGPT in your own work.

Chapter 2 - Getting Started with ChatGPT

In this chapter, we will provide you with a comprehensive guide on how to get started with ChatGPT. We understand that starting a new project can be overwhelming, so we've made sure to include all the essential steps to ensure you have a smooth and successful integration process.

First, we'll start by identifying the tools and knowledge you need to effectively utilize this powerful AI language model in your projects. We'll cover the basics of setting up your development environment and integrating the ChatGPT API.

In addition to the basics, we'll also delve into the more advanced features and parameters available to customize your ChatGPT experience. This includes learning how to interact with the ChatGPT API and the various features available to you.

As you progress through this chapter, you'll learn about the intricacies of configuring your development environment, understanding the ChatGPT API, and navigating the different features available to you. We'll offer practical advice and clear examples to make sure you have a complete understanding of ChatGPT.

By the end of this chapter, you'll be well-equipped to harness the capabilities of ChatGPT and begin implementing it into your applications, projects, or business processes. You'll have a deep understanding of the integration process and be able to use ChatGPT to its fullest potential.

2.1. Setting Up Your Development Environment

Before you can start working with ChatGPT, it is crucial to understand the importance of creating a well-structured development environment. A well-structured development environment ensures that your workflow is optimized, making it easier for you to focus on the task at hand.

The first step towards creating a well-structured development environment is to install the necessary software. This process involves ensuring that you have the correct version of the software and that your system specifications meet the requirements.

Once you have installed the necessary software, the next step is to create an OpenAI API key. An API key is a unique identifier that is used to authenticate requests made to an API. In the case of ChatGPT, the API key is used to access the OpenAI API, which is a critical component of the ChatGPT system.

After creating the API key, the next step is to configure your environment to interact with the ChatGPT API. This process involves ensuring that your API key is correctly configured and that your environment is set up to send and receive requests to and from the ChatGPT API.

In this section, we will walk you through each step in detail, ensuring that your development environment is optimized for seamless integration with ChatGPT. By following these steps, you can be confident that your development environment is set up correctly and that you are ready to start working with ChatGPT.

2.1.1. Installing Required Software

To work with ChatGPT, you will need to have the following software installed on your computer:

Python

ChatGPT is designed to work with Python, a popular programming language for AI and machine learning applications. Make sure you have the latest version of Python installed.

If you are a beginner with Python, we recommend our book "Python Programming Unlocked for Beginners." You can find more information about the book on https://books.cuantum.tech

To install Python on your computer, follow the following steps:

Step 1: Go to www.python.org

Step 2: Select 'Downloads' from the toolbar

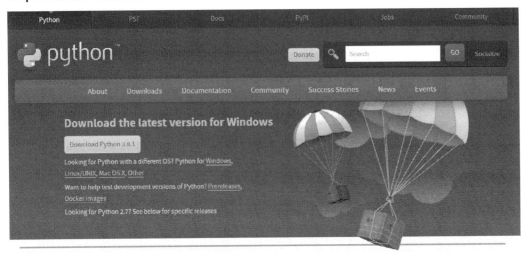

Step 3: Click on 'Download Python 3.8.1' or the latest version available

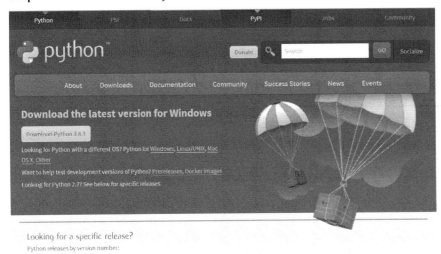

Step 4: Then, go to the **Fil**e option. After that, a security dialog box will appear as shown below. Click on 'Run' to continue the installation process

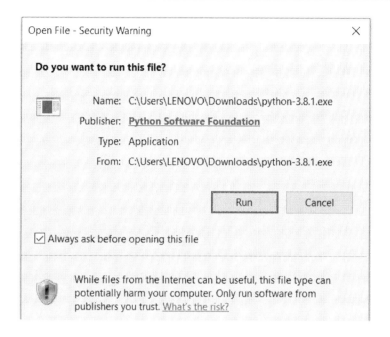

Step 5: Click on 'Install Now'

Once you do that, you can see the setup in progress as in the below screenshot:

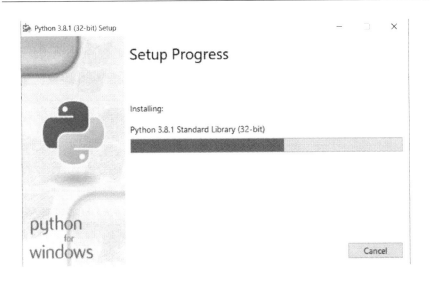

Step 6: After the installation of Python, when you see a window with the message 'Setup was successful', click on the 'Close' button.

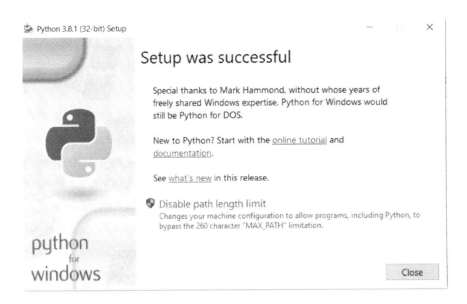

Now, you are ready with Python 3.8.1 installed in your system.

Further, we will move on to the installation of PyCharm.

There are several IDEs and code editors available for Python development. Here, we'll discuss setting up three popular options: PyCharm, Visual Studio Code (VSCode), and Jupyter Notebook.

PyCharm

Step 1: To download PyCharm, visit the official website of JetBrains: http://www.jetbrains.com/pycharm/

Step 2: Click on the 'Download" button

Step 3: After that, you will see the below window with two options, **Professional** and **Community**

Step 4: Download the **Community** version

Note: If you are interested to work with the Professional version, then you can download the **Professional** version and avail a free trial.

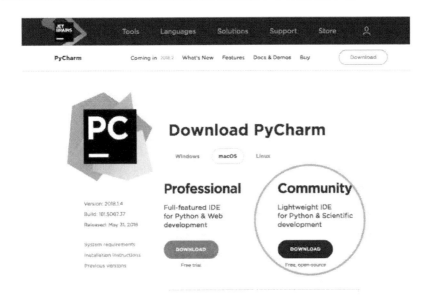

Step 5: After downloading the file, click on it

Step 6: When the following window appears, click on **Next** and the installation process will start

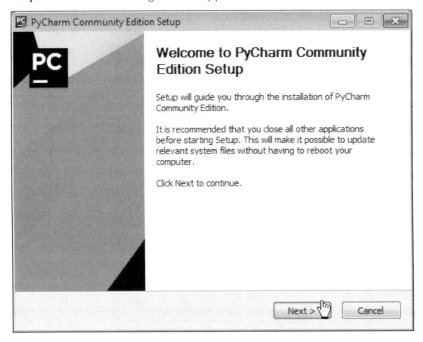

Step 7: After clicking on **Next**, first, a window for setting up the installation location will appear.

Note: You can either select a folder for the installation location or retain the default path.

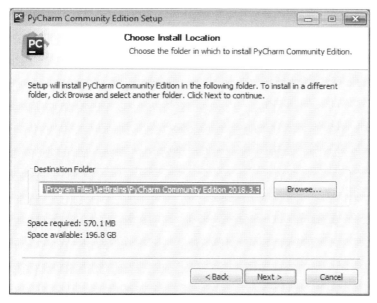

Step 8: In the next step, you can set the **Installation Options** as per requirements, and then, click on the **Next** button to proceed

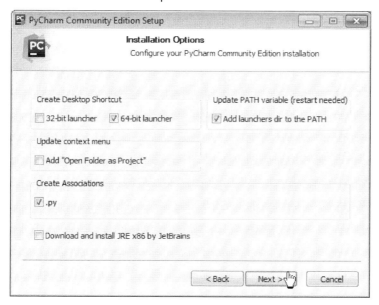

Step 9: Now, you have to select the Start Menu folder, or you can leave it as default

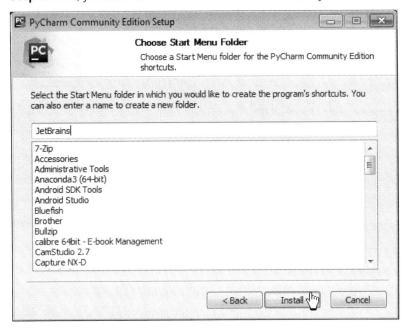

Step 10: After these steps, click on the **Install** button as above to start the installation process

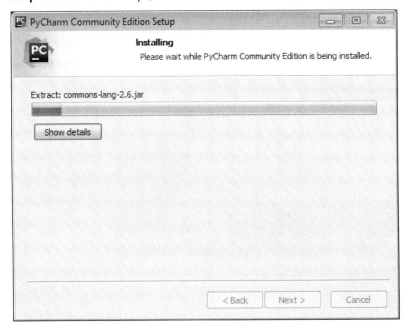

Step 11: When you click on the Finish button, your PyCharm installation completes

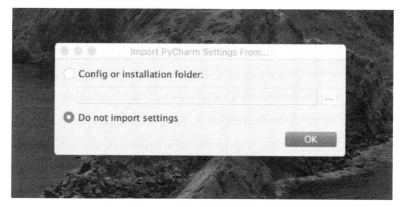

Now, you have successfully installed PyCharm and Python both in your system.

Configuring PyCharm

The first time PyCharm launches, it will offer you the chance to import older settings (from a previous PyCharm installation).

If you are installing PyCharm for the first time, you don't need to import settings. The next screen will ask you to customize PyCharm. The first question is to select a keymap scheme. Keymap scheme refers to keyboard shortcuts, check the different examples in the figure. You can leave it as it if you never used PyCharm before, and it is updated for newer Mac OS versions.

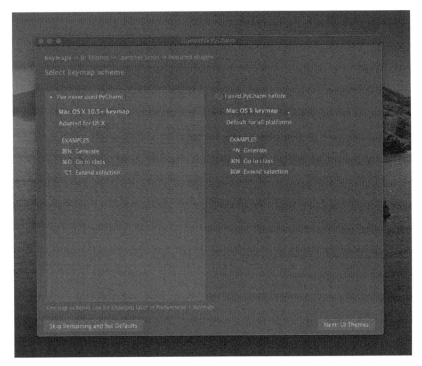

I click on Next: UI Themes. On the following page, I opted for the dark 'Darcula' theme. Don't be disappointed if you don't like any of the themes right now. Later you can add a plugin that allows you to choose between several other beautiful options 😄 *(hint: it's a plugin called Material UI Theme)*. After you chose, click on Next: Launcher Script. A Launcher script adds a small terminal program that can launch PyCharm from your terminal in any given directory. What I mean is that it allows you to do the following:

charm ~/DeveloperProjects/MyNewPythonApplication

In that line, I am launching PyCharm in the directory called 'MyNewPythonApplication' that is a sub-directory of 'DeveloperProjects.' If you like this feature, check the box. To continue, click on Next: Featured plugins.

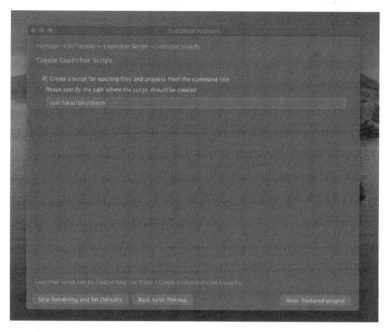

On the next screen, Pycharm suggests popular plugins. That's a personal choice. The configuration is almost ready, now click on Start using PyCharm.

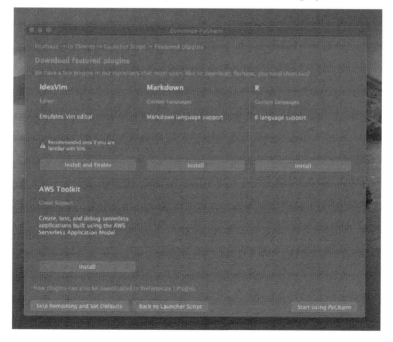

Creating a new project in PyCharm

Now, the next step is to either open an old project (from a repository on your local machine or version control) or create a new project. Let's suppose you want to start a new project. Then, click on + Create New Project.

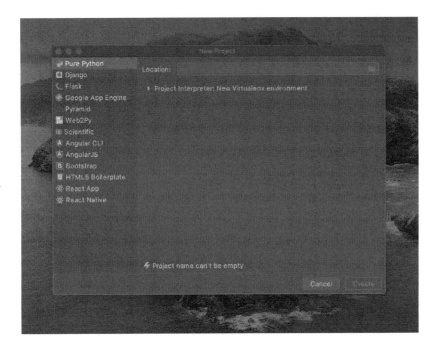

If you chose the professional version of PyCharm, you can select among several project options from the left sidebar. Or, in case you have the free version, you won't have these options, so you can only open a new Pure Python project. You can create a new project in the same way, though. Chose the location (directory) where you want to save your project.

By clicking on Project Interpreter: New Virtualenv environment, you can choose the environment options for your new project. When you are coding in Python, you will probably make use of several libraries. The environment will hold all the libraries you will install for that project. There are two options 1) New environment or 2) Existing interpreter.

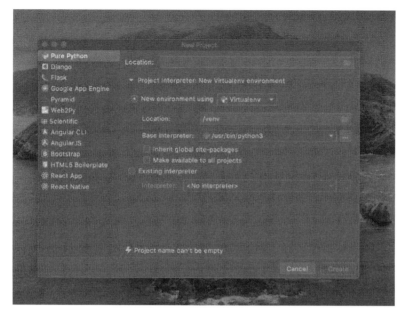

The new environment (first) option gives yet three possibilities, Virtualenv, Pipenv, or Conda. Virtualenv is the default option. Pipenv is newer, and it is supposed to have extra functionalities. To make use of Conda, you need to have installed the Anaconda or Miniconda on your machine. You can use the default Virtualenv. Besides, you can choose the Base interpreter (Python 3 recommended). Click on Create to continue.

Before you can start coding, PyCharm suggests a 'Tip of the Day' option with tricks on how to increase your productivity by using keyboard shortcuts. If you think you don't need them, you can uncheck this option on the bottom left corner of the pop-up. After that, close the pop-up.

Now you can create a new file by clicking Cmd + N (on Mac) or clicking on File > New > File or clicking File > New > Python File (from templates). If you chose the last option, PyCharm will create a file with the .py extension.

You can finally write your code! After you are ready, you can run your script by clicking Run on the main menu (the green arrow on the top right corner) or pressing Ctrl + Option + R on the keyboard. PyCharm offers several features to help you code.

Visual Studio Code (VSCode)

Getting up and running with **Visual Studio Code** is swift and straightforward. It is a small download so you can install it quickly and give the VS Code a try. VS Code is a free code editor. Additionally, it runs on the **macOS, Linux, and Windows** operating systems. Let's see how we can set up the same in the different platforms we use.

The first step is shared across all the platforms irrespective of any OS you are using.

Download Visual Studio Code:

You can download Visual Studio code from URL **_"https://code.visualstudio.com/download"_** by selecting the right platform:

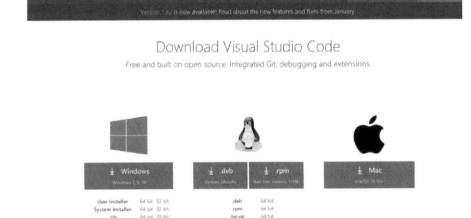

You can click any of the icons mentioned above, depending on the operating system for which you are planning to download the visual studio code editor.

How to install Visual Studio Code on macOS?

Follow the below steps*(shown in gif file and mentioned in bullet points)* to install the VS Code on macOS:

1. *Download Visual Studio Code for macOS.*

2. *After clicking on the Mac option on the download site, it will download a zip file, as shown below:*

3. *Double-click on the downloaded zip to expand the contents. It will give a file, as shown below:*

4. *Drag **"Visual Studio Code.app"** to the **"Applications"** folder, so as it available in the **"Launchpad."***

5. *Double click on the **"Visual Studio Code"** to open.*

6. *Add VS Code to your Dock by right-clicking on the icon to bring up the context menu and choosing **Options => Keep in Dock.***

How to Install Visual Studio Code on Windows?

Firstly, download the Visual Studio Code installer for Windows. Once it is downloaded, run the installer *(VSCodeUserSetup-{version}.exe)*. It will only take a minute.

Secondly, accept the agreement and click on next.

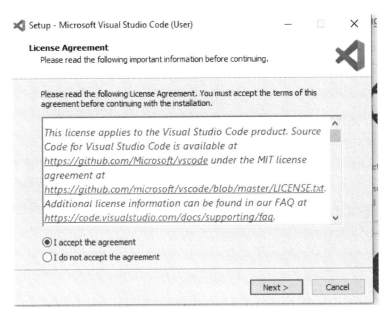

Thirdly, click on **"create a desktop icon"** so that it can be accessed from desktop and click on Next.

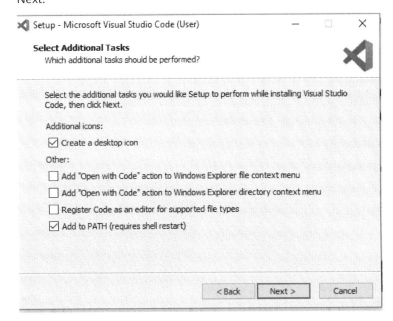

After that, click on the install button.

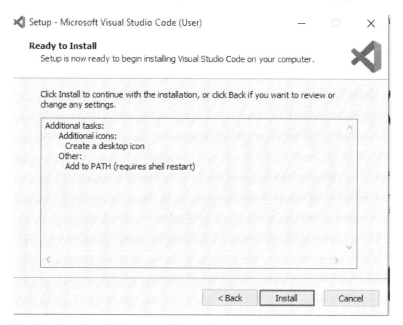

Finally, after installation completes, click on the finish button, and the visual studio code will get open.

By default, VS Code installs under C:\users{username}\AppData\Local\Programs\Microsoft VS Code.

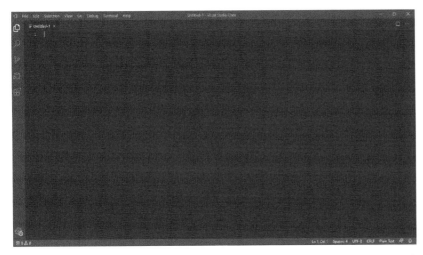

After the successful installation, let's move to the next section to understand the various components of the User Interface of Visual Studio Code Editor.

What are the essential components of the VS Code?

Visual Studio Code is a code editor at its core. Like many other code editors, VS Code adopts a standard user interface and layout of an explorer on the left, showing all of the files and folders you have access to. Additionally, it has an editor on the right, showing the content of the files you have opened. Below are a few of the most critical components the VSCode editor:

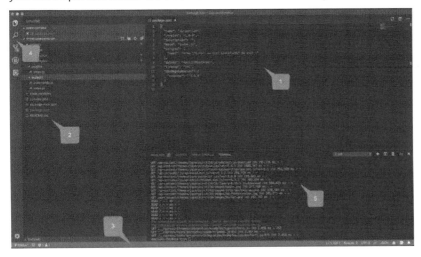

VS Code comes with a straight-forward and intuitive layout that maximizes the space provided for the editor while leaving ample room to browse. Additionally, it allows access to the full context of your folder or project. The UI is divided into five areas, as highlighted in the above image.

1. **Editor** - *It is the main area to edit your files. You can open as many editors as possible side by side vertically and horizontally.*

2. **SideBar** - *Contains different views like the Explorer to assist you while working on your project.*

3. **Status Bar** - *It contains the information about the opened project and the files you edit.*

4. **Activity Bar** - *It is located on the far left-hand side. It lets you switch between views and gives you additional context-specific indicators, like the number of outgoing changes when Git is enabled.*

5. **Panels** - *It displays different panels below the editor region for output or debug information, errors, and warnings, or an integrated terminal. Additionally, the panel can also move to the right for more vertical space.*

VS Code opens up in the same state it was last in, every time you start it. It also preserves folder, layout, and opened files.

Jupyter Notebook

1. To install Jupyter Notebook, open a command prompt (Windows) or terminal (macOS or Linux) and run the following command:

```
pip install notebook
```

Code block: 1.7

2. Once the installation is complete, launch Jupyter Notebook by running the following command:

```
jupyter notebook
```

Code block: 1.8

This will open a new browser window with the Jupyter Notebook interface.

3. To create a new Python notebook, click on "New" in the upper-right corner and select "Python 3" (or the appropriate Python version) from the dropdown menu.

4. You can now write Python code in the notebook cells and execute them by clicking "Run" or pressing **Shift+Enter**. Jupyter Notebook allows you to mix code, text, and multimedia content, making it an excellent tool for interactive data exploration and documentation.

With Python installed and your development environment set up, you're now ready to start writing and executing Python code.

Git (optional)

Git is a widely-used version control system that can help you manage your code and collaborate with other developers. While not strictly necessary for working with ChatGPT, it can be helpful if you plan to work on larger projects or collaborate with a team.

GitHub is a web-based platform that is widely used by developers for version control and collaborative software development. It provides a place for developers to store their code and collaborate with others on a project. GitHub is built on top of Git, which is a distributed version control system that allows developers to keep track of changes made to their code over time.

One of the main benefits of GitHub is its ease of collaboration. Developers can easily share their code with others and work together on a project, regardless of their physical location. This makes it much easier for developers to work together on a project, especially if they are spread out across different locations or time zones.

Another key benefit of GitHub is its powerful version control features. This means that developers can keep track of changes made to their code over time, and easily roll back to a previous version if necessary. This is particularly useful when working on complex projects with multiple developers, where changes to the code can be difficult to keep track of.

GitHub also allows developers to easily share their code with others, and even collaborate on open source projects. This means that developers can contribute to projects that they are interested in, and learn from others in the community.

To get started with GitHub, you'll need to create an account and set up a repository for your project. Once you've done this, you can start adding files and making changes to your code, and collaborate with others on your project. Overall, GitHub is an incredibly useful tool for developers, and is widely used in the industry for collaborative software development.

2.2. Accessing the ChatGPT API

To access the ChatGPT API, you will need an API key from OpenAI. Obtaining an API key is a simple four-step process that we will outline below:

1. The first step is to sign up for an OpenAI account. You can sign up by visiting the following URL: **https://www.openai.com/signup/**. This process takes just a few minutes and requires you to provide some basic information about yourself.
2. After signing up, you will be directed to the OpenAI Dashboard. From there, navigate to the API Keys section. This section contains all of the API keys associated with your OpenAI account.
3. In the API Keys section, you will see a button labeled "Create API Key". Click this button to create a new API key. When prompted, give your API key a descriptive name so that you can easily identify it later.
4. After you have named your API key, OpenAI will generate a new key for you. This key is a long string of characters that is unique to your account. It is important to keep this key secure, as it grants access to your OpenAI account and its associated services. We recommend that you store your API key in a safe and secure location, such as a password manager.

By following these four steps, you can obtain your API key and start using the ChatGPT API.

2.2.1. Configuring Your Development Environment

With the required software installed and your OpenAI API key obtained, it's time to configure your development environment to interact with the ChatGPT API. Follow these steps to set up your environment:

Install the OpenAI Python package: In your terminal or command prompt, run the following command to install the OpenAI Python package:

```
pip install openai
```

This package will allow you to interact with the ChatGPT API using Python.

Set up your API key: Create a new Python file in your code editor and add the following lines, replacing "your_api_key" with the API key you obtained from OpenAI:

```
import openai

openai.api_key = "your_api_key"
```

With these steps completed, your development environment is now set up and ready to interact with the ChatGPT API. In the following sections, we will guide you through the process of making API requests, handling responses, and customizing your interactions with ChatGPT to suit your specific needs and use cases.

2.2.2. Testing Your Development Environment

Before moving forward with the development process, it is essential to test your development environment to ensure everything is set up correctly. This ensures that the rest of the development process can proceed smoothly without any unnecessary delays or issues. To do this, you can create a simple Python script that sends a request to the ChatGPT API and prints the response.

This is a straightforward process that will help you identify any potential issues with your development environment before you begin writing more complex code. Additionally, testing your development environment will allow you to become familiar with the ChatGPT API, which will be beneficial later in the development process.

Create a new Python file called **chatgpt_test.py** and add the following code:

```python
import openai

openai.api_key = "your_api_key"

def test_chatgpt(prompt):
    response = openai.Completion.create(
        engine="text-davinci-002",
        prompt=prompt,
        max_tokens=50,
        n=1,
        stop=None,
        temperature=0.7,
    )
    message = response.choices[0].text.strip()
    return message

prompt = "What is the capital of Italy?"
response = test_chatgpt(prompt)
print(response)
```

Replace "your_api_key" with your OpenAI API key, and then run the script. If everything is set up correctly, you should see the response from ChatGPT, which should be something like "The capital of Italy is Rome."

2.2.3. Understanding API Rate Limits

When it comes to working with the ChatGPT API, it's crucial to keep in mind the API rate limits that OpenAI imposes. These limits are put in place to prevent excessive requests within a given timeframe, and they can vary depending on the subscription plan you have with OpenAI.

But how can you ensure that your application stays within these limits? One approach is to design your application to handle retries and backoffs, meaning that it can wait for a certain amount of time before sending another request. This way, you can avoid hitting the rate limits and ensure that your application runs smoothly.

To do this, you can use Python libraries like **retry** or **tenacity**, which can help you manage your API requests and ensure that you stay within the rate limits. By implementing these strategies, you can ensure that your application is optimized for success and can handle any potential issues that may arise.

With these steps in mind, you can confidently set up your development environment to work with ChatGPT and start integrating the API into your projects. As you move forward, you'll learn more about making API requests, interpreting API responses, and customizing the ChatGPT experience to suit your specific needs. By taking these steps, you'll be well on your way to building robust, effective applications that leverage the power of AI to achieve your goals.

2.2.4. Exploring the OpenAI Python Package Documentation

As you continue to work with the ChatGPT API, it is crucial to familiarize yourself with the OpenAI Python package documentation. The documentation will serve as a valuable resource, providing detailed information on the package's features, functions, and parameters. This knowledge will empower you to fully harness the capabilities of the ChatGPT API and make the most of its potential.

Furthermore, the OpenAI Python package documentation offers additional resources, such as examples and tutorials, that can help you better understand how to use the package in your projects. By studying these resources, you can gain a deeper understanding of the package's functionality and learn how to customize it to meet your specific needs.

Another benefit of familiarizing yourself with the OpenAI Python package documentation is that it can help you troubleshoot any issues you may encounter while using the ChatGPT API. The documentation provides detailed information on common errors and their solutions, which can save you valuable time and effort.

Taking the time to read and understand the OpenAI Python package documentation is essential if you want to get the most out of the ChatGPT API. The documentation offers a wealth of information that can help you use the package more effectively, troubleshoot issues, and customize it to meet your needs.

You can access the OpenAI Python package documentation here: https://beta.openai.com/docs/

2.2.5. Setting Up a Virtual Environment (Optional)

For developers working on multiple projects or collaborating with a team, it is important to set up a virtual environment for your ChatGPT integration. A virtual environment is an isolated Python workspace that allows you to manage dependencies and package versions specific to your project without interfering with other projects or your system's Python installation.

This is particularly useful when working with multiple projects that have different dependencies or versions of packages. With a virtual environment, you can easily switch between projects without having to worry about conflicts between versions of packages or dependencies.

Additionally, virtual environments are often used to test code in a clean and controlled environment, ensuring that your code works as expected before deploying it to production. Setting up a virtual environment may seem like an extra step, but it can save you a lot of time and headaches in the long run.

To set up a virtual environment for your ChatGPT project, follow these steps:

1. Install the **virtualenv** package using the following command:

```
pip install virtualenv
```

2. Create a new virtual environment for your project by running the following command in your project directory:

```
virtualenv chatgpt_env
```

3. Activate the virtual environment:

   - On Windows, run the following command:

```
chatgpt_env\Scripts\activate
```

   - On macOS and Linux, run the following command:

```
source chatgpt_env/bin/activate
```

4. With the virtual environment activated, you can now install the OpenAI Python package and any other required packages within the isolated environment:

```
pip install openai
```

By following the comprehensive steps and guidelines outlined in this section, you have successfully set up your development environment to work with ChatGPT. Additionally, you have learned about best practices such as working with virtual environments and exploring the official documentation. These practices are essential in ensuring that you can seamlessly integrate the ChatGPT API into your projects and applications.

With the help of this foundation, you can unlock the power of AI-driven language understanding and generation. This will enable you to develop more sophisticated and intelligent applications that can provide value to your users and stakeholders. By leveraging the ChatGPT API, you can create chatbots, question-answering systems, and other language-based applications that can help you achieve your goals.

Moreover, you can confidently proceed with the development process, knowing that you have thoroughly tested your development environment to ensure that everything is set up correctly. This will help you avoid any potential issues that may arise later in the development process, saving you valuable time and effort.

It is also essential to familiarize yourself with the OpenAI Python package documentation, which serves as a valuable resource that provides detailed information on the package's features, functions, and parameters. This knowledge will empower you to fully harness the capabilities of the ChatGPT API and make the most of its potential.

Lastly, we recommend setting up a virtual environment for your ChatGPT project, especially if you are working on multiple projects with different dependencies or versions of packages. This will enable you to manage dependencies and package versions specific to your project without interfering with other projects or your system's Python installation.

By following these steps, you can build robust, effective applications that leverage the power of AI to achieve your goals.

Chapter 3 - Basic Usage of ChatGPT API

Now that you have completed the initial setup of your development environment and familiarized yourself with the available ChatGPT API libraries, it is time to delve into the basic usage of the ChatGPT API and explore its capabilities further. This chapter will provide you with a detailed overview of the various ways in which you can interact with the API, including how to send text prompts to ChatGPT, format these prompts for desired outputs, and experiment with different prompt types to achieve a variety of results.

Additionally, we will cover some advanced techniques that can help you get the most out of ChatGPT, such as using custom parameters to fine-tune your results, leveraging pre-trained models for specific use cases, and integrating other machine learning tools to enhance your chatbot's functionality. By mastering these fundamental and advanced techniques, you will be well-equipped to build highly effective chatbots that can provide exceptional value to your users and customers.

3.1. Sending Text Prompts

In order to interact with ChatGPT, you can send text prompts to the API. Once the API receives the prompt, it processes the information and generates a relevant response based on the given input. This is a quick and easy way to get the information you need, without having to spend a lot of time searching for it yourself.

To get started, you simply need to send a text prompt to the API. This can be done using a variety of methods, including through a web browser, a mobile app, or a chatbot interface. Once the API receives your prompt, it will begin processing the information and generating a response.

There are a number of parameters you can use to customize the API's behavior. For example, you can specify the language of the prompt, the type of response you want, and the level of detail you require. By using these parameters, you can tailor the API's behavior to your specific needs and get the most out of your interactions with ChatGPT.

```
import openai

openai.api_key = "your_api_key"

response = openai.Completion.create(
    engine="text-davinci-002",
    prompt="What is the capital of France?",
    max_tokens=50,
    n=1,
    stop=None,
    temperature=0.7,
)
```

3.1.1. Formatting Prompts for Desired Output

To help ChatGPT generate the desired output, you can incorporate various formatting techniques into your prompts. These formatting techniques can aid in clarifying the expected response while preserving the key ideas. Here are a few of the techniques to consider:

Provide context

When you ask a question or make a request to ChatGPT, it can be helpful to provide some additional information at the start. For example, you could give a brief overview or context to help ChatGPT understand what you're looking for. This could include details about the topic, specific keywords, or any other relevant information. By doing this, ChatGPT will be better equipped to provide a more accurate and helpful response.

In the case of geography questions, starting with a brief context can be especially important. For example, you might say "As an AI designed to answer geography questions, please tell me the capital city of France." This provides ChatGPT with clear information about the type of question you're asking and the specific information you're looking for.

Overall, taking a moment to provide context can help ensure that you get the most useful response possible from ChatGPT.

Specify the format

When sending a prompt to ChatGPT, it can be helpful to specify the format in which you'd like to receive your answer. This can be done by outlining the desired response or providing specific instructions on the format you'd like to receive.

By doing so, you can ensure that ChatGPT provides you with a response that is structured in a way that meets your needs, saving you time and effort in the process. For example, if you're looking for a list of items, you could specify that you'd like the response to be in bullet points or numbered list format. Or, if you're looking for a paragraph response, you could specify that you'd like the response to be in complete sentences.

Providing clear instructions on the format can also help ChatGPT better understand your needs and expectations, resulting in more accurate and relevant responses. This is especially important for complex or technical queries, where the format of the response can significantly impact understanding and usability.

So, the next time you send a prompt to ChatGPT, consider specifying the format in which you'd like to receive your answer. This simple step can help you get the most out of your interactions with ChatGPT, and ultimately, enable you to achieve your goals more efficiently.

Use examples

To help ChatGPT better understand the desired format, it is recommended to provide examples of inputs and outputs. This technique is known as 'prompt engineering.' For example, if the question is "What is the capital city of Italy?", the expected response would be "Rome." By providing clear examples, ChatGPT will be able to provide a more accurate response that meets your needs. Additionally, it is important to note that prompt engineering can be especially helpful in cases where the desired response format is complex or specific. Therefore, it is always a good idea to provide examples whenever possible to ensure that ChatGPT is able to provide the best possible response.

If you want expand your knowledge about Prompt Engineering, we recommend our book: **"Mastering ChatGPT and Prompt Engineering"** you can get more info about this book visiting https://books.cuantum.tech

3.1.2. Experimenting with Different Prompt Types

Different types of prompts can elicit various responses from ChatGPT. Here are some prompt types you can experiment with:

1. **Open-ended prompts**: These prompts are designed to inspire more creative and elaborate responses. They provide a starting point for writers to delve into their imaginations and develop a unique story or idea. For instance, "Write a short story about a talking cat" could lead to a tale about a feline detective who solves mysteries, or a heartwarming story about a lonely cat who finds a new friend. By using open-ended prompts, writers are encouraged to think outside the box and explore new ideas, resulting in a more engaging and interesting piece of writing.

2. **Closed-ended prompts**: These prompts are designed to elicit specific information, such as a fact or a numerical value, and typically require a short, concise response. An example of a closed-ended prompt is "What is the boiling point of water?" which requires a specific temperature as an answer. While these prompts can be useful for gathering specific information quickly, they may not always provide the opportunity for more in-depth exploration or discussion of a topic.

3. **Conversational prompts**: One way to make your prompts more engaging is to format them as a dialogue. By alternating between questions and answers, you can create a more interactive experience for your audience. This can be especially effective when you are trying to build rapport with your readers or encourage them to take action. For example:

User: What is a black hole?

AI: A black hole is a region of spacetime exhibiting gravitational acceleration so strong that nothing—no particles or even electromagnetic radiation such as light—can escape from it.

User: How are black holes formed?

AI: Black holes are typically formed when a massive star reaches the end of its life and undergoes gravitational collapse. The star's core collapses under its own gravity, and if the mass of the core is above a certain threshold, it forms a black hole.

By mastering the techniques discussed in this section, you will be able to effectively use the ChatGPT API for a wide range of tasks and applications, from generating creative text to answering factual questions and engaging in interactive conversations.

3.1.3. Adjusting API Parameters

You can customize the API's behavior by adjusting various parameters. Some key parameters include:

- **temperature**: This parameter allows you to adjust the level of randomness in the output. The value of this parameter directly affects the level of variability in the results. By increasing the temperature value (to, for example, 1.0), the output will become more random and unpredictable. Conversely, by decreasing the temperature value (to, for example, 0.1), the output will become more focused and predictable. This parameter can be a useful tool when generating creative content, as it allows you to balance the need for novelty and the need for coherence in the output.
- **top_p**: This parameter is used for controlling the amount of randomness in the output. It is an implementation of nucleus sampling, which means that the model selects tokens from the top **p** probability mass. In other words, the model chooses from a subset of the most likely tokens, thus ensuring that the generated output is still relevant to the input. Using **top_p** as an alternative to **temperature** can provide more precise control over the output.
- **max_tokens**: Limits the response length by setting the maximum number of tokens in the generated output. The max_tokens parameter can be used to control the length of the generated text. By setting a higher value for max_tokens, you can generate longer responses, while setting a lower value will result in shorter responses. It is important to note that max_tokens is not an exact measurement of the length of the generated text, as different tokens may have different lengths. However, it can be used as a rough guideline for controlling the length of the output.
- **n**: The n parameter is a crucial aspect of controlling the number of responses that the model generates in response to a single prompt. By setting n to a higher value, the model can explore a greater range of possible responses, leading to potentially more

diverse and nuanced output. It is important to note, however, that setting n too high can lead to an increase in computational resources required to generate the responses, as well as potentially sacrificing the quality and coherence of the generated text. Therefore, it is recommended to experiment with different values of n to find the optimal balance between response diversity and computational efficiency.

- The **stop** parameter is a useful feature provided in the API to specify a sequence of tokens at which the text generation should stop. For example, we can set **stop=["\\\\n"]** to stop the generation at the first occurrence of a newline character. This can be particularly helpful when we want to generate text up until a specific point in the document, such as the end of a paragraph or section. By setting the stop parameter appropriately, we can ensure that the generated text is of the desired length and contains only the relevant information.

Example

```python
import openai

openai.api_key = "your_api_key"

response = openai.Completion.create(
    engine="text-davinci-002",
    prompt="What is the capital of France?",
    max_tokens=50,
    n=1,
    stop=None,
    temperature=0.5,  # Adjust the temperature value
    top_p=0.9,  # Add the top_p parameter for nucleus sampling
)
```

3.1.4. Dealing with Inappropriate or Unsafe Content

ChatGPT is an incredibly advanced language model that has been programmed to produce high-quality content. It can generate content on a wide range of topics, from science and technology to literature and philosophy. However, there may be instances where the content it generates is not suitable for work, or it is considered inappropriate. In such cases, it is important to take steps to ensure that the content you receive is appropriate for your intended audience.

One effective way to do this is to use OpenAI's content filter, which is available through the API. The content filter is designed to detect and filter out any content that violates the usage policies

set forth by OpenAI. By using the content filter, you can ensure that the content you receive is free from any offensive or inappropriate material that could potentially harm your reputation.

In addition to using the content filter, there are other steps you can take to ensure that the content generated by ChatGPT is appropriate for your needs. For example, you can provide the model with clear guidelines and instructions on the type of content you are looking for, and the tone and style you prefer. You can also provide feedback to the model on the content it generates, helping it to learn and improve over time.

By taking these steps, you can ensure that ChatGPT generates high-quality content that meets your needs and is appropriate for your intended audience.

Example:

```python
import openai

def content_filter(prompt, generated_text):
    # Add the moderation prompt
    moderation_prompt = f"{{text:{generated_text}}} Moderation: Is this text safe for work and follows OpenAI's usage policies?"

    # Make an API request for the moderation prompt
    response = openai.Completion.create(
        engine="text-davinci-002",
        prompt=moderation_prompt,
        max_tokens=10,
        n=1,
        stop=None,
        temperature=0.7,
    )

    # Check the generated response and return True if the content is safe
    return response.choices[0].text.strip().lower() == "yes"

generated_text = "This is an example of generated text."
if content_filter("What is the capital of France?", generated_text):
    print("The generated text is safe.")
else:
    print("The generated text is not safe.")
```

3.1.5. Iterative Refinement and Feedback Loops

When working with ChatGPT, you might need to refine your prompts and parameters iteratively to achieve the desired output. This is because the AI model is trained on a vast corpus of text and may generate responses that are not relevant or accurate. Therefore, it's essential to review the generated content and experiment with different approaches to improve the quality of the results. One way to do this is by adjusting the prompts and parameters to optimize the AI's response. However, this can be a time-consuming process, and it may take several attempts to get the desired output.

Another way to improve the quality of the results is by creating feedback loops in your applications. This means allowing users to rate or provide feedback on the generated content. By doing so, you can collect valuable data on how well the AI is performing and use this information to fine-tune your prompts and API parameters over time. This iterative process can help you achieve the desired output, and it can also help you to discover new uses for ChatGPT in your applications.

Example:

A code example for this topic would involve collecting user feedback and adjusting the API parameters or prompts accordingly. Here's a simple example using Python:

```python
import openai

openai.api_key = "your_api_key"

def generate_text(prompt, temperature):
    response = openai.Completion.create(
        engine="text-davinci-002",
        prompt=prompt,
        max_tokens=50,
        n=1,
        stop=None,
        temperature=temperature,
    )
    return response.choices[0].text.strip()

def collect_feedback():
    feedback = input("Please rate the response (1-5): ")
    return int(feedback)

def main():
    prompt = "Write a brief introduction to machine learning."
    temperature = 0.7
    user_feedback = 0

    while user_feedback < 4:
        generated_text = generate_text(prompt, temperature)
        print("\nGenerated Text:")
        print(generated_text)

        user_feedback = collect_feedback()

        if user_feedback < 4:
            # Adjust the temperature based on user feedback
            if user_feedback < 3:
                temperature += 0.1
            else:
                temperature -= 0.1

    print("Final Generated Text:")
    print(generated_text)

if __name__ == "__main__":
    main()
```

In this example, we generate text based on a prompt and ask the user to rate the response on a scale of 1 to 5. If the user's rating is less than 4, we adjust the temperature parameter and generate a new response. We continue this process until the user provides a rating of 4 or higher.

Please note that this example is relatively simple and may not cover all possible scenarios. You might need to adapt it to your specific use case, taking into account various API parameters, prompts, and other factors.

3.2. Controlling the Output

To achieve the best possible results with ChatGPT, it's important to have fine-grained control over the generated output. This allows you to not only adjust the response length, creativity, and sampling strategies, but also to tailor the generated text to your specific needs. By using a combination of various techniques and parameters, you can achieve a wide range of outputs, from short and to-the-point responses to more verbose, elaborated ones that provide more context and detail.

One of the key aspects to consider is the response length. By default, ChatGPT generates responses that are between one and three sentences long, which can be useful for quick, simple interactions. However, in certain contexts, you might need longer responses that provide more information and context. In these cases, you can adjust the length of the generated text by specifying a minimum and maximum length for the output.

Another important parameter to consider is creativity. By default, ChatGPT generates responses that are relatively conservative and safe, in order to avoid generating inappropriate or offensive content. However, in some cases, you might want to increase the creativity of the generated text, to produce more surprising or unexpected outputs. This can be done by adjusting the temperature parameter, which controls the randomness and diversity of the generated text.

Sampling strategies can also play an important role in determining the quality and relevance of the generated text. ChatGPT supports several sampling strategies, including top-k sampling, nucleus sampling, and beam search, each with its own advantages and drawbacks. By experimenting with different sampling techniques, you can find the one that best suits your needs and preferences, and generates the most accurate and relevant responses.

3.2.1. Adjusting Response Length and Creativity

ChatGPT's response length and creativity can be controlled by modifying the **max_tokens**, **temperature**, and **top_p** parameters.

max_tokens: This parameter sets the maximum number of tokens in the generated response. By increasing or decreasing this value, you can control the length of the output. The **max_tokens** parameter determines the maximum number of tokens that the model can generate in its response. A higher value will result in longer responses, while a lower value will result in shorter responses.

temperature: This parameter influences the randomness of the generated text. A higher temperature value (e.g., 1.0) will make the output more creative and diverse, while a lower value (e.g., 0.1) will make it more focused and deterministic. The **temperature** parameter controls the "creativity" of the model. A higher value will result in more surprising and diverse responses, while a lower value will result in more predictable responses.

The **top_p** parameter is used to control the diversity of the generated responses by restricting the probability mass to the top p tokens. A lower value of p will result in more conservative responses, while a higher value of p will result in more varied responses.

Here's an explanation of each parameter and an example of how to use them:

Example:

```python
import openai

openai.api_key = "your_api_key"

response = openai.Completion.create(
    engine="text-davinci-002",
    prompt="Write a short introduction to artificial intelligence.",
    max_tokens=100,  # Adjust the max_tokens value to control response length
    n=1,
    stop=None,
    temperature=0.5,  # Adjust the temperature value to control creativity
)
```

3.2.2. Temperature and Top-k Sampling

There are two primary sampling strategies for controlling the randomness of ChatGPT's output: temperature sampling and top-k sampling.

temperature: As mentioned earlier, this parameter influences the randomness of the generated text. A higher temperature value will produce more diverse and creative output, while a lower value will generate more focused and deterministic text.

top_k: This parameter controls the top-k sampling strategy that is used during the text generation process. As you may know, the model selects the next token from the top-k most likely tokens. However, by adjusting the value of **top_k**, you can control the diversity of the generated output. In other words, a lower **top_k** value will result in a more conservative and predictable output, while a higher **top_k** value will result in a more diverse and surprising output.

Therefore, it is important to experiment with different values of **top_k** to find the one that best suits your needs. Additionally, keep in mind that other parameters, such as **temperature** and **length_penalty**, may also affect the quality and diversity of the generated output, so it is important to consider them as well when fine-tuning your model.

Here's an example of using both the **temperature** and **top_k** parameters:

```
import openai

openai.api_key = "your_api_key"

response = openai.Completion.create(
    engine="text-davinci-002",
    prompt="Describe the process of photosynthesis.",
    max_tokens=150,
    n=1,
    stop=None,
    temperature=0.7,  # Adjust the temperature value
    top_k=50,  # Add the top_k parameter for top-k sampling
)
```

3.2.3. Using the stop Parameter

The **stop** parameter is a useful feature that enables you to specify a list of tokens at which the API should stop generating text. This can be especially helpful when you want to customize the output structure and ensure that the response ends at a logical point. By using the stop

parameter, you can create more complex and nuanced outputs that better reflect the context and purpose of your text.

Furthermore, the stop parameter allows you to refine your text generation process by providing more detailed control over the content and structure of your responses. With this powerful tool at your disposal, you can create more engaging, informative, and compelling content that resonates with your audience and achieves your goals.

```python
import openai

openai.api_key = "your_api_key"

response = openai.Completion.create(
    engine="text-davinci-002",
    prompt="List the benefits of exercise:",
    max_tokens=50,
    n=1,
    stop=["\n"],  # Stop generating text at the first newline character
    temperature=0.5,
)
```

3.2.4. Generating Multiple Responses with n

The **n** parameter is an extremely useful tool that enables you to generate multiple responses for a single prompt. This is particularly helpful when you want to explore different ideas or provide users with a wide variety of options.

With the n parameter, you can easily fine-tune the output to generate exactly the kind of content you need. Whether you're looking to brainstorm new ideas or provide users with a range of choices, the n parameter is an essential tool in your arsenal.

By leveraging this powerful feature, you'll be able to take your content creation to the next level and achieve remarkable results with your audience.

To generate multiple responses, simply set the **n** parameter to the desired number of responses:

```python
import openai

openai.api_key = "your_api_key"

response = openai.Completion.create(
    engine="text-davinci-002",
    prompt="What are some creative ways to reuse plastic bottles?",
    max_tokens=100,
    n=3,   # Generate 3 different responses
    stop=None,
    temperature=0.7,
)

for i, choice in enumerate(response.choices):
    print(f"Response {i + 1}:")
    print(choice.text.strip())
    print()
```

3.2.5. Prompt Engineering

Prompt engineering involves crafting the input text in such a way that it encourages the model to generate the desired output. One way to do this is by asking the model to think step-by-step. For example, you can break down a complex question into smaller sub-questions, and ask the model to answer each one in sequence.

Alternatively, you could ask the model to debate pros and cons, where it is required to weigh the advantages and disadvantages of a given topic. You could also ask the model to provide a summary before giving a detailed answer, which can help it to focus on the key points and avoid meandering. By using these techniques, you can obtain more focused and relevant responses from ChatGPT, which can be useful in a variety of settings, such as customer service, research, or entertainment.

Example:

```python
import openai

openai.api_key = "your_api_key"

# Craft the prompt to encourage a more structured response
prompt = ("Imagine you are an AI tutor. First, briefly explain the concept of "
          "machine learning. Then, describe three common types of machine learni
ng.")

response = openai.Completion.create(
    engine="text-davinci-002",
    prompt=prompt,
    max_tokens=200,
    n=1,
    stop=None,
    temperature=0.5,
)

print(response.choices[0].text.strip())
```

One way to improve the effectiveness of ChatGPT is to experiment with different prompt structures and incorporate control techniques. By doing this, you can gain greater control over the output of ChatGPT and guide it to match specific use cases and requirements.

For example, you might try using more complex prompts that include multiple questions or directions. Another approach could be to use more nuanced control techniques, such as adjusting the response length or using keyword prompts. With these strategies, you can optimize ChatGPT's output to better meet your needs and achieve your desired outcomes.

If you want expand your knowledge about Prompt Engineering, we recommend our book: **"Mastering ChatGPT and Prompt Engineering"** you can get more info about this book visiting https://books.cuantum.tech

3.3. Managing API Rate Limits

When using the ChatGPT API, it's important to be aware of and manage the API rate limits. Rate limiting is a mechanism used by APIs to control the amount of traffic sent to the server at any given time. The ChatGPT API has a limit on the number of requests that can be made in a given time period. Therefore, it's important to use the API efficiently to prevent hitting these limits and avoid any interruptions in service.

One way to manage API rate limits is by implementing caching. Caching stores the API response locally and retrieves it from the cache instead of making a new request to the server. This can help reduce the number of API requests made and, in turn, reduce the likelihood of hitting the rate limits.

Another strategy for efficient API usage is to batch requests. Instead of making multiple requests for each individual task, batching allows you to combine multiple tasks into a single request. This can also help reduce the number of API requests made, which can help prevent hitting the rate limits.

By understanding these strategies and employing them in your use of the ChatGPT API, you can ensure a smooth experience while interacting with the API, even when dealing with large amounts of data.

3.3.1. Understanding Rate Limiting

Rate limiting is a crucial mechanism used by APIs to regulate the number of requests a user can send within a specific time frame. This helps to ensure that OpenAI's services are used in a fair and optimal manner. The rate limits for ChatGPT API can vary depending on your subscription tier and can differ across various engines.

For instance, free trial users are typically provided with a rate limit of 20 requests per minute (RPM) and 40,000 tokens per minute (TPM). However, pay-as-you-go users may have different limits during their first 48 hours, with a rate limit of 60 RPM and 60,000 TPM. After this period, the limits could increase to 3,500 RPM and 90,000 TPM, which is quite a significant difference from the free trial limit.

It's important to note that while these limits may seem restrictive, they are put in place to ensure that the API remains accessible and available for all users. By limiting the number of requests that can be made, OpenAI can better manage the resources available to them and provide a smoother experience to their users.

Example:

```python
import openai
import time

openai.api_key = "your_api_key"

def generate_text(prompt):
    response = None
    while response is None:
        try:
            response = openai.Completion.create(
                engine="text-davinci-002",
                prompt=prompt,
                max_tokens=50,
                n=1,
                stop=None,
                temperature=0.5,
            )
        except openai.error.RateLimitError as e:
            print(f"Rate limit exceeded. Retrying in {e.retry_after} seconds.")
            time.sleep(e.retry_after + 1)

    return response.choices[0].text.strip()

generated_text = generate_text("What are the benefits of exercise?")
print(generated_text)
```

This example demonstrates how to handle a **RateLimitError** when calling the ChatGPT API. When the rate limit is exceeded, the program prints a message and waits for the recommended time before retrying the request.

3.3.2. Strategies for Efficient API Usage

To manage rate limits effectively and make the most of your available tokens, consider the following strategies:

Batching requests

If you have multiple prompts to process, you can use the **n** parameter to generate multiple responses in a single API call. This can help you reduce the number of requests and make better use of your available rate limit.

Additionally, batching requests can help reduce the amount of time it takes to process a large number of prompts. By sending multiple prompts in a single API call, you can streamline your workflow and improve your overall efficiency.

Furthermore, using the n parameter can also help you better manage your resources. Instead of making multiple API calls and potentially exceeding your rate limit, you can consolidate your requests and make more efficient use of your available resources. This can be especially useful if you are working with a large dataset or processing a high volume of prompts.

In summary, batching requests using the n parameter is a powerful technique for improving your workflow and making better use of your available resources. By consolidating multiple prompts into a single API call, you can save time, reduce the number of requests you need to make, and improve your overall efficiency.

Handling rate limit errors

When making requests to an API, it is important to keep in mind that the server might limit the number of requests you can make over a certain period of time. If you exceed this limit, the API will return a **429 Too Many Requests** error. In order to avoid this error, it is important to implement error handling in your code that can intelligently deal with these rate limit errors.

One way to do this is to catch the 429 Too Many Requests error and pause for an appropriate duration before retrying the request. An appropriate duration can be calculated based on the rate limit information provided by the API. Some APIs might return the duration of the rate limit

as part of the error response, while others might require you to make a separate request to retrieve this information.

Another way to deal with rate limit errors is to implement a queuing system that can throttle your requests to ensure that you don't exceed the rate limit. This can be especially useful if you need to make a large number of requests or if you are working with a slow API that requires long pauses between requests.

Regardless of the method you choose to deal with rate limit errors, it is important to make sure that your code is robust and can handle unexpected errors that might arise. By implementing error handling and rate limiting strategies, you can ensure that your code is reliable and can handle the demands of working with APIs over the long term.

Here's an example of handling rate limit errors using Python and the **time** module:

```python
import openai
import time

openai.api_key = "your_api_key"

def generate_text(prompt):
    while True:
        try:
            response = openai.Completion.create(
                engine="text-davinci-002",
                prompt=prompt,
                max_tokens=50,
                n=1,
                stop=None,
                temperature=0.5,
            )
            return response.choices[0].text.strip()
        except openai.error.RateLimitError as e:
            print(f"Rate limit exceeded. Retrying in {e.retry_after} seconds.")
            time.sleep(e.retry_after + 1)

generated_text = generate_text("What are the benefits of exercise?")
print(generated_text)
```

Here's another code example that demonstrates a simple technique to track the number of tokens used in your requests to avoid exceeding your tokens per minute (TPM) limit:

```python
import openai

openai.api_key = "your_api_key"

def count_tokens(text):
    return len(openai.Tokenizer().encode(text))

def generate_text(prompt, token_budget):
    tokens_used = count_tokens(prompt)

    if tokens_used > token_budget:
        print("Token budget exceeded.")
        return None

    response = openai.Completion.create(
        engine="text-davinci-002",
        prompt=prompt,
        max_tokens=50,
        n=1,
        stop=None,
        temperature=0.5,
    )

    tokens_used += response.choices[0].usage["total_tokens"]

    if tokens_used > token_budget:
        print("Token budget exceeded after generating response.")
        return None

    return response.choices[0].text.strip(), tokens_used

token_budget = 10000
prompt = "What are the benefits of exercise?"
generated_text, tokens_used = generate_text(prompt, token_budget)

if generated_text is not None:
    print(f"Generated text: {generated_text}")
    print(f"Tokens used: {tokens_used}")
```

In this example, we define a **token_budget** to represent the maximum number of tokens we want to use in a certain period. We then use the **count_tokens** function to count the tokens in both the prompt and the response. If the combined tokens exceed our budget, we print a message and return **None**.

Token tracking is a crucial aspect of managing your token usage, especially if you're working with TPM limits. By tracking your tokens, you can keep a closer eye on your token usage and prevent accidental overuse.

Furthermore, you can identify patterns in your token usage and optimize your code accordingly. This can help you not only stay under your TPM limit, but also improve the performance of your code. Overall, token tracking is a simple yet powerful tool that can make a big difference in your token usage and overall code quality.

3.3.3. Monitoring and Managing Token Usage

Tracking your token usage is one of the most important things you can do to ensure that you are using APIs effectively. By carefully monitoring your token usage, you can avoid the risk of encountering unexpected errors caused by exceeding rate limits, which can cause significant delays and even result in the temporary suspension of your account.

In addition, taking the time to understand how your API tokens are being used can help you to identify areas where your application may be overutilizing certain APIs, allowing you to fine-tune your usage and optimize performance.

Overall, making a habit of tracking your token usage is a simple yet effective way to ensure that you are getting the most out of your API integration and avoiding any potential issues down the line.

Here are a few tips to help you monitor and manage your token usage:

1. **Check token usage in API responses**

To ensure you have a clear understanding of your token consumption when using the ChatGPT API, the response object includes a **usage** attribute that provides detailed information on token usage. This attribute can be accessed by users to monitor their token usage, and ensure they have sufficient tokens available for their needs. By keeping a close eye on token usage, users can ensure they have the necessary resources to use the ChatGPT API effectively and efficiently, without running into any issues or limitations.

Example:

```python
import openai

openai.api_key = "your_api_key"

response = openai.Completion.create(
    engine="text-davinci-002",
    prompt="What are the benefits of exercise?",
    max_tokens=50,
    n=1,
    stop=None,
    temperature=0.5,
)

tokens_used = response.choices[0].usage["total_tokens"]
print(f"Tokens used: {tokens_used}")
```

2. **Implement token usage alerts**

One of the most important things to do when working with tokens is to set up alerts that tell you when your token usage approaches a certain threshold. By doing this, you can avoid hitting rate limits unexpectedly and proactively manage your consumption.

There are several ways to set up these alerts, including email notifications or automated messages in your code. You can also consider creating a dashboard that provides real-time information about your token usage, so you can quickly identify any potential issues.

Additionally, it's important to regularly review your token usage and adjust your alerts as needed. By taking these steps, you can ensure that your token usage is always optimized and that you have the information you need to make informed decisions about your API integration.

Example:

In this example, we'll set up an alert to notify when the total token usage reaches a certain threshold:

```python
import openai

openai.api_key = "your_api_key"

# Set a token usage threshold
token_threshold = 10000
total_tokens_used = 0

# Example prompts
prompts = ["What are the benefits of exercise?",
           "What is the difference between aerobic and anaerobic exercise?",
           "How often should one exercise?"]

for prompt in prompts:
    response = openai.Completion.create(
        engine="text-davinci-002",
        prompt=prompt,
        max_tokens=50,
        n=1,
        stop=None,
        temperature=0.5,
    )

    tokens_used = response.choices[0].usage["total_tokens"]
    total_tokens_used += tokens_used

    # Check if the total token usage exceeds the threshold
    if total_tokens_used >= token_threshold:
        print(f"Token usage threshold reached: {total_tokens_used}/{token_threshold}")

    print(f"Response: {response.choices[0].text.strip()}")
```

3. **Optimize token usage**

One thing that can really help when designing your application is taking a close look at your prompts and responses. By optimizing these to be more concise, you can help to minimize the number of tokens used in each request.

For instance, you might consider using shorter prompts or carefully setting **max_tokens** values that will limit the length of each response. This can help to ensure that your application is running smoothly and efficiently, while also making it easier for users to interact with and enjoy.

Example:

In this example, we'll demonstrate how to optimize token usage by using concise prompts and limiting response length with the **max_tokens** parameter:

```python
import openai

openai.api_key = "your_api_key"

# Example prompts
prompts = ["Benefits of exercise?",
           "Aerobic vs anaerobic exercise?",
           "How often to exercise?"]

for prompt in prompts:
    response = openai.Completion.create(
        engine="text-davinci-002",
        prompt=prompt,
        max_tokens=30,  # Limit response length
        n=1,
        stop=None,
        temperature=0.5,
    )

    print(f"Response: {response.choices[0].text.strip()}")
```

3.3.4. Handling Long Conversations

When working with ChatGPT, you may need to handle long conversations with multiple back-and-forth exchanges. To ensure that you stay within rate limits and manage tokens effectively in such scenarios, you can adopt the following strategies:

1. **Truncate or omit less relevant parts**

If a conversation exceeds the maximum token limit for a single API call (e.g., 4096 tokens for some engines), you may need to truncate or omit parts of the conversation that are less relevant. However, it is important to note that removing a message might cause the model to lose context about that message. This can lead to inaccurate responses or misunderstandings.

Therefore, it is recommended to carefully consider which parts of the conversation to truncate or omit and to do so in a way that preserves the key ideas and context of the conversation. Additionally, in some cases, it may be useful to split the conversation into multiple API calls to ensure that all the relevant information is included.

By doing so, you can ensure that the model has access to all the necessary context and can provide accurate responses.

Example:

In this example, we truncate the conversation to fit within the token limit:

```python
import openai

openai.api_key = "your_api_key"

def truncate_conversation(conversation, max_tokens):
    tokens = openai.Tokenizer().encode(conversation)
    if len(tokens) > max_tokens:
        tokens = tokens[-max_tokens:]
        truncated_conversation = openai.Tokenizer().decode(tokens)
        return truncated_conversation
    return conversation

conversation = "A long conversation that exceeds the maximum token limit..."
max_tokens = 4096

truncated_conversation = truncate_conversation(conversation, max_tokens)

response = openai.Completion.create(
    engine="text-davinci-002",
    prompt=truncated_conversation,
    max_tokens=50,
    n=1,
    stop=None,
    temperature=0.5,
)

print(response.choices[0].text.strip())
```

2. **Use continuation tokens**

To prevent exceeding token limits, it is always a good idea to break long conversations into smaller segments. By using continuation tokens, you can ensure that the conversation can be resumed where it left off, even if it crosses the token limit. When the conversation continues beyond the token limit, you can store the last few tokens from the current response and use them as a starting point for the next API call.

This way, the conversation can continue seamlessly without any interruption or loss of data. It is important to note that using continuation tokens not only helps prevent token limits but also ensures that the conversation is more manageable and easier to work with.

Example:

In this example, we demonstrate breaking a long conversation into smaller segments using continuation tokens:

```python
import openai

openai.api_key = "your_api_key"

conversation = "A long conversation that exceeds the maximum token limit..."
max_tokens_per_call = 1000
continuation_length = 5

tokens = openai.Tokenizer().encode(conversation)
num_segments = (len(tokens) + max_tokens_per_call - 1) // max_tokens_per_call

responses = []

for i in range(num_segments):
    start = i * max_tokens_per_call
    end = (i + 1) * max_tokens_per_call

    if i > 0:
        start -= continuation_length

    segment = openai.Tokenizer().decode(tokens[start:end])

    response = openai.Completion.create(
        engine="text-davinci-002",
        prompt=segment,
        max_tokens=50,
        n=1,
        stop=None,
        temperature=0.5,
    )
    responses.append(response.choices[0].text.strip())

print("\n".join(responses))
```

3. Minimize tokens in prompts

It can be beneficial to keep prompts and instructions brief when engaging in conversation in order to preserve tokens for more meaningful content. However, it is important to strike a balance between brevity and thoroughness. By providing clear and detailed prompts and instructions, you can ensure that all necessary information is conveyed and that everyone involved in the conversation is on the same page.

Additionally, taking the time to explain things in depth can help to foster a deeper understanding and promote more productive discussions. Therefore, while it is important to be concise, it is equally important to be thorough and provide enough information to facilitate effective communication.

Example:

In this example, we demonstrate how to minimize tokens in prompts:

```python
import openai

openai.api_key = "your_api_key"

concise_prompts = [
    "Benefits of exercise?",
    "Aerobic vs anaerobic?",
    "How often to exercise?",
]

for prompt in concise_prompts:
    response = openai.Completion.create(
        engine="text-davinci-002",
        prompt=prompt,
        max_tokens=50,
        n=1,
        stop=None,
        temperature=0.5,
    )

    print(f"Response: {response.choices[0].text.strip()}")
```

When it comes to managing long conversations, it's important to have a few strategies in place to ensure that you don't run into any issues with rate limits or token usage. One approach is to break up the conversation into smaller, more manageable chunks. This can be done by setting a maximum message length or by limiting the number of messages that can be sent in a given amount of time.

Another strategy is to use more efficient communication methods, such as sending condensed or summarized messages that still convey the main ideas. Additionally, it's important to be aware of any external factors that could impact the conversation, such as network connectivity or server downtime, and to plan accordingly. By implementing these strategies, you can ensure that your long conversations are both effective and efficient, without running into any unnecessary roadblocks or limitations.

3.4. Error Handling and Troubleshooting

When working with the ChatGPT API, it is important to be aware of the various errors and issues that you may encounter. Being familiar with the most common API errors and their solutions, as well as debugging and logging techniques, can help you troubleshoot issues effectively.

In this section, we will explore some of the most common errors you may encounter when using the ChatGPT API, such as rate limiting errors, authentication errors, and server errors. We will also provide detailed information on how to diagnose and resolve these errors, as well as how to configure logging to help you track down any issues.

By following the guidelines and recommendations outlined in this section, you can ensure that you are able to use the ChatGPT API effectively and efficiently, without any unnecessary downtime or delays.

3.4.1. Common API Errors and Solutions

Here are some common API errors you may encounter when using the ChatGPT API, along with their solutions:

1. **Authentication Error**

This error occurs when you provide an incorrect or expired API key. Make sure to use a valid API key and keep it secure.

API keys are an important part of application security. They are used to authenticate requests between applications and servers, ensuring that only authorized requests are processed. To

keep your API keys safe, it is important to store them securely and to avoid sharing them with unauthorized parties.

In addition to using a valid API key, there are other steps you can take to prevent authentication errors. For example, you can implement rate limiting to prevent excessive requests and ensure that your API is not overloaded. You can also monitor your API logs to detect and respond to any suspicious activity.

Example:

```python
import openai

try:
    openai.api_key = "your_api_key"
    response = openai.Completion.create(engine="text-davinci-002", prompt="Examp
le prompt")
except openai.error.AuthenticationError as e:
    print("Error: Invalid API key. Please check your key.")
```

2. **Rate Limit Error**

This error message is received when the number of requests per time period has been exceeded. In order to resolve the issue, you need to ensure that the number of requests made falls within the allowed limit.

If you have already exceeded the limit, you will need to wait for the specified time period before making more requests. It is also important to ensure that the requests are being made in a reasonable and efficient manner in order to prevent future rate limit errors.

Example:

```python
import openai
import time

openai.api_key = "your_api_key"

while True:
    try:
        response = openai.Completion.create(engine="text-davinci-002", prompt="E
xample prompt")
        print(response.choices[0].text.strip())
    except openai.error.RateLimitError as e:
        print(f"Rate limit exceeded. Retrying in {e.retry_after} seconds.")
        time.sleep(e.retry_after)
```

3. **Request Error**

This error occurs when the provided request parameters are incorrect, such as an invalid engine name or exceeding the maximum token limit. Check the API documentation to ensure your parameters are correct.

When encountering this error, it is important to double-check that the engine name provided is valid and that the maximum token limit has not been exceeded. Additionally, it may be helpful to review the API documentation for guidance on how to properly format your request parameters. By ensuring that all parameters are correct, you can minimize the risk of encountering this error and ensure that your requests are processed smoothly.

Example:

```python
import openai

openai.api_key = "your_api_key"

try:
    response = openai.Completion.create(engine="invalid-engine", prompt="Example
prompt")
except openai.error.RequestError as e:
    print("Error: Invalid request. Please check your parameters.")
```

3.4.2. Debugging and Logging Techniques

To help troubleshoot issues, you can use debugging and logging techniques to monitor the API's behavior:

1. **Print API responses**

Printing API responses can be a useful debugging tool that can help you understand the model's output and identify any issues. By printing the response, you can see the details of the output and examine it more closely. You may also be able to determine whether there are any underlying patterns or trends in the data that could be affecting the model's performance.

Furthermore, by analyzing the response, you can gain insight into the model's decision-making process and potentially identify areas for improvement. Therefore, it is highly recommended that you print API responses whenever possible, as it can provide valuable information that will help you optimize your model and ensure that it is functioning as intended.

Example:

```python
import openai

openai.api_key = "your_api_key"
response = openai.Completion.create(engine="text-davinci-002", prompt="Example prompt")

print("Full API response:")
print(response)
```

2. **Enable OpenAI's debug mode**

In order to gain more information about your API requests and responses, you can enable OpenAI's debug mode. This feature logs additional information and can be especially helpful in troubleshooting issues with your API calls. By using this mode, you will be able to access detailed reports that can provide insight into potential problems that may be affecting your system's performance. So don't hesitate to take advantage of this useful feature in your work with OpenAI's API.

Example:

```python
import openai

openai.api_key = "your_api_key"
openai.debug = True

response = openai.Completion.create(engine="text-davinci-002", prompt="Example p
rompt")
```

3. Implementation of custom logging

To have finer control over logging, it is possible to create custom logging functions to store and manage log entries related to API usage. This can be useful in situations where the default logging methods do not provide sufficient information. By customizing the logging functionality, developers can track specific events and create more detailed reports.

For example, one might use custom logging to create a log of all the unique endpoints that are accessed by the API. Alternatively, one could use custom logging to track user behavior and identify potential issues or inefficiencies.

The possibilities are endless when it comes to custom logging, and the benefits can be significant in terms of improving the overall performance and reliability of the API.

Example:

```python
import openai
import logging

logging.basicConfig(filename='chatgpt_api.log', level=logging.INFO, format='%(as
ctime)s %(levelname)s: %(message)s')

openai.api_key = "your_api_key"

def log_api_call(response):
    logging.info(f"API call: engine={response.engine}, tokens={response.choices
[0].usage['total_tokens']}")

def log_api_error(error_type, error_message):
    logging.error(f"{error_type}: {error_message}")

try:
    response = openai.Completion.create(engine="text-davinci-002", prompt="Examp
le prompt")
    log_api_call(response)
except openai.error.OpenAIError as e:
    log_api_error(type(e).__name__, str(e))
```

In this example, we have two custom logging functions: **log_api_call()** for logging successful API calls and **log_api_error()** for logging API errors. When an error occurs, the **log_api_error()** function logs the error type and message.

4. **Resource not found**

This error occurs when a specified resource, such as an engine or model, is not found. The most common reasons for this error are typos or incorrect file paths.

To resolve this issue, double-check the resource name and make sure it exists. If the resource is a file, ensure that it is in the correct location and that the file path is accurate. Additionally, check the permissions of the resource and make sure that the user has the necessary access rights to view it. If all else fails, try reinstalling the resource or contacting the vendor for assistance.

Example:

```python
import openai

openai.api_key = "your_api_key"

try:
    response = openai.Completion.create(engine="nonexistent-engine", prompt="Exa
mple prompt")
except openai.error.ResourceNotFoundError as e:
    print("Error: Resource not found. Please check the resource name.")
```

5. API connection error

This error message is usually displayed when your system is unable to establish a connection with the API server. This issue can be caused by various factors, including network problems or server-side issues. If you encounter this error, you can try implementing a retry mechanism with exponential backoff.

This means that if the first attempt fails, you can try again after a short delay. If that fails as well, you can try again after a longer delay, and so on. This will help reduce the likelihood of recurring errors and improve the overall performance of your system.

Example:

```
import openai
import time

openai.api_key = "your_api_key"

def make_request_with_retries(prompt, retries=3, backoff_factor=2):
    for i in range(retries):
        try:
            response = openai.Completion.create(engine="text-davinci-002", prompt=prompt)
            return response
        except openai.error.APIConnectionError as e:
            sleep_time = backoff_factor ** i
            print(f"API connection error. Retrying in {sleep_time} seconds.")
            time.sleep(sleep_time)
    raise Exception("Failed to connect to the API after multiple retries.")

response = make_request_with_retries("Example prompt")
```

3.4.3. Handling Errors in Asynchronous API Calls

When making asynchronous API calls, a slightly different error handling approach is required. In contrast to synchronous calls, where an error is returned immediately, asynchronous calls require you to poll the API for the completion of a task. This means that you will need to set up a loop that periodically checks whether the task has completed, and handle any errors based on the status that is returned.

This approach can be more complex than synchronous error handling, but it can be necessary for long-running tasks or for situations where performance is a concern. Additionally, as with any error handling approach, it is important to consider the specific requirements of your application and to choose an approach that is appropriate for your use case.

Check task status

When using asynchronous API calls, it is important to periodically poll the API to check the status of the task. This ensures that the task is progressing as expected and that any errors or issues are caught early on. Additionally, it can be helpful to implement a system that sends

notifications or alerts to the appropriate parties when the task has completed or encountered an issue. This can help to ensure that everyone is kept up-to-date and that any necessary actions are taken in a timely manner.

```python
import openai
import time

openai.api_key = "your_api_key"

task = openai.Completion.create(engine="text-davinci-002", prompt="Example promp
t", n=1, max_tokens=50, stop=None, return_prompt=True, echo=True, use_cache=Fals
e)

while task.status != "succeeded":
    time.sleep(5)
    task = openai.Task.retrieve(task.id)

    if task.status == "failed":
        print("Task failed. Error details:", task.error)
        break

if task.status == "succeeded":
    print("Task succeeded. Response:", task.get_result())
```

In this example, we poll the API every 5 seconds to check the status of the task. If the task has failed, we print the error details, and if the task has succeeded, we print the response.

3.4.4. Proactive Error Prevention

While handling errors is essential, taking proactive measures to prevent errors in the first place can save time and effort. Here are some tips for proactive error prevention:

1. **Validate input data**

Before sending a request to the API, it is important to validate the user inputs and data to ensure that they meet the API's requirements. This can be done by performing a series of checks and tests to verify that the data is in the correct format and that it contains the required information.

For example, you could check that the user has entered a valid email address, or that a numeric value is within a certain range. By validating the data in this way, you can help to prevent errors and ensure that the API is able to process the request as intended.

Example:

```python
import openai

openai.api_key = "your_api_key"

def validate_prompt(prompt):
    if len(prompt) > 2048:
        raise ValueError("Prompt is too long. Maximum length is 2048 characters.")
    return prompt

prompt = "A long prompt exceeding 2048 characters..."

try:
    prompt = validate_prompt(prompt)
    response = openai.Completion.create(engine="text-davinci-002", prompt=prompt)
except ValueError as e:
    print("Error:", e)
```

In this example, we have a function **validate_prompt()** to check if the prompt length exceeds the allowed limit. If it does, an error is raised.

2. Use helper libraries

One of the best ways to ease the development of your API requests is by using official or community-supported helper libraries. These libraries are designed to simplify the process by providing a range of features tailored to the specific needs of the developer.

For instance, they often include built-in error handling mechanisms, which can help you avoid common pitfalls and streamline your workflow. Moreover, they can save you time and effort by providing pre-written code that you can use to build your requests, instead of having to write the code from scratch. Overall, using helper libraries is an excellent strategy for making your API requests more efficient and less error-prone.

Example:

```python
import openai
from openai.util import prompt_tokens

openai.api_key = "your_api_key"

prompt = "Example prompt"

try:
    if prompt_tokens(prompt) <= openai.Engine.get("text-davinci-002").max_token
s:
        response = openai.Completion.create(engine="text-davinci-002", prompt=pr
ompt)
    else:
        print("Prompt is too long. Reduce the length and try again.")
except openai.error.OpenAIError as e:
    print("Error:", e)
```

In this example, we use the **prompt_tokens()** function from the **openai.util** module to count the tokens in the prompt. This helps to ensure that the prompt does not exceed the maximum tokens allowed by the engine.

3. **Monitor API usage**

To ensure that your API is working optimally, it is important to regularly monitor your API usage. This involves keeping an eye on the rate limits, response times, and error rates.

By monitoring these metrics, you can identify patterns and trends in your API usage, which can help you to proactively address any issues that may arise. In addition to monitoring these metrics, it is also important to regularly review your API documentation and test your API endpoints to ensure that they are functioning as expected.

By taking a proactive approach to monitoring and testing your API, you can help to avoid errors and ensure that your API is delivering the best possible user experience.

4. **Keep up-to-date with API changes**

One of the most important things to do when working with APIs is to stay informed about any changes or updates. This can help you ensure that your integration remains functional and that your application continues to provide value to users.

To keep up-to-date with API changes, you should regularly check the API documentation for any changes or updates. Additionally, you may want to consider subscribing to the API provider's mailing list or RSS feeds, as this can help you stay informed about any changes or updates that may affect your integration.

Finally, following the API provider's blog or social media channels is also a great way to stay informed about any changes or updates. Often, API providers will use these channels to announce changes or updates to their API, which can help you stay ahead of the curve and ensure that your integration remains up-to-date and functional.

By incorporating these proactive error prevention measures and the error handling, debugging, and logging techniques discussed earlier, you can effectively minimize issues when working with the ChatGPT API and ensure a smooth development experience.

3.5: Enhancing Output Quality

In this section, we will delve into some techniques that can be employed to enhance the quality of the output generated by ChatGPT. These techniques can be applied to better suit your specific use cases. In the following paragraphs, we will discuss some of these techniques in detail.

One of the techniques that can be employed is post-processing. This method involves applying additional processing to the output generated by ChatGPT. This can include techniques such as grammar checking, spell checking, and sentence restructuring. By applying these techniques, the quality and accuracy of the output can be significantly improved.

Another technique that can be used is content filtering and moderation. This involves identifying inappropriate or irrelevant content generated by ChatGPT and removing it from the output. This can be done by setting up rules and filters to detect such content and either remove it or flag it for further review.

By using these techniques, you can ensure that the output generated by ChatGPT is of the highest quality and is best suited to your specific use cases.

3.5.1. Post-processing Techniques

Post-processing techniques involve modifying the generated text after receiving it from the API. These techniques are an essential part of the natural language processing pipeline, and they help to improve the output by refining it, fixing inconsistencies, or applying custom formatting.

One common post-processing technique is to use named entity recognition to identify and label entities such as people, places, and organizations in the text. Another technique is to use sentiment analysis to determine the emotional tone of the text and adjust it accordingly.

Additionally, post-processing techniques can be used to add or remove information from the text, such as adding background information or removing irrelevant details. Overall, post-processing techniques play a crucial role in ensuring that the output generated by NLP models is accurate, coherent, and easy to understand. Here are a few examples:

Truncating responses

When you are working with large datasets, it is often necessary to limit the amount of data that is returned in your query response for performance reasons. This can be accomplished by truncating the response to a specific length or by removing any extra information that is not relevant to your particular use case.

However, it is important to keep in mind that this approach can potentially impact the accuracy of your results, especially if the removed data contains important information that is required for your analysis. Therefore, it is important to carefully consider the trade-offs between performance and accuracy when deciding how to handle large datasets in your queries.

Example:

```
response_text = response.choices[0].text
truncated_text = response_text[:50]
print(truncated_text)
```

Removing unwanted characters

One useful technique for improving the quality of generated text is to use regular expressions to remove or replace unwanted characters or patterns. This can be especially helpful when

working with large datasets or when trying to clean up text that has been generated through automated processes.

By identifying and removing these unwanted characters, you can ensure that the resulting text is more readable and easier to work with. Additionally, regular expressions can be used to reformat text in a variety of ways, such as changing the case of words or adding punctuation where it is missing. Overall, using regular expressions to clean and format generated text is an essential step in the data processing pipeline.

Example:

```python
import re

response_text = response.choices[0].text
clean_text = re.sub(r'\s+', ' ', response_text).strip()
print(clean_text)
```

Implementing custom formatting

One of the most useful features of this tool is the ability to apply custom formatting to your output. This means you can add bullet points, change the font size or color, or even convert your text to uppercase.

By taking advantage of this feature, you can make your content more visually appealing and easier to read. In addition, custom formatting can help you emphasize important points and make them stand out from the rest of your text. So next time you use this tool, don't forget to experiment with custom formatting and see how it can enhance your content.

```python
response_text = response.choices[0].text
formatted_text = "- " + response_text.upper()
print(formatted_text)
```

3.5.2. Implementing Content Filters and Moderation

Content filtering and moderation is a crucial aspect of ensuring that your content is appropriate for your intended audience. By implementing content filtering and moderation, you can help to ensure that the generated text aligns with your desired content guidelines or restrictions. This can include various measures such as keyword filtering, image recognition, and manual moderation.

Additionally, content filtering and moderation can help to improve your brand reputation and prevent any potential legal issues that may arise from inappropriate content. So if you want to ensure that your content is of the highest quality, it's important to implement a comprehensive content filtering and moderation strategy. Here are a few examples:

Filtering out profanity

When generating text, it's important to keep in mind the potential for generating inappropriate content. One way to avoid this is by filtering out profanity. Third-party libraries or custom functions can be utilized to accomplish this. It's important to carefully consider the chosen method for filtering, as some may be more effective than others.

Additionally, it's important to consider the potential impact on performance, as some methods may be more resource-intensive than others. Overall, it's crucial to take steps to ensure that generated content is appropriate for the intended audience.

Example:

```python
from profanity_filter import ProfanityFilter

pf = ProfanityFilter()

response_text = response.choices[0].text
censored_text = pf.censor(response_text)
print(censored_text)
```

Using a custom moderation function

When generating text, it is important to ensure that it meets your specific content requirements. One way to do this is by implementing a custom function that moderates the generated text. This function can take into account factors such as tone, length, and keyword usage to ensure that the text is suitable for your needs.

Additionally, by incorporating a custom function, you have greater control over the final output, allowing you to fine-tune the text to better align with your goals and objectives. So, if you find that the generated text is not quite hitting the mark, consider implementing a custom function to help bring it in line with your requirements.

Example:

```python
def custom_moderation(text):
    forbidden_words = ["word1", "word2", "word3"]
    if any(word in text.lower() for word in forbidden_words):
        return False
    return True

response_text = response.choices[0].text

if custom_moderation(response_text):
    print(response_text)
else:
    print("Generated text violates content guidelines.")
```

3.5.3. Evaluating Output Quality with Metrics

Evaluating the quality of the generated text using metrics can help you identify areas for improvement and guide your adjustments. One way to do this is by utilizing automated tools that can provide insight into the readability and coherence of the text.

Additionally, you can also gather feedback from human evaluators to gain a more nuanced understanding of the text's strengths and weaknesses. By incorporating both quantitative and qualitative measures, you can ensure that your text meets the needs of your audience and effectively communicates your message.

Commonly used metrics include:

BLEU (Bilingual Evaluation Understudy)

BLEU is a metric for evaluating the similarity between generated text and a reference text. It has been widely used in the field of natural language processing, particularly in machine translation tasks, although it can be applied to any text generation problem. BLEU was proposed as a more objective measure of translation quality than human evaluation, which is subjective and time-consuming.

It works by comparing the n-grams (contiguous sequences of words) in the generated text to those in the reference text, and assigning a score based on the overlap. BLEU has several variants, such as smoothed BLEU, which adjusts for the fact that some n-grams may not occur in the reference text. Despite its widespread use, BLEU has been criticized for its limitations, such as its inability to capture the semantic content of the text or to distinguish between grammatically correct but semantically meaningless sentences and grammatically incorrect but semantically meaningful sentences.

Example:

Calculating BLEU score using the **nltk** library:

```python
from nltk.translate.bleu_score import sentence_bleu

reference = ["This is a sample reference sentence.".split()]
candidate = "This is a generated candidate sentence.".split()

bleu_score = sentence_bleu(reference, candidate)
print("BLEU Score:", bleu_score)
```

ROUGE (Recall-Oriented Understudy for Gisting Evaluation)

ROUGE is a set of metrics commonly used in natural language processing, particularly in the evaluation of text summaries. It is designed to compare the quality of machine-generated summaries to reference summaries written by humans.

However, its use is not limited to text summarization and has been applied to other text generation tasks, such as paraphrasing. ROUGE is based on the calculation of recall, precision, and F-measure scores, which are widely used in information retrieval.

The scores are calculated by comparing the n-gram overlap between the system-generated summary and the reference summary. ROUGE has been used extensively in research and is considered a standard evaluation metric in the field of natural language processing.

Example:

Calculating ROUGE score using the **rouge** library:

First, install the library with:

```
pip install rouge
```

Then, you can use the following code to calculate ROUGE scores:

```
from rouge import Rouge

reference = "This is a sample reference text."
candidate = "This is a generated candidate text."

rouge = Rouge()
rouge_scores = rouge.get_scores(candidate, reference, avg=True)

print("ROUGE Scores:", rouge_scores)
```

Perplexity

Perplexity is a widely used metric in natural language processing that measures the quality of language models. It evaluates how well a model can predict the next token in a given sequence of words. A lower perplexity score is an indication of better predictive performance, as the model can more accurately predict the next word in a sequence.

This is important in various applications, including speech recognition, machine translation, and text generation. Therefore, improving perplexity scores is a key goal of language modelers as they strive to build more accurate and efficient models.

Example:

Calculating Perplexity using a pre-trained GPT-4 model:

To calculate perplexity, you'll need to have a pre-trained GPT-4 model and tokenizer available. Here's an example using the Hugging Face Transformers library:

First, install the library with:

```
pip install transformers
```

Then, you can use the following code to calculate perplexity:

```python
import torch
from transformers import GPT4LMHeadModel, GPT4Tokenizer

model_name = "gpt4-model"  # Replace with the actual model name
tokenizer = GPT4Tokenizer.from_pretrained(model_name)
model = GPT4LMHeadModel.from_pretrained(model_name)

def calculate_perplexity(text):
    input_ids = tokenizer.encode(text, return_tensors="pt")
    with torch.no_grad():
        outputs = model(input_ids, labels=input_ids)
    loss = outputs.loss
    perplexity = torch.exp(loss)
    return perplexity.item()

text = "This is a sample text to calculate perplexity."
perplexity = calculate_perplexity(text)
print("Perplexity:", perplexity)
```

Please note that the code provided assumes the availability of a GPT-4 model and tokenizer. Replace **gpt4-model** with the actual model name or the path to your GPT-4 model.

While these metrics can provide useful insights, it's essential to remember that they do not always align with human perception of quality. Use them as a reference, but make sure to consider human evaluation for a comprehensive understanding of the output quality.

3.5.4. Iteratively Fine-tuning the Model

It is important to remember that machine learning models are not static and require constant attention. Continuously fine-tuning your model based on feedback and newly available data can help improve output quality.

However, it is also important to consider the potential downsides of overfitting your model to the training data. One way to avoid this is by regularly testing your model on new data to ensure that it is still performing well.

Additionally, exploring new features or data sources can help to further improve the accuracy and reliability of your model. All of these factors should be taken into account when developing and refining a machine learning model.Iterative fine-tuning involves:

Collecting user feedback

One important aspect to consider when generating text is to encourage users to give feedback on the output. It is essential to create an open and welcoming environment where users can feel comfortable pointing out issues or suggesting improvements to the generated text. This can be done by providing clear instructions on how to give feedback, or by setting up a system where users can easily report any problems they encounter.

Additionally, it is crucial to take user feedback seriously and make changes accordingly to improve the quality of the generated text. By doing so, we can create a better user experience and ensure that the generated text meets the needs and expectations of our users.

Example:

Here's an example of how to collect user feedback for a conversation with a ChatGPT model using Python:

```python
import json
import requests

# Function to interact with ChatGPT API
def chatgpt_request(prompt, access_token):
    headers = {
        "Authorization": f"Bearer {access_token}",
        "Content-Type": "application/json"
    }

    data = json.dumps({
        "prompt": prompt,
        "max_tokens": 50
    })

    response = requests.post("https://api.openai.com/v1/engines/davinci-codex/co
mpletions", headers=headers, data=data)
    response_json = response.json()

    if response.status_code == 200:
        generated_text = response_json["choices"][0]["text"].strip()
        return generated_text
    else:
        raise Exception(f"ChatGPT API returned an error: {response_json['erro
r']}")

# Function to collect user feedback
def collect_user_feedback(prompt, generated_text):
    print(f"Input: {prompt}")
    print(f"Generated Text: {generated_text}")

    feedback = input("Please provide your feedback on the generated text: ")
    return feedback

# Example usage
access_token = "your_access_token"  # Replace with your actual API access token
prompt = "What is the capital of France?"
generated_text = chatgpt_request(prompt, access_token)

feedback = collect_user_feedback(prompt, generated_text)
print(f"User feedback: {feedback}")
```

This code example demonstrates how to interact with the ChatGPT API and collect user feedback on the generated text. The **chatgpt_request** function sends a prompt to the ChatGPT API and returns the generated text. The **collect_user_feedback** function displays the input prompt and generated text to the user and collects their feedback.

Please replace **"your_access_token"** with your actual API access token, and modify the API URL and headers as needed to match the specific API endpoint you are using. This example uses the OpenAI API; however, you may need to adjust the URL and headers for your specific ChatGPT instance.

Incorporating new data

One of the most important things you can do to keep your machine learning models up-to-date and accurate is to regularly update your training dataset with new examples. This is particularly important because as your model continues to learn and make predictions, new patterns and trends in the data will inevitably emerge.

By incorporating these new examples into your training dataset, you can help ensure that your model stays ahead of the curve and is able to accurately predict future outcomes. Additionally, it's important to periodically remove outdated or irrelevant data from your training dataset to help improve the accuracy of your model.

This can be done by carefully analyzing your existing dataset and identifying any examples that are no longer relevant or useful for training your model. By taking these steps to regularly update and maintain your training dataset, you can help ensure that your machine learning models are always working at their best and delivering the most accurate results possible.

Example:

Assuming you have a dataset in a CSV file with columns "prompt" and "response", you can read and preprocess the data using the following code:

```python
import pandas as pd
from transformers import GPT4Tokenizer

model_name = "gpt4-model"  # Replace with the actual model name
tokenizer = GPT4Tokenizer.from_pretrained(model_name)

def preprocess_data(file_path):
    data = pd.read_csv(file_path)
    input_texts = data["prompt"].tolist()
    target_texts = data["response"].tolist()
    input_ids = tokenizer(input_texts, return_tensors="pt", padding=True, trunca
tion=True)["input_ids"]
    labels = tokenizer(target_texts, return_tensors="pt", padding=True, truncati
on=True)["input_ids"]
    return input_ids, labels

file_path = "new_data.csv"
input_ids, labels = preprocess_data(file_path)
```

Adjusting hyperparameters

One thing you can do during the fine-tuning process is to experiment with different hyperparameters. This allows you to find the optimal configuration for your use case. For instance, you could try adjusting the learning rate, batch size, or number of epochs to see how they affect the performance of your model.

By doing so, you can gain a deeper understanding of the impact that each hyperparameter has on your results, which can help you make more informed decisions about how to fine-tune your model in the future.

Example:

Here's an example of adjusting hyperparameters during model fine-tuning using the Hugging Face Transformers library:

```python
from transformers import GPT4LMHeadModel, GPT4Tokenizer, Trainer, TrainingArgume
nts

# Load the model, tokenizer, and data
model = GPT4LMHeadModel.from_pretrained(model_name)
tokenizer = GPT4Tokenizer.from_pretrained(model_name)

input_ids, labels = preprocess_data(file_path)

# Create a PyTorch dataset
from torch.utils.data import Dataset

class CustomDataset(Dataset):
    def __init__(self, input_ids, labels):
        self.input_ids = input_ids
        self.labels = labels

    def __getitem__(self, idx):
        return {"input_ids": self.input_ids[idx], "labels": self.labels[idx]}

    def __len__(self):
        return len(self.input_ids)

train_dataset = CustomDataset(input_ids, labels)

# Define training arguments
training_args = TrainingArguments(
    output_dir="./outputs",
    overwrite_output_dir=True,
    num_train_epochs=3,
    per_device_train_batch_size=4,
    learning_rate=5e-5,
    weight_decay=0.01,
    save_steps=100,
    save_total_limit=2,
)

# Create a Trainer instance
trainer = Trainer(
    model=model,
    args=training_args,
    train_dataset=train_dataset,
)

# Fine-tune the model
trainer.train()

# Save the fine-tuned model
trainer.save_model("./outputs")
```

Repeating the process:

It is important to note that iteration is key to the fine-tuning process. By regularly revisiting the process and monitoring its performance, you can make the necessary adjustments to ensure that it remains effective over time.

This will help you to stay on track and achieve your goals, while also allowing you to adapt to changing circumstances as needed. Remember that the fine-tuning process is an ongoing one, and that it requires your attention and effort in order to be successful.

Example:

To repeat the process of incorporating new data, adjusting hyperparameters, and fine-tuning the model, you can create a loop that iterates through different versions of your dataset and adjusts hyperparameters accordingly. You can also include monitoring and evaluation steps to assess the model's performance during each iteration.

```
# Replace `gpt4-model` with the actual model name or the path to your GPT-4 mode
l.
model_name = "gpt4-model"

file_paths = ["new_data_v1.csv", "new_data_v2.csv", "new_data_v3.csv"]

for file_path in file_paths:
    # Preprocess the data
    input_ids, labels = preprocess_data(file_path)
    train_dataset = CustomDataset(input_ids, labels)

    # Update the train_dataset in the Trainer instance
    trainer.train_dataset = train_dataset

    # Fine-tune the model
    trainer.train()

    # Save the fine-tuned model
    trainer.save_model(f"./outputs/{file_path.split('.')[0]}")

    # Evaluate the model performance and adjust hyperparameters as needed
    # ...
```

This code will save each fine-tuned model in a separate output directory based on the corresponding input data file's name (e.g., "outputs/new_data_v1" for "new_data_v1.csv").

Remember that these code examples assume you have a pre-trained GPT-4 model and tokenizer, and you have installed the Hugging Face Transformers library. Replace **gpt4-model** with the actual model name or the path to your GPT-4 model.

By incorporating these additional strategies, you can further enhance the quality of the output generated by ChatGPT and make it more suitable for your specific needs.

Chapter 3 Conclusion

In conclusion, this chapter has taken a deep dive into the basic usage of the ChatGPT API, providing readers with the necessary knowledge and tools to get started with their own projects. The discussion has spanned a range of topics, from sending text prompts and controlling output, to managing API rate limits and handling errors, as well as enhancing output quality. With each topic, we have explored the nuances and provided detailed explanations along with relevant code examples to help readers apply the concepts in practice.

Starting with sending text prompts, we discussed how to format prompts for desired output and experiment with different prompt types. We highlighted the importance of understanding the various prompt structures to better control the model's responses, making it more suitable for diverse applications.

Next, we delved into controlling the output of ChatGPT API. We introduced methods to adjust response length and creativity, and explored key concepts like temperature and top-k sampling. These techniques enable users to fine-tune the generated text based on their specific requirements, striking the right balance between creativity and relevance.

We then discussed managing API rate limits, an essential aspect of working with APIs, especially in production environments. Understanding rate limiting is crucial to ensure efficient and uninterrupted use of the API. We also shared strategies for efficient API usage, such as caching, batching, and prioritizing requests, allowing developers to optimize their applications and stay within rate limits.

Error handling and troubleshooting were covered in detail, as well. We listed common API errors and their solutions, helping developers identify and resolve issues quickly. Additionally, we introduced debugging and logging techniques, enabling readers to monitor and maintain their applications effectively.

Finally, we explored techniques to enhance the output quality of ChatGPT-generated text. Post-processing techniques, content filters, and moderation were discussed to ensure the generated content is relevant, accurate, and adheres to the desired guidelines. This section also touched upon ways to improve the model's performance by incorporating user feedback and adjusting hyperparameters iteratively.

Throughout the chapter, code examples were provided to illustrate the concepts and enable readers to implement the techniques in their own projects. These examples serve as a foundation for developers to build upon and adapt to their specific use cases.

In summary, this chapter has laid a solid foundation for working with the ChatGPT API, equipping developers with the knowledge and tools required to create effective and efficient applications using ChatGPT. The topics discussed in this chapter are critical for anyone looking to leverage the power of GPT-4 for various tasks and industries. With this information in hand, readers are now prepared to advance to more complex and specialized topics in the following chapters, where we will explore fine-tuning, integration with other systems, and real-world applications across various industries.

Chapter 4 - Advanced API Features

Welcome to the fourth chapter of our journey through the ChatGPT API. In the previous chapter, we covered the basics of using the API, and now we're ready to take things to the next level. This chapter will explore some of the more advanced features of the ChatGPT API, which will allow you to create even more powerful applications.

In this chapter, we will focus on four key areas: context and message handling, conditional statements, external data sources, and multilingual support. These features will enable you to create advanced applications that can provide more relevant and tailored responses to your users.

Firstly, we'll discuss context and message handling. When working with conversational AI models like ChatGPT, it's essential to maintain the context of the conversation to ensure coherent and relevant responses. We will explore how to provide context using the Hugging Face Transformers library and how to manage user inputs and model responses effectively.

Secondly, we'll delve into conditional statements, which allow you to create more complex and dynamic conversations. We will show you how to use if-else statements to implement conditional logic in your applications.

Thirdly, we will look at incorporating external data sources into your ChatGPT application. This will enable you to provide more accurate and up-to-date information to your users, making your application even more valuable.

Finally, we will explore how to use the ChatGPT API for multilingual support. In today's globalized world, providing multilingual support is becoming increasingly important. We will show you how to use the API to support multiple languages in your application.

By mastering these advanced features, you will be able to create truly sophisticated applications powered by ChatGPT. So let's get started and take your ChatGPT application to the next level!

4.1. Context and Message Handling

In Python, context refers to the state of a program at a given point in time. It includes things like variables, objects, and other data structures that are currently in memory. Context is important because it determines how a program behaves and what actions it can take.

Message handling refers to the process of receiving and processing messages within a program. In the context of ChatGPT API, message handling involves receiving messages from users, processing them, and generating responses. This is typically done using natural language processing (NLP) techniques to understand the user's intent and generate an appropriate response.

To handle messages in ChatGPT API, you can use the API's built-in message-handling functions or write your own custom functions. These functions typically involve parsing the user's message, generating a response, and sending the response back to the user.

Overall, context and message handling are important concepts in both Python and ChatGPT API, as they determine how programs behave and how users interact with them.

4.1.1. Maintaining Conversation Context

When working with conversational AI models such as ChatGPT, it is essential to maintain the context of the conversation to ensure that responses are both coherent and relevant. To do so, the model relies on the information it has gathered from previous messages or turns in the conversation; this information is referred to as "context." Context can take many forms, such as the subject of the conversation, the person the model is speaking to, or the user's stated preferences.

In the case of ChatGPT, context is provided through a series of messages supplied as input. These messages are carefully crafted to include all relevant information from previous turns in the conversation, allowing the model to understand the user's intent and respond appropriately. By maintaining context in this way, ChatGPT is able to generate more accurate and helpful responses, leading to a better user experience overall.

Here's an example of how to provide context using the Hugging Face Transformers library:

```python
from transformers import GPT2LMHeadModel, GPT2Tokenizer

tokenizer = GPT2Tokenizer.from_pretrained("gpt2")
model = GPT2LMHeadModel.from_pretrained("gpt2")

# Replace these example messages with your own conversation
messages = [
    {"role": "system", "content": "You are a helpful assistant."},
    {"role": "user", "content": "What's the weather like today?"},
    {"role": "assistant", "content": "The weather today is sunny with a high of
25°C."},
    {"role": "user", "content": "How about tomorrow?"}
]

# Concatenate the conversation messages
conversation = ""
for message in messages:
    conversation += f"{message['role']}:{message['content']}\n"

# Generate a response
input_ids = tokenizer.encode(conversation, return_tensors="pt")
output = model.generate(input_ids, max_length=250, pad_token_id=tokenizer.eos_to
ken_id)
response = tokenizer.decode(output[:, input_ids.shape[-1]:][0], skip_special_tok
ens=True)

print(response)
```

This code demonstrates how to concatenate messages into a single conversation string and pass it as input to the model to maintain context.

4.1.2. Managing User Inputs and Model Responses

When building an application with ChatGPT, it is important to ensure a smooth user experience by managing user inputs and model responses effectively. One effective way to achieve this is by storing the conversation history and updating it with each new user input and model response.

This approach has the added benefit of allowing the application to personalize its responses based on the user's previous inputs, thereby creating a more engaging and interactive

experience. In addition, by analyzing the conversation history, developers can gain valuable insights into user behavior and preferences, which can inform future updates and improvements to the application.

Therefore, it is highly recommended that developers implement a conversation history feature when building applications with ChatGPT.

Example:

Here's an example of managing user inputs and model responses:

```python
def add_message(conversation, role, content):
    conversation.append({"role": role, "content": content})
    return conversation

def generate_response(conversation, tokenizer, model):
    conversation_text = ""
    for message in conversation:
        conversation_text += f"{message['role']}:{message['content']}\n"

    input_ids = tokenizer.encode(conversation_text, return_tensors="pt")
    output = model.generate(input_ids, max_length=250, pad_token_id=tokenizer.eo
s_token_id)
    response = tokenizer.decode(output[:, input_ids.shape[-1]:][0], skip_special
_tokens=True)

    return response

# Example usage
conversation = [{"role": "system", "content": "You are a helpful assistant."}]
user_input = "What's the weather like today?"

conversation = add_message(conversation, "user", user_input)
response = generate_response(conversation, tokenizer, model)
conversation = add_message(conversation, "assistant", response)

print(conversation)
```

In this example, we define two functions: **add_message** to add a message to the conversation and **generate_response** to generate a model response based on the conversation history. These functions help manage user inputs and model responses effectively.

By using these functions, you can seamlessly manage the conversation flow and ensure that the context is preserved throughout the interaction with the user. This approach helps maintain the model's understanding of the conversation, resulting in more coherent and accurate responses.

In addition to the examples provided, you can also consider the following points to further enhance the management of user inputs and model responses in your application:

Sanitizing user inputs

One important step to consider before feeding user inputs into the model is sanitizing the text. This involves removing unwanted characters, emojis, or symbols that may be present in the text. Sanitization has been shown to improve the quality of the model's responses by reducing the potential for confusion.

For instance, imagine a user inputs a message with an emoji, such as a smiley face, at the end. Without sanitization, the model may interpret this as a signal to respond in a positive manner, even if the message itself is negative in tone. Sanitization can help prevent these types of errors from occurring and ensure that the model produces accurate and appropriate responses. In addition to improving model performance, sanitization can also have broader implications for user experience and engagement.

By ensuring that the model understands user inputs more accurately, sanitization can help increase user trust in the system and encourage greater use and adoption over time.

Limiting conversation length

Due to the token limitations of ChatGPT, excessively long conversations may cause truncation or removal of important context. To avoid this, there are several strategies that can be used to limit the length of the conversation.

One way is to shorten older messages that may no longer be relevant to the current discussion. Another approach is to remove less relevant parts of the conversation that may not be contributing to the overall topic. In any case, it is important to ensure that the conversation remains focused on the key ideas and that any important contextual information is preserved.

By limiting the length of the conversation in this way, you can help ensure that all participants are able to fully engage in the discussion and that important insights are not lost due to truncation or other limitations.

Implementing a cache

To further optimize your application's performance and reduce API usage, you can implement caching mechanisms to store not only recent model responses but also previous user inputs. Caching can be particularly useful in scenarios where your application receives a large number of similar or repeated user queries, allowing your application to return results more quickly by retrieving previously processed data rather than making the same API calls repeatedly.

Additionally, implementing a cache can also help reduce the impact of network latency and connection disruptions, as your application can continue to operate offline or with limited connectivity by retrieving cached data instead of relying solely on API responses.

Handling multiple users

If your application supports multiple users, you can maintain separate conversation contexts for each user. This ensures that the model provides personalized and relevant responses to each individual user. One way to enhance the user experience is to allow users to customize their own conversation settings. For instance, users could choose a preferred language or tone of voice that they want the chatbot to use.

Additionally, the chatbot could keep track of the user's preferences and adapt its responses accordingly. This allows the chatbot to build a stronger relationship with the user and make the interaction more engaging. Furthermore, the chatbot could offer personalized recommendations based on the user's history and preferences.

For example, if the user frequently asks about pizza, the chatbot could suggest nearby pizza places or offer discounts for pizza delivery. This feature not only provides value to the user but also encourages them to continue using the chatbot.

By incorporating these additional techniques, you can further improve the effectiveness and user experience of your ChatGPT-powered application.

4.1.3. Conversation Tokens and Model Limits

ChatGPT models are designed to be efficient and effective for processing text. However, there are token limits that must be considered when processing longer conversations. These token

limits restrict the number of tokens that can be processed in a single request, which can impact the effectiveness of the model. In order to ensure that the model is able to effectively process longer conversations, it is important to carefully consider these token limits and adjust the conversation accordingly.

This might involve breaking longer conversations into smaller segments that can be processed more easily by the model, or making use of other techniques to ensure that the conversation remains within the token limits. Despite these limitations, ChatGPT models remain a powerful tool for processing text and generating meaningful responses.

By carefully managing token limits and working to optimize the conversation, it is possible to achieve excellent results with these models.Strategies for handling conversations that exceed model limits include:

Truncation

Truncating conversations is a technique used to reduce the length of a conversation to fit within the model's token limit. This technique can be useful in certain situations, but it may result in losing important context from earlier parts of the conversation.

For instance, if a conversation is truncated too much, it may be difficult to understand the overall meaning or intent of the conversation. Therefore, it is important to use this technique judiciously and to ensure that the key ideas are still preserved after truncation.

Additionally, it may be helpful to provide a summary or recap of the earlier parts of the conversation to provide context for the truncated portion.

Summarization

Summarize longer conversation segments to preserve essential information while reducing the overall token count. In order to achieve this, one can use techniques such as abstraction, generalization and paraphrasing.

Abstraction involves omitting less important details and focusing on the main points of the conversation. Generalization involves summarizing the conversation into broader concepts that cover multiple aspects. Paraphrasing involves rephrasing the conversation in a simpler manner without changing the meaning.

Omitting less relevant information

One way to ensure that important context is maintained and that your text fits within the token limit is to selectively remove less relevant parts of the conversation. However, it is important to be careful when doing so, as removing too much information can change the meaning of the conversation. It is also helpful to provide a summary of the removed information to ensure that the context is not lost. By doing so, you can maintain the necessary context while still adhering to the token limit.

Example:

For token counting, you can use the **tokenizer** provided by the Transformers library:

```python
from transformers import GPT2Tokenizer

tokenizer = GPT2Tokenizer.from_pretrained("gpt2")

def count_tokens(text):
    tokens = tokenizer.encode(text)
    return len(tokens)

conversation = "some long conversation text ..."
token_count = count_tokens(conversation)
print("Token count:", token_count)
```

4.1.4. Multi-turn Conversations and Context Forgetting

Context forgetting can be a significant challenge in multi-turn conversations. As the conversation progresses, the model may lose track of important context or relevant information, which can lead to misunderstandings and a breakdown in communication.

In order to mitigate this issue, it is important to develop strategies that help the model retain important information from previous turns. One approach is to use memory networks, which can store information from previous turns and retrieve it as needed. Another approach is to incorporate context-aware attention mechanisms, which can help the model focus on the most relevant information in the current turn while still taking previous context into account.

By using these techniques, we can improve the ability of models to handle multi-turn conversations and maintain a coherent dialogue with users.To reduce context forgetting, you can consider the following techniques:

Reiterating important information

One of the most effective ways to ensure that critical information is understood and remembered is to repeat it throughout the conversation. This can be done by rephrasing the information in different ways or by emphasizing it in subsequent conversation turns. By doing so, the listener is more likely to retain the information and understand its significance.

In addition, reiteration can help to reinforce the context of the conversation and ensure that all parties are on the same page. Thus, it is important to make use of this technique when communicating important information.

External memory mechanisms

External memory mechanisms can be implemented to store essential information and refer to it when necessary. This helps maintain context consistency throughout the conversation, which can be particularly important in long and complex exchanges. By utilizing external memory mechanisms, you can ensure that key points and relevant details are not forgotten or overlooked.

Additionally, these mechanisms can help facilitate more effective communication between parties, as they allow for a more seamless transition between topics. Overall, the use of external memory mechanisms can be a valuable tool for improving communication and ensuring that important information is not lost or forgotten during conversations.

Example:

For reiterating important information, you can append the essential context at the beginning of each conversation turn:

```
important_info = "User is looking for a pizza restaurant in New York City."

user_input = "Can you recommend a place?"
prompt = f"{important_info} {user_input}"
# Send the prompt to ChatGPT for a response
```

4.1.5. Conversational AI Metrics

Evaluating the performance of conversational AI systems is a crucial aspect of optimizing user experiences. These systems have become increasingly popular in recent years, with businesses incorporating them into their customer service strategies.

As such, it is important to ensure that the AI is performing at its best, providing users with the highest quality experience possible. One way to achieve this is by analyzing the system's performance metrics, such as accuracy and response time. Additionally, user feedback can be invaluable in improving the AI's performance. By gathering feedback from users, businesses can gain insight into how the AI is perceived and identify areas that may need improvement.

Overall, continuous evaluation and improvement of conversational AI systems is key to ensuring a positive user experience and maintaining customer satisfaction.

Some metrics to consider include:

Consistency

AI systems should be able to provide consistent responses across different user inputs and conversation turns. This means that the system should be able to provide the same response to similar or repeated prompts. Ensuring consistency is important for building trust with users and making sure that the system is reliable.

One way to measure consistency is to compare the similarity of responses to different prompts. By doing so, we can identify any areas where the system may be inconsistent and work to improve it.

Relevance

One important aspect of assessing the model's responses is to evaluate their relevance to the user's inputs. This can be done using various techniques, such as cosine similarity or other text similarity algorithms. These approaches aim to measure the degree of similarity between the user's inputs and the model's responses, and therefore provide a quantitative measure of relevance.

By using these techniques, we can gain a deeper understanding of how well the model is able to understand and respond to user queries, and identify areas for improvement. Additionally, it is important to consider the context of the user's inputs when evaluating relevance. For example, if the user is asking a question about a specific topic, it may be more relevant to

provide a response that is focused on that topic, even if it is not the most similar to the user's input overall.

Thus, it is important to take a holistic approach to assessing relevance, considering both the similarity of the model's responses to the user's inputs, as well as the broader context in which those inputs are given.

Engagement

Evaluating the level of user engagement with the AI system, based on factors like conversation length, response time, and user satisfaction ratings. It is important to measure user engagement in order to improve the AI system's ability to interact with users and provide relevant information.

One way to increase user engagement is to personalize the system's responses to each user based on their interests and preferences. Another way is to make the conversation more interactive and engaging by incorporating multimedia elements such as images, videos, and audio. Additionally, providing users with incentives such as rewards or discounts can also increase their engagement and encourage them to use the AI system more frequently.

By continuously monitoring and improving user engagement, the AI system can become more effective and valuable for users.

To measure these metrics, you can collect user feedback, use automated evaluation techniques, or employ a combination of both.

Example:

For measuring text similarity using cosine similarity, you can use the **SentenceTransformer** library:

```
from sentence_transformers import SentenceTransformer
from sklearn.metrics.pairwise import cosine_similarity

model = SentenceTransformer('paraphrase-MiniLM-L6-v2')

def get_similarity(text1, text2):
    embeddings = model.encode([text1, text2])
    similarity = cosine_similarity(embeddings[0].reshape(1, -1), embeddings[1].r
eshape(1, -1))
    return similarity[0][0]

text1 = "The pizza restaurant is located in Manhattan."
text2 = "The pizzeria is in Manhattan."

similarity = get_similarity(text1, text2)
print("Similarity:", similarity)
```

In summary, there are several key challenges to effectively utilizing conversation tokens and addressing model limits, context forgetting, and performance evaluation. To tackle these challenges, it is important to combine various examples and techniques.

For instance, one can consider utilizing multiple models with different strengths and weaknesses to ensure that the conversation remains engaging and on-topic. Additionally, it may be useful to incorporate context-specific information into the conversation, such as the user's preferences or previous interactions.

Furthermore, conducting regular performance evaluations and making necessary adjustments can help ensure that the conversation remains effective over time. By combining these and other strategies, it is possible to effectively address the challenges posed by conversation tokens and model limits, context forgetting, and performance evaluation while maintaining engaging and effective conversations.

4.2. User Attributes and Personalization

Incorporating user attributes into your ChatGPT application can greatly enhance the user experience. By understanding the user's preferences and profile data, ChatGPT can give personalized and relevant responses to each user. This not only helps the user receive the information they need but can also lead to increased engagement with the application.

To start, you can capture basic user information such as age, gender, and location. This information can be used to provide location-specific recommendations or gender-specific language in the responses. Additionally, you can capture user preferences such as favorite topics or preferred communication style. This information can be used to tailor the output of the model and ensure that the user is receiving information that they find interesting and engaging.

Another way to enhance the user experience is to track user behavior within the application. By analyzing how users interact with the application, you can identify areas where users may be struggling or where they are finding the most value. This can help you optimize the application and ensure that users are receiving the information they need in the most effective way possible.

Incorporating user attributes into your ChatGPT application requires effort and time, but can lead to a significant improvement in the user experience. By understanding the needs and preferences of your users, you can provide personalized and relevant responses that keep them engaged with the application and coming back for more.

4.2.1. Capturing User Preferences and Profile Data

To capture user preferences and profile data, you can create a comprehensive user profile management system that stores essential information about each user. This can include a wide range of data such as their interests, preferences, location, demographics, and past interactions with the application. For instance, you can collect their age, gender, education, occupation, or income level to provide more personalized recommendations and content. Moreover, the system can also gather information about their social media activities, browsing history, or purchase behavior to better understand their needs and preferences.

There are several ways to obtain this information, including user input, third-party integrations, or data analysis. For example, you may ask users to fill out a form with their personal information and preferences when they register or create an account. Alternatively, you can integrate your application with other platforms or services that already have this data, such as Facebook, LinkedIn, or Google. Another option is to analyze users' behavior and interactions with your application over time, using tools such as Google Analytics, heatmaps, or A/B testing. By combining these methods, you can create a robust and dynamic user profile management system that adapts to users' changing needs and preferences over time.

Example:

Here's an example of a simple user profile structure in Python:

```python
user_profile = {
    "user_id": "12345",
    "name": "Alice",
    "location": "New York City",
    "interests": ["technology", "travel", "music"],
    "preferences": {
        "response_length": "short",
        "formality": "casual",
    }
}
```

4.2.2. Adapting Responses for Personalized Experiences

Once you've collected user preferences and profile data, there are several ways to utilize this information to personalize the model's responses. One approach is to incorporate user attributes into the conversation context. For instance, if the user has a preference for a certain type of music, the AI model can be adjusted to respond with music-related content. Additionally, user preferences could be used to tailor the API parameters.

For example, if the user has indicated a preference for shorter responses, the API could be adjusted to generate shorter responses. There are other ways to utilize user data as well, such as creating personalized recommendations based on their preferences, or using the data to improve the accuracy of the model.

Example:

For example, you can include user attributes in the conversation context like this:

```python
user_input = "Tell me about the latest technology news."
context = f"User {user_profile['name']} is interested in {', '.join(user_profile['interests'])}. {user_input}"
# Send the context to ChatGPT for a response
```

Additionally, you can adjust the API parameters based on user preferences:

```
api_parameters = {
    "temperature": 0.8,
    "max_tokens": 50,
    "top_p": 1
}

if user_profile["preferences"]["response_length"] == "short":
    api_parameters["max_tokens"] = 25

if user_profile["preferences"]["formality"] == "formal":
    api_parameters["temperature"] = 0.5
```

4.2.3. Learning User Preferences Over Time

To further improve personalization, your application can learn user preferences in a more comprehensive way over time. One way to achieve this is by analyzing user behavior and feedback, as well as updating their profile data accordingly. Additionally, you could consider tracking user activity outside of your application, such as on social media or other platforms, to get a more complete picture of their preferences.

Another way to improve personalization is to implement a feedback mechanism that allows users to rate or provide comments on the model's responses. By collecting this data, you can not only fine-tune the user's preferences, but also gain insights into how the model is performing and what areas could be improved.

Furthermore, you could consider using machine learning algorithms to analyze user data and identify patterns or trends that may not be immediately apparent. This could help to further refine the personalization process and ensure that your application is providing the best possible experience for each individual user.

In summary, there are multiple ways to improve personalization in your application, including analyzing user behavior and feedback, tracking user activity outside of your application, implementing a feedback mechanism, and using machine learning algorithms to identify patterns and trends. By taking advantage of these techniques, you can create a more personalized and engaging experience for your users.

Example:

For this example, we will simulate a user rating the response on a scale of 1 to 5. Based on the rating, we will adjust the temperature parameter to improve future responses.

```python
# Simulate user rating for a response
user_rating = 4

# Update user preferences based on rating
if user_rating >= 4:
    user_profile["preferences"]["temperature"] -= 0.1
else:
    user_profile["preferences"]["temperature"] += 0.1

# Ensure temperature is within the valid range
user_profile["preferences"]["temperature"] = min(max(user_profile["preferences"]
["temperature"], 0.0), 1.0)
```

4.2.4. Personalized Content Recommendations

ChatGPT is a powerful tool for generating personalized content recommendations based on user preferences and profile data. By taking into account a user's interests, ChatGPT can provide a vast array of news articles, blog posts, and other content on topics that pique their curiosity. Whether a user is interested in technology, travel, or any other subject, ChatGPT can generate suggestions that are tailored to their individual tastes.

The process of generating these recommendations is made possible by the integration of user interests into the prompts that are sent to the ChatGPT API. By providing ChatGPT with detailed information about a user's preferences, the API can use this data to search through its vast database of content and provide recommendations that are highly relevant to the user. This not only helps to keep users engaged with your application but also ensures that they are receiving content that is of genuine interest to them.

There are many ways in which ChatGPT can be used to generate content recommendations. For example, if a user is interested in technology, ChatGPT can provide them with articles about the latest gadgets, software releases, and industry news. Similarly, if a user is interested in travel, ChatGPT can suggest articles about popular destinations, travel tips, and cultural experiences.

By providing users with a diverse range of content that is tailored to their interests, ChatGPT can help to keep them engaged and coming back for more.

Overall, ChatGPT is an incredibly powerful tool for generating personalized content recommendations. By taking into account a user's interests and profile data, it can provide a wide array of content that is highly relevant to their individual tastes. By integrating this technology into your application, you can help to keep users engaged and ensure that they are receiving content that is of genuine interest to them.

Example:

```
content_recommendation_prompt = f"Find interesting articles about {', '.join(use
r_profile['interests'])}."
# Send the prompt to ChatGPT for a response
```

4.2.5. Adapting to Different Communication Styles

Different users might prefer different communication styles, such as formal or informal language, concise or elaborate responses, or even the use of emojis. The choice of communication style depends on the context and the relationship between the users. For example, in a professional setting, formal language might be more appropriate, while informal language might be more suitable for a personal conversation. Similarly, some users might prefer concise responses that get straight to the point, while others might appreciate more elaborate answers that provide additional context or examples.

To enhance personalization, it's important to adapt the model's output to match the user's preferred communication style. This can be achieved by adjusting the API parameters, such as the temperature and max tokens, or by applying post-processing techniques to modify the model's responses. For instance, you could use a filter that replaces formal words with informal ones, or vice versa, depending on the user's preference. Alternatively, you could add emojis or other visual elements to make the response more engaging and personalized.

By taking the user's communication style into account, you can create a more meaningful and enjoyable interaction that fosters trust and engagement. This, in turn, can lead to better outcomes and more satisfied users. So, don't underestimate the power of personalization when it comes to communication, and always strive to adapt your message to your audience.

Example:

In this example, we will adapt the ChatGPT response based on the user's preferred communication style (formal or informal) and their preference for using emojis.

```python
def add_emojis(text):
    # Simulate adding emojis to the text
    return text + " 😊"

# Set user preferences for communication style and emoji usage
user_profile["preferences"]["communication_style"] = "informal"
user_profile["preferences"]["use_emojis"] = True

# Adjust API parameters based on communication style
if user_profile["preferences"]["communication_style"] == "formal":
    api_parameters["temperature"] = 0.5
else:
    api_parameters["temperature"] = 0.8

# Send the prompt to ChatGPT for a response
response_text = "This is a sample response from ChatGPT."

# Apply post-processing based on user preferences
if user_profile["preferences"]["use_emojis"]:
    response_text = add_emojis(response_text)

print(response_text)
```

In summary, user attributes and personalization are essential for creating engaging and relevant experiences with ChatGPT. By understanding individual user preferences and profile data, we can tailor the model's responses to better suit each user. This involves capturing user preferences, adjusting API parameters, and incorporating user-specific information into prompts.

Furthermore, it is crucial to learn and adapt to user preferences over time by analyzing user feedback and behavior, which helps improve the personalization process. Providing personalized content recommendations and adapting to different communication styles, such as formal or informal language, adds another layer of customization to the user experience.

By focusing on these personalization strategies, we can create a more enjoyable and satisfying experience for users, ensuring that the ChatGPT model aligns more closely with their expectations and requirements.

4.3. System Level Instructions

System level instructions refer to the method of guiding the ChatGPT model's behavior by providing specific instructions or prompts. These instructions can be explicit or implicit, helping users achieve desired responses and outcomes from the model. Explicit instructions provide a clearer picture of what the user wants to achieve, and as a result, the model can give more relevant and accurate responses. In contrast, implicit instructions are not specific and may lead to vague or irrelevant responses from the model.

In order to guide the model with explicit instructions, it's important to consider the specific task or goal the user wants to achieve. This could involve asking the model specific questions, providing specific details or examples, or even giving the model a hypothetical scenario to respond to. For instance, if the user wants to ask the model about a particular movie, they could provide information about the genre, director, actors, or plot to help the model understand what kind of response is expected.

Experimenting with different prompt types can also help improve the model's performance. Some prompt types to consider include "fill in the blank" prompts, where the user provides a sentence with a missing word for the model to complete, or "story completion" prompts, where the user provides the beginning of a story for the model to continue. By varying the types of prompts used, users can help the model learn how to respond to a wider range of inputs and produce more nuanced and complex responses.

Overall, guiding the ChatGPT model with specific instructions and prompts can help users achieve more accurate and relevant responses from the model. By considering the specific task or goal at hand and experimenting with different prompt types, users can help the model learn how to respond to a wider range of inputs and produce more nuanced and complex responses.

4.3.1. Guiding the Model with Explicit Instructions

Explicit instructions are a critical aspect of obtaining accurate and specific responses from ChatGPT. When drafting instructions, it is important to provide the model with clear and direct commands that allow it to fully understand the desired output.

One way to achieve this is to be as detailed as possible when explaining the desired outcome. This could include specifying the tone of the response, the length of the response, or the specific topic you want the response to address.

Additionally, it is important to remember that the more information you provide, the better equipped ChatGPT will be to generate a response that meets your specific needs. For example, if you are looking for a response that is related to a particular industry or topic, it can be helpful to provide relevant background information in your instructions.

Explicit instructions can also help to reduce the likelihood of errors or misunderstandings, which can save you time and frustration in the long run. By investing a little extra time in crafting explicit instructions, you can ensure that you get the most out of ChatGPT and that you receive responses that are tailored to your unique needs and preferences.

Example:

For instance, if you want the model to list three benefits of exercise, you can provide an explicit instruction as follows:

```
prompt = "List three benefits of regular exercise."
response = chat_gpt(prompt)
print(response)
```

By using explicit instructions, you can minimize confusion and guide the model towards producing the desired output. Explicit instructions can include detailed descriptions of the task, clear guidelines for how the task should be completed, and examples of what the final output should look like.

Providing explicit instructions can also help to ensure that the model understands the task at hand and is able to produce accurate results. In addition, using explicit instructions can help to minimize errors and reduce the time and effort required to correct mistakes. Therefore, it is important to take the time to provide clear and detailed instructions to ensure the success of your project.

4.3.2. Experimenting with Implicit and Explicit Prompts

Incorporating user attributes and personalization into your ChatGPT application can greatly enhance the user experience. By understanding the user's preferences and profile data, ChatGPT can give personalized and relevant responses to each user. This not only helps the user receive the information they need but can also lead to increased engagement with the application.

To start, you can capture basic user information such as age, gender, and location. This information can be used to provide location-specific recommendations or gender-specific language in the responses. Additionally, you can capture user preferences such as favorite topics or preferred communication style. This information can be used to tailor the output of the model and ensure that the user is receiving information that they find interesting and engaging.

Another way to enhance the user experience is to track user behavior within the application. By analyzing how users interact with the application, you can identify areas where users may be struggling or where they are finding the most value. This can help you optimize the application and ensure that users are receiving the information they need in the most effective way possible.

Incorporating user attributes into your ChatGPT application requires effort and time, but can lead to a significant improvement in the user experience. By understanding the needs and preferences of your users, you can provide personalized and relevant responses that keep them engaged with the application and coming back for more.

To capture user preferences and profile data, you can create a comprehensive user profile management system that stores essential information about each user. This can include a wide range of data such as their interests, preferences, location, demographics, and past interactions with the application. For instance, you can collect their age, gender, education, occupation, or income level to provide more personalized recommendations and content. Moreover, the system can also gather information about their social media activities, browsing history, or purchase behavior to better understand their needs and preferences.

There are several ways to obtain this information, including user input, third-party integrations, or data analysis. For example, you may ask users to fill out a form with their personal information and preferences when they register or create an account. Alternatively, you can integrate your application with other platforms or services that already have this data, such as Facebook, LinkedIn, or Google. Another option is to analyze users' behavior and interactions with your application over time, using tools such as Google Analytics, heatmaps, or A/B testing.

By combining these methods, you can create a robust and dynamic user profile management system that adapts to users' changing needs and preferences over time.

Once you've collected user preferences and profile data, there are several ways to utilize this information to personalize the model's responses. One approach is to incorporate user attributes into the conversation context. For instance, if the user has a preference for a certain type of music, the AI model can be adjusted to respond with music-related content. Additionally, user preferences could be used to tailor the API parameters.

For example, if the user has indicated a preference for shorter responses, the API could be adjusted to generate shorter responses. There are other ways to utilize user data as well, such as creating personalized recommendations based on their preferences, or using the data to improve the accuracy of the model.

To further improve personalization, your application can learn user preferences in a more comprehensive way over time. One way to achieve this is by analyzing user behavior and feedback, as well as updating their profile data accordingly. Additionally, you could consider tracking user activity outside of your application, such as on social media or other platforms, to get a more complete picture of their preferences.

Another way to improve personalization is to implement a feedback mechanism that allows users to rate or provide comments on the model's responses. By collecting this data, you can not only fine-tune the user's preferences, but also gain insights into how the model is performing and what areas could be improved.

Furthermore, you could consider using machine learning algorithms to analyze user data and identify patterns or trends that may not be immediately apparent. This could help to further refine the personalization process and ensure that your application is providing the best possible experience for each individual user.

In summary, there are multiple ways to improve personalization in your application, including analyzing user behavior and feedback, tracking user activity outside of your application, implementing a feedback mechanism, and using machine learning algorithms to identify patterns and trends. By taking advantage of these techniques, you can create a more personalized and engaging experience for your users.

Example:

For example, let's consider a scenario where you want to know the benefits of exercise. You can try both implicit and explicit prompts:

```
# Implicit prompt
implicit_prompt = "Why should someone exercise regularly?"
implicit_response = chat_gpt(implicit_prompt)
print("Implicit response:", implicit_response)

# Explicit prompt
explicit_prompt = "List three benefits of regular exercise."
explicit_response = chat_gpt(explicit_prompt)
print("Explicit response:", explicit_response)
```

By comparing the responses, you can determine which type of prompt is more effective in guiding the model towards the desired outcome.

4.3.3. Balancing Explicitness and Creativity

The balance between explicitness and creativity is a crucial aspect of using ChatGPT effectively. Explicit instructions can provide more specific guidance to the model and help it produce more accurate and relevant outputs. However, being too specific can limit the model's range of responses, leading to outputs that may lack creativity or originality. It's important to find the right balance between the two, allowing for enough freedom and creativity while still providing enough guidance to ensure that the output meets your needs.

One way to find this balance is to experiment with different levels of explicitness in your instructions. For example, you could try providing a general prompt that allows for more creativity and flexibility, such as "Write a story about a magical adventure." Alternatively, you could provide a more specific prompt that gives the model a clearer idea of what you're looking for, such as "Write a story about a young wizard who discovers a hidden treasure in a mysterious forest." By varying the level of specificity in your prompts, you can find the right balance that allows for maximum creativity and accuracy.

Another way to find the right balance is to consider the context of your prompt and the intended audience. For example, if you're using ChatGPT for a professional setting, it may be more appropriate to provide more specific instructions that align with the expectations of the audience. On the other hand, if you're using ChatGPT for a creative writing exercise, it may be more appropriate to provide a more general prompt that allows for more creativity.

Ultimately, finding the right balance between explicitness and creativity requires a bit of trial and error. It's important to experiment with different prompts and levels of specificity to find

what works best for your use case. By finding the optimal balance, you can harness the full potential of ChatGPT and generate high-quality outputs that meet your needs, while still allowing for enough creativity and originality to engage your audience.

Example:

For example, let's consider a scenario where you want a creative story about an adventure in a fantasy world. You can try varying levels of explicitness:

```
# Less explicit prompt
less_explicit_prompt = "Write a short story about an adventure in a fantasy worl
d."
less_explicit_response = chat_gpt(less_explicit_prompt)
print("Less explicit response:", less_explicit_response)

# More explicit prompt
more_explicit_prompt = "Write a short story about a brave knight and a cunning s
orcerer who embark on a quest to find a hidden treasure in a magical forest."
more_explicit_response = chat_gpt(more_explicit_prompt)
print("More explicit response:", more_explicit_response)
```

By experimenting with the level of explicitness, you can find the right balance between specific guidance and creative freedom, resulting in a more engaging and tailored output from the ChatGPT model.

4.3.4. Gradual Refinement of Instructions

In addition to refining instructions in a step-by-step manner, it is also important to consider the context and intended audience when providing prompts to the ChatGPT model. For example, if the model is being used in a professional setting, it may be more appropriate to provide more specific instructions and guidance, as this can help to ensure that the output is aligned with the expectations of the audience. On the other hand, if the model is being used for a creative writing exercise, a more open-ended prompt may be more appropriate, as this can encourage the model to generate more imaginative and original output.

Another approach to improving the model's responses is to experiment with different types of prompts and instructions. For instance, rather than providing the model with a traditional prompt, such as "Write a story about X", it may be useful to try more unconventional prompts,

such as "Write a story backwards" or "Write a story using only one word per sentence". By varying the type of prompt used, it is possible to encourage the model to generate output that is more diverse and interesting.

It is also important to consider the balance between explicitness and creativity when providing prompts to the model. Providing too much guidance and specificity can limit the model's range of responses and result in output that lacks originality, whereas providing too little guidance can result in output that is irrelevant or unhelpful. Finding the right balance between the two is key to achieving the desired output.

It is important to continually analyze the model's output and refine the prompts and instructions as needed. By analyzing the output, it is possible to identify areas where the model is struggling or where the prompts and instructions could be improved. By continually refining the prompts and instructions, it is possible to improve the model's performance and achieve better results overall.

There are many ways to improve the quality of the ChatGPT model's responses by refining the instructions and prompts provided to it. By taking a step-by-step approach, considering the context and intended audience, experimenting with different types of prompts, finding the right balance between explicitness and creativity, and continually refining the prompts and instructions, it is possible to achieve more accurate and relevant output from the model.

Example:

For example, if you're looking for a detailed description of a fictional character, you can start with a broad instruction and then refine it based on the model's response:

```python
# Broad instruction
broad_prompt = "Describe a character from a fantasy novel."
broad_response = chat_gpt(broad_prompt)
print("Broad response:", broad_response)

# Refined instruction
refined_prompt = f"Expand on the character's background, personality traits, and
magical abilities, based on the previous response: {broad_response}"
refined_response = chat_gpt(refined_prompt)
print("Refined response:", refined_response)
```

This iterative approach allows you to guide the model more effectively, enabling it to generate more accurate and relevant responses while still maintaining a degree of creative freedom.

4.3.5. Using Instruction Tokens for Fine-grained Control

Instruction tokens are a powerful tool that can be used to guide the behavior of the ChatGPT model with a high degree of precision. These tokens can be used to provide the model with more specific guidance, ensuring that the generated output is more accurate and relevant to the user's needs.

One of the main advantages of using instruction tokens is that they allow you to control the structure and content of the generated output. For example, by using the **<list>** token, you can instruct the model to generate a list of items, while the **<description>** token can be used to generate a more detailed description of a particular topic. Similarly, the **<cause>** and **<effect>** tokens can be used to generate output that highlights the causal relationship between different factors.

Another advantage of instruction tokens is that they allow you to generate output that aligns with specific goals or objectives. This can be particularly useful when working with marketing or advertising copy, where the goal is to generate content that is engaging and persuasive to the target audience. By using tokens such as **<benefit>** or **<testimonial>**, you can generate content that highlights the key benefits of a product or service, or that includes testimonials from satisfied customers.

In addition to these benefits, instruction tokens also allow you to fine-tune the model's behavior in response to user feedback or changing requirements. By monitoring the quality of the generated output and adjusting the instruction tokens as needed, you can ensure that the model is delivering the best possible results for your particular use case.

Overall, instruction tokens are an essential tool for anyone looking to get the most out of the ChatGPT model. By providing more specific guidance and control over the generated output, these tokens can help you achieve your goals and generate high-quality text that is tailored to your specific needs. Whether you're working on marketing copy, instructional material, or any other type of text generation project, instruction tokens can help you achieve the results you're looking for.

Example:

For example, you can use tokens like **<opinion>**, **<summary>**, or **<explain>** to specify the type of response you want from the model:

```
# Opinion-based instruction
opinion_prompt = "<opinion> What do you think about the impact of artificial int
elligence on the job market?"
opinion_response = chat_gpt(opinion_prompt)
print("Opinion response:", opinion_response)

# Summary-based instruction
summary_prompt = "<summary> Summarize the key points of the book 'The Catcher in
the Rye'."
summary_response = chat_gpt(summary_prompt)
print("Summary response:", summary_response)

# Explanation-based instruction
explain_prompt = "<explain> What is the greenhouse effect and its impact on clim
ate change?"
explain_response = chat_gpt(explain_prompt)
print("Explain response:", explain_response)
```

These tokens, which are essentially predefined structures that convey specific information to the model, play a crucial role in enabling ChatGPT to generate more accurate responses. By providing clearer instructions to the model, the tokens help the system better understand the desired output format and refine its responses accordingly. This leads to a more natural and coherent conversation between ChatGPT and the user, enhancing the overall user experience.

In conclusion, leveraging system level instructions effectively can result in more targeted and relevant outputs from ChatGPT. By experimenting with a variety of techniques, such as balancing explicitness and creativity, using gradual refinement, adjusting between implicit and explicit prompts, and incorporating instruction tokens, you can optimize the model's behavior and achieve the desired output for your specific use case.

4.4. Multi-turn Conversations and Dialogue Systems

Multi-turn conversations are a crucial aspect of building effective dialogue systems that can engage users and provide them with the information they need. These types of conversations are particularly useful when working with complex topics that require multiple exchanges to fully explore. However, designing effective multi-turn conversations can be challenging, as it requires careful planning and consideration of various factors, such as the user's goals, the context of the conversation, and the model's capabilities.

One of the most important aspects of designing effective multi-turn conversations is crafting clear and concise messages that are easy to understand. This includes using simple language, avoiding jargon, and breaking down complex concepts into smaller, more manageable pieces. Additionally, it is important to anticipate user responses and provide helpful prompts to guide the conversation in the right direction. This can include asking open-ended questions, providing multiple-choice options, or offering relevant resources for further exploration.

Another important factor in designing effective multi-turn conversations is understanding the user's goals and needs. This requires a deep understanding of the user's motivations, preferences, and pain points, as well as an awareness of their level of knowledge and expertise on the topic at hand. By tailoring the conversation to the user's specific needs, we can create a more engaging and relevant experience that is better suited to their unique requirements.

In addition to these factors, it is important to consider the context of the conversation when designing multi-turn interactions. This includes understanding the user's situation, the environment in which they are interacting with the system, and any other relevant factors that may impact the conversation. For example, if the user is in a noisy environment, it may be necessary to use shorter, more direct messages to ensure that they can understand the conversation.

It is important to leverage the capabilities of the ChatGPT model to create engaging and dynamic multi-turn conversations. This includes using advanced techniques such as adaptive prompting, conversation branching, and turn-taking management to guide the conversation and keep the user engaged. By using these techniques, we can create more natural and coherent conversations that feel like genuine interactions between the user and the system.

Designing effective multi-turn conversations is a complex and multifaceted process that requires careful planning and consideration of various factors. By crafting clear and concise messages, understanding the user's goals and needs, considering the context of the conversation, and leveraging the capabilities of the ChatGPT model, we can create engaging and meaningful interactions that leave users satisfied and eager to explore further.

4.4.1. Designing Effective Multi-turn Conversations

To create a successful multi-turn conversation, consider the following best practices:

Use conversation history

To ensure that the model generates contextually relevant responses, it's important to provide it with the necessary information. One way to do this is to maintain the conversation context by including the user's messages and the model's responses in the input to the API. In doing so,

the model is made aware of the previous exchanges, which allows it to generate responses that are more relevant and meaningful to the user.

In addition, providing the model with this context enables it to better understand the user's needs and preferences, which can help to improve the overall quality of the conversation. By taking these steps, we can help to ensure that the model is able to provide the best possible experience for users, and that they are able to get the information they need in a timely and efficient manner.

Example:

```
conversation_history = [
    {"role": "user", "content": "Tell me a joke."},
    {"role": "assistant", "content": "Why did the chicken cross the road? To get
to the other side!"},
    {"role": "user", "content": "That's funny! Tell me another one."},
]

response = chat_gpt(conversation_history)
```

Define user roles

It is important to clearly specify the role of each participant in the conversation, such as "user" and "assistant". This helps the model understand the context and generate appropriate responses. By doing so, the model can differentiate between the user's inputs and the assistant's responses, and provide more accurate and relevant feedback.

In addition, specifying the role of each participant helps to establish a clear and structured conversation. This can be particularly useful when discussing complex topics or when multiple people are involved in the conversation. It can also help to avoid confusion and misunderstandings, as everyone knows who is speaking and what their role is in the discussion.

Therefore, it is recommended to always specify the role of each participant in the conversation, especially when dealing with automated systems or machine learning models. This allows for a more effective and efficient communication, and can ultimately lead to better outcomes and results.

Set conversation objectives

It is important to establish the goals of the conversation to ensure that all parties involved are on the same page. This can be done by clearly outlining the desired outcomes and aligning the prompts and responses with these objectives. By doing so, participants can ensure that the conversation stays focused and productive.

Additionally, having set conversation objectives can help to prevent misunderstandings and ensure that all parties involved are able to effectively communicate their ideas and perspectives. Overall, taking the time to set clear conversation objectives is an important step in facilitating successful and productive discussions.

4.4.2. Techniques for Conversation Flow Management

When it comes to managing a conversation, it's not just about what you say, but how you say it. One aspect of this is controlling the pace of the conversation. This can mean slowing down and taking more time to communicate important information, or speeding up the conversation to keep things moving quickly.

Another important aspect of conversation management is controlling the direction of the conversation. This can involve asking strategic questions to steer the conversation in a certain direction, or gently redirecting it if it veers off course. Finally, managing engagement level is crucial to ensure that all participants feel involved and invested in the conversation.

This can involve using active listening techniques to show that you are fully present and engaged with the conversation, or encouraging participation from quieter participants to prevent the conversation from becoming one-sided.

Here are some techniques to achieve this:

1. **Conversation timeouts**: Implementing timeouts is a great way to improve the user experience. If conversations go on for too long, users may lose interest and engagement may suffer. By setting timeouts, you can ensure that conversations don't drag on for too long, while still allowing for meaningful discussions. Additionally, timeouts can help prevent any potential miscommunications that may arise from prolonged conversation. Overall, implementing conversation timeouts is a simple and effective way to improve the effectiveness of your conversations with users.
2. **Turn-taking management**: One important aspect of maintaining a balanced and engaging conversation is controlling the number of turns taken by the user and the model. This can help to avoid one-sided interactions and ensure that both parties have an equal opportunity to participate in the conversation. To achieve this, it may be

helpful to establish guidelines or rules around turn-taking, such as limiting the number of turns each person can take or establishing specific topics or areas of discussion for each turn. Additionally, using tools such as timers or prompts can help to ensure that turn-taking is managed effectively and that the conversation remains engaging and productive for both parties.

3. **Adaptive prompting** is a feature that allows the prompts to be tailored to the user's inputs and previous responses. This is done to steer the conversation towards the intended goal. By using machine learning algorithms, the system can accurately track and analyze the user's behavior and preferences, and adjust the prompts accordingly. This makes for a more personalized and engaging experience that can ultimately lead to a more successful outcome. The power of adaptive prompting lies in its ability to anticipate the user's needs and respond accordingly, making it an invaluable tool for anyone looking to improve their conversational skills.

4. **Conversation branching**: One way to design a great chatbot is to create a conversation flow that includes multiple paths. By doing this, users can explore different topics and engage in more complex interactions. This approach can help increase user engagement and satisfaction, as it allows them to have a more personalized experience. Additionally, it can help to make the chatbot feel more human-like, as it mimics the way humans converse by allowing for tangents and digressions. In order to create a successful conversation branching design, it's important to consider the user's goals and needs, and to anticipate the various paths they might take. By doing so, you can create a chatbot that is not only useful, but also enjoyable to use.

Example:

For example, you can implement adaptive prompting and conversation branching as follows:

```
# Starting prompt
initial_prompt = "Let's discuss the environmental impact of electric cars."

# User input
user_input = "What are the main benefits of electric cars?"

# Adaptive prompting
if "benefits" in user_input.lower():
    adaptive_prompt = "Discuss the environmental benefits of electric cars."
else:
    adaptive_prompt = "Discuss the environmental drawbacks of electric cars."

response = chat_gpt(adaptive_prompt)
```

In summary, designing effective multi-turn conversations and managing the dialogue flow are crucial components of building a robust and engaging dialogue system with ChatGPT. One way to design effective conversations is to create a clear conversation structure with a beginning, middle, and end.

This structure can help keep users engaged and make it easier to manage the flow of the conversation. Additionally, it's important to leverage conversation history to provide users with a personalized experience. For example, you could use previous user responses to inform the questions you ask next. Finally, implementing various flow management techniques can help ensure that the conversation stays on track and doesn't become too repetitive or confusing.

By following best practices for conversation design, leveraging conversation history, and implementing various flow management techniques, you can create rich, interactive experiences for your users that keep them engaged and coming back for more.

4.4.3. Evaluating and Optimizing Dialogue Systems

Evaluating and optimizing dialogue systems is a critical aspect of ensuring that they perform well and provide a positive user experience. One common approach to evaluate dialogue systems is to use human evaluations, where human judges interact with the system and rate its performance based on various metrics such as relevance, coherence, and fluency. In addition, another approach is to use automatic metrics such as perplexity, response quality, and user satisfaction scores. These methods are crucial in providing a comprehensive evaluation of the system's performance and identifying areas of improvement.

To optimize dialogue systems, there are various techniques that can be used to improve their performance. One technique is to train the system on more data, which can help it better understand the nuances of natural language and improve its ability to generate relevant responses. Additionally, fine-tuning the model can also help improve the system's performance by adjusting its parameters to better suit the task at hand. Furthermore, improving the system's architecture can also contribute to its optimization by providing a more efficient framework for generating responses.

However, it's not just about optimizing the system based on metrics alone. It's also essential to consider the user's feedback and iterate on the system based on their needs and preferences. This can involve incorporating features that users find useful or adapting the system's responses to better match their language patterns. By doing so, dialogue systems can provide more personalized and engaging experiences to users.

Evaluating and optimizing dialogue systems is an ongoing process that requires a combination of human evaluations, automatic metrics, and user feedback. By continually improving the system's performance, dialogue systems can provide the best possible user experience and help users achieve their goals more efficiently.

Quantitative Metrics

To measure the performance of your dialogue system, you may want to consider using quantitative metrics such as precision, recall, F1-score, and BLEU (Bilingual Evaluation Understudy) scores. These metrics can help you assess the accuracy and relevance of your model's responses.

Precision is a metric that measures the proportion of true positives (correctly identified relevant responses) to the total number of positives (all identified relevant responses). Recall, on the other hand, measures the proportion of true positives to the total number of actual positives (all relevant responses in the data set). F1-score is a weighted average of precision and recall, and is useful for comparing systems that have different trade-offs between precision and recall. Finally, BLEU scores are used to evaluate the quality of machine translation systems by comparing the machine-generated translations to a set of reference translations.

By using these quantitative metrics, you can gain a more nuanced understanding of your model's performance. However, keep in mind that these metrics only provide one aspect of your system's performance, and should be supplemented with qualitative evaluations as well.

Qualitative Analysis

In order to improve your dialogue system and gain a better understanding of the user experience, it is important to perform a thorough qualitative analysis. This can involve gathering feedback from users, observing their interactions with the system, and analyzing data from these interactions.

By carefully examining the results of this analysis, you can identify areas of improvement and develop strategies to enhance the overall user experience. Some techniques that can be used in qualitative analysis include user surveys, focus groups, and usability testing. Additionally, it can be helpful to conduct a competitive analysis to see how your system compares to similar products on the market. By taking a comprehensive approach to qualitative analysis, you can gain valuable insights into your users' needs and preferences, and develop a more effective and user-friendly dialogue system.

A/B Testing

One approach to improve your dialogue system is by conducting A/B testing. This method allows you to compare different versions of the system and identify the best-performing setup.

During the A/B testing, you can measure various metrics such as response time, user satisfaction, and conversion rate. By analyzing the results, you can gain insights into which version of the system is most effective and make informed decisions about how to optimize its performance.

This process is iterative, so you can continue to refine and improve the dialogue system over time.

Reinforcement Learning

Incorporating reinforcement learning techniques to train your model based on user feedback is a great way to ensure that your model is always learning and improving. By analyzing user feedback, you can identify patterns that may not have been apparent before and make changes to your model to better adapt to user preferences.

Additionally, this approach allows your model to continually improve and adapt to new scenarios, making it more versatile and effective over time. By incorporating reinforcement learning into your model, you can ensure that it remains up-to-date and relevant in an ever-changing technological landscape.

Model Fine-tuning

In order to achieve better performance in the context of your application, you can fine-tune your model on a domain-specific dataset or task-specific prompts. This allows the model to adapt to the nuances and intricacies of the specific domain or task, resulting in improved accuracy and performance.

Fine-tuning involves adjusting the pre-trained weights of the model to fit the new dataset or prompts, allowing it to make more accurate predictions and produce more relevant outputs. By fine-tuning your model, you can tailor it to your specific needs and ensure that it performs optimally in your particular use case.

Example:

```python
def evaluate_accuracy(system_responses, true_responses):
    correct_responses = 0
    total_responses = len(system_responses)

    for i in range(total_responses):
        if system_responses[i] == true_responses[i]:
            correct_responses += 1

    accuracy = correct_responses / total_responses
    return accuracy

# Example dataset
system_responses = [
    "Yes, I can help you with that.",
    "I'm sorry, I don't understand your question.",
    "The nearest restaurant is 5 miles away.",
    "It's currently 25 degrees Celsius outside.",
]

true_responses = [
    "Yes, I can help you with that.",
    "I apologize, but I don't understand your question.",
    "The closest restaurant is 5 miles away.",
    "It's currently 25 degrees Celsius outside.",
]

accuracy = evaluate_accuracy(system_responses, true_responses)
print(f"Accuracy: {accuracy:.2f}")
```

In this code example, we define a function **evaluate_accuracy** that takes the system-generated responses and the true responses as input. The function compares each system response with the corresponding true response and calculates the accuracy as the proportion of correct responses.

While this example uses a simple accuracy metric, it's important to note that evaluating and optimizing dialogue systems often requires more sophisticated techniques and metrics that consider the context and semantics of the conversation.

You can integrate this evaluation function into your dialogue system to measure its performance and identify areas for improvement.

4.4.4. Integrating External Data Sources and APIs in Dialogue Systems

Integrating external data sources and APIs is an important aspect of building a robust and effective dialogue system. In Python, this can be done using packages like requests, which allows you to make HTTP requests to external APIs and retrieve data in JSON format.

To integrate an external API into your dialogue system using ChatGPT API, you would first need to identify the API you want to use and obtain an API key or access token. Once you have this, you can use the requests package in Python to make requests to the API and retrieve data.

For example, if you wanted to integrate a weather API into your dialogue system, you could use requests to retrieve the current weather conditions for a given location and incorporate this information into your responses.

Overall, integrating external data sources and APIs is an important step in building a more useful and engaging dialogue system, and Python provides a range of tools and libraries to make this process easier.

1. **API Integration**: In today's world, where users expect quick and accurate information at their fingertips, it is essential for dialogue systems to be integrated with external APIs. By connecting your system with APIs, you can provide real-time information or perform actions on behalf of the user without having to build the functionality from scratch. For instance, you could integrate a weather API to provide up-to-date weather forecasts, or a calendar API to create and manage events. By leveraging the power of APIs, you can enhance the capabilities of your dialogue system and provide a seamless user experience.

2. **Data Preprocessing**: It is crucial to understand the importance of preprocessing external data to make it compatible with your dialogue system. This step involves cleaning, formatting, or transforming the data to ensure a smooth integration with the conversation flow. For instance, cleaning the data may include removing irrelevant or redundant information, correcting spelling or grammatical errors, or standardizing the data format. Formatting the data may involve converting the data into a specific structure or file type that is compatible with the dialogue system, such as JSON or CSV. Transforming the data may require applying algorithms or models to extract relevant features or insights from the data, such as sentiment analysis or topic modeling. Overall, data preprocessing is an essential step in building a robust and effective dialogue system that can handle various types of external data and provide meaningful and accurate responses to users.

3. **Contextual Information**: One possible area of research is to investigate the utilization of external data to provide more contextually relevant responses. For example, we could potentially use user location data to recommend nearby restaurants or events. Additionally, we could also explore the possibility of incorporating historical user data, such as past search queries or user preferences, into our response generation process. By leveraging this data, we could potentially provide more personalized and tailored responses to each individual user. Furthermore, we could also explore the use of sentiment analysis or other NLP techniques to better understand the user's state of mind and provide more empathetic and supportive responses. Overall, there are many exciting directions we can take in terms of utilizing external data to enhance the relevance and effectiveness of our responses.

4. **Data Security and Privacy**: It's important to make sure that your team is well-versed in the best practices for handling user data. This includes not only ensuring data security, but also respecting user privacy. One way to do this is by staying up-to-date with the latest guidelines and regulations, such as GDPR and HIPAA. These regulations provide a framework for ensuring that sensitive user data is kept safe and that user privacy is respected. In addition to these regulations, there are a number of best practices that can help organizations to ensure that they are handling user data in a responsible manner. Some of these best practices include implementing strong access controls, regularly conducting security audits, and educating employees about the importance of data security and privacy. By following these best practices and staying up-to-date with the latest regulations, your team can help to ensure that user data is always kept safe and that user privacy is always respected.

5. **Handling API Errors**: In order to ensure smooth integration with external APIs, it is important to know how to handle errors or unexpected responses gracefully. It is essential to develop effective strategies to provide alternative information or suggestions in case of API failures. Additionally, it is recommended to monitor API usage and performance regularly to identify and address potential issues before they become significant problems. By following these best practices, you can ensure reliable and efficient communication between your application and external APIs.

Example:

Here's an example demonstrating the integration of the OpenWeatherMap API into a dialogue system to provide weather information. In this example, we assume that the user has asked for the current weather in a given city.

First, you'll need an API key from OpenWeatherMap. You can get one for free by signing up at <u>https://openweathermap.org/appid</u>.

```python
import requests

def get_weather(city, api_key):
    base_url = "http://api.openweathermap.org/data/2.5/weather?"
    complete_url = f"{base_url}appid={api_key}&q={city}"

    response = requests.get(complete_url)
    data = response.json()

    if data["cod"] != "404":
        main_data = data["main"]
        weather_data = data["weather"][0]
        temperature = main_data["temp"]
        description = weather_data["description"]

        return f"The current temperature in {city} is {temperature} Kelvin, and
the weather is {description}."
    else:
        return "City not found. Please try again."

# Replace YOUR_API_KEY with your actual API key from OpenWeatherMap
api_key = "YOUR_API_KEY"
city = "San Francisco"
weather_response = get_weather(city, api_key)
print(weather_response)
```

This code defines a function **get_weather** that takes a city name and an API key as input. It then constructs the API request URL, sends the request, and processes the response. If the city is found and the data is retrieved successfully, it returns a string describing the current weather. If the city is not found, it returns an error message.

You can integrate this function into your dialogue system to handle user queries related to weather information.

4.5: Multilingual Support and Translation

As our world becomes increasingly interconnected through the ever-growing use of technology, there is a growing need for AI-driven applications to support multilingual communication. The current trend of globalization has made it necessary for many businesses to cater to a global audience and provide support in multiple languages. ChatGPT is a cutting-edge tool designed

to help developers address this challenge by providing support for multiple languages. With ChatGPT, developers can create applications that cater to a diverse range of users, regardless of their language.

This chapter will explore the various ways in which ChatGPT can be used to facilitate language translation for AI-driven applications. With ChatGPT's advanced capabilities, developers can fine-tune the model to support non-English languages as well. This opens up a world of possibilities for businesses and organizations looking to expand their reach and connect with a wider audience. By leveraging ChatGPT's powerful features, developers can create applications that are truly global in scope and cater to the needs of a diverse user base.

4.5.1. Leveraging ChatGPT for Language Translation

ChatGPT is a powerful tool that can be used for a wide range of language translation tasks. Whether you need to translate a document, a website, or just a simple phrase, ChatGPT is up to the task. One of the key features of ChatGPT is its ability to generate translations on the fly. This means that you can get accurate translations in real-time, without having to wait for a human translator to manually translate the text.

To use ChatGPT for language translation, all you need to do is provide it with a text prompt formatted as a translation request. You'll need to specify the source language, target language, and the text to translate. Once you've done that, ChatGPT will get to work, using its advanced algorithms and machine learning models to generate accurate translations that are tailored to your specific needs.

Whether you're translating a business document, a personal letter, or just a simple message, ChatGPT is the perfect tool for the job. And with its intuitive interface and easy-to-use features, you'll be able to get started right away, without any special training or expertise required.

Example:

Here's an example of how you can use ChatGPT to translate text from English to Spanish:

```python
import openai

prompt = "Translate the following English text to Spanish: 'Hello, how are you?'"

response = openai.Completion.create(
    engine="text-davinci-002",
    prompt=prompt,
    max_tokens=50,
    n=1,
    stop=None,
    temperature=0.8,
)

translated_text = response.choices[0].text.strip()
print(translated_text)
```

This code snippet sends a translation request to ChatGPT, which translates the given English text into Spanish. You can adapt this approach for other language pairs as well.

4.5.2. Fine-tuning for Non-English Languages

While ChatGPT is pre-trained on a diverse dataset that includes multiple languages, its performance on non-English languages might not be as strong as on English. However, this doesn't mean that ChatGPT can't be used effectively for non-English languages. In fact, you can still use ChatGPT for non-English languages and get great results, especially if you fine-tune the model using additional training data in that language.

Fine-tuning ChatGPT is a process of training the model on additional data that is specific to the language you want to improve its performance on. This additional data can be in the form of text in that language, and it can be obtained from various sources such as books, news articles, and social media posts. By fine-tuning the model using this additional data, you can teach ChatGPT to better understand the nuances of that language, and as a result, improve its performance on that language.

So, if you want to use ChatGPT for a non-English language, don't hesitate to do so. With the right approach and additional training data, you can make ChatGPT work effectively for any language. Here's an outline of the fine-tuning process:

Collect a dataset

The first step is to collect a dataset that contains text in the target language. It is important to gather text from various sources like websites, books, and news articles. The dataset should also be representative of the domain you want the model to excel in. For example, if the model is meant to be used for medical text, the dataset should include medical journals and articles.

In addition, it is important to ensure that the dataset is of a sufficient size and quality in order to create a robust and accurate model. Once you have gathered the dataset, you can move on to the next step in the process.

Preprocess the data

To ensure accurate and reliable analysis, it is important to first clean and preprocess the data. This involves removing any irrelevant or low-quality content that could skew the results. However, it is also important to be mindful of potential biases that may arise from this process, and to address them accordingly.

Once the data has been cleaned and preprocessed, the next step is to split the dataset into training and validation sets. This allows us to train our model on a subset of the data, while still being able to evaluate its accuracy on an independent set of data. By doing so, we can ensure that our model is not simply memorizing the training data, but is instead able to generalize to new, unseen data.

Overall, taking the time to properly clean, preprocess, and split the data is crucial for any successful data analysis project. By doing so, we can ensure that our results are accurate, reliable, and unbiased.

Fine-tune the model

To improve the performance of ChatGPT, we can fine-tune it on the training set using the OpenAI API or a compatible fine-tuning library. This will allow us to customize the model to our specific use case and achieve better results. During the fine-tuning process, we should monitor the validation loss to ensure that the model is not overfitting to the training data.

To prevent overfitting, we can use techniques such as early stopping, which stops the training process when the validation loss starts to increase. By implementing these strategies, we can create a more robust and effective model that will better serve our needs.

Evaluate the model

The process of evaluating the model is crucial to determine its effectiveness. Once the fine-tuning process is complete, it is recommended to evaluate the model's performance on a separate test set. This will help us understand the model's ability to generalize to new data and make sure that it is not overfitting.

There are different evaluation metrics that can be used to measure the model's performance, such as BLEU, ROUGE, or Perplexity. BLEU, for example, measures the similarity between the generated output and the reference output based on n-gram matching. ROUGE, on the other hand, is a set of metrics that evaluate the quality of text summaries. Perplexity, meanwhile, calculates the degree of uncertainty of a language model when predicting the next word in a sequence.

All of these metrics are useful in different ways, and the choice of which ones to use will depend on the specific task at hand. Regardless of the chosen metrics, it is important to carefully analyze the results and use them to inform future iterations of the model.

Iterate and improve

One way to further enhance the model's performance is to experiment with different hyperparameters, training dataset sizes, or other optimization techniques. For instance, you could try tweaking the learning rate, adjusting the batch size, or fine-tuning the model's architecture.

Additionally, it may be beneficial to gather more data, refine your data preprocessing pipeline, or incorporate additional features to improve the model's accuracy. By iteratively testing and refining your model, you can create a more robust and accurate solution that better captures the underlying patterns in the data.

By following these steps, you can adapt ChatGPT to support non-English languages effectively and build applications that cater to a global audience.

Example:

Here's an example of fine-tuning ChatGPT for a non-English language, in this case, French, using the Hugging Face Transformers library:

1. Install the necessary libraries:

```
pip install transformers datasets
```

2. Prepare a French dataset:

    Let's assume you have a French dataset in a text file named **french_data.txt**. Load and preprocess the dataset using the Hugging Face **datasets** library:

```
from datasets import Dataset

with open("french_data.txt", "r") as f:
    french_data = f.readlines()

data = {"text": french_data}
dataset = Dataset.from_dict(data)
dataset = dataset.train_test_split(test_size=0.1)
train_dataset, test_dataset = dataset["train"], dataset["test"]
```

3. Tokenize the data:

```
from transformers import GPT2Tokenizer

tokenizer = GPT2Tokenizer.from_pretrained("gpt2")
train_dataset = train_dataset.map(lambda e: tokenizer(e["text"]), batched=True)
test_dataset = test_dataset.map(lambda e: tokenizer(e["text"]), batched=True)
```

4. Fine-tune the model:

```python
from transformers import GPT2LMHeadModel, Trainer, TrainingArguments

model = GPT2LMHeadModel.from_pretrained("gpt2")
training_args = TrainingArguments(
    output_dir="fine-tuned",
    num_train_epochs=3,
    per_device_train_batch_size=4,
    per_device_eval_batch_size=4,
    logging_dir="logs",
    logging_steps=10,
    save_steps=0,
    eval_steps=100,
)

trainer = Trainer(
    model=model,
    args=training_args,
    train_dataset=train_dataset,
    eval_dataset=test_dataset,
)

trainer.train()
```

5. Evaluate the model:

After training, you can use the fine-tuned model to generate text in French or perform other tasks in the target language.

```python
french_prompt = "Bonjour, comment ça va ?"
encoded_prompt = tokenizer.encode(french_prompt, return_tensors="pt")
generated_tokens = model.generate(encoded_prompt)
generated_text = tokenizer.decode(generated_tokens[0], skip_special_tokens=True)
print(generated_text)
```

This example demonstrates the process of fine-tuning ChatGPT using the Hugging Face Transformers library to support the French language better. You can adapt this approach for other languages by providing a dataset in the target language and using the same fine-tuning process.

4.5.3. Handling Code-switching and Multilingual Inputs

Code-switching is a common practice among multilingual speakers where they alternate between different languages within the same conversation. It can be observed in various settings, such as in casual conversations with friends or in more formal contexts, like in business meetings. Since code-switching is prevalent among many individuals, it is necessary to address this aspect to ensure that AI systems can handle it effectively.

Doing so will enable the AI system to provide appropriate and contextually relevant responses in a multilingual environment. In this regard, we will explore various techniques that can help manage code-switching efficiently. For example, one approach is to use language identification models that can automatically detect the language being spoken and switch to the appropriate language model for generating responses.

Another technique is to use code-switching language models that can generate responses that incorporate multiple languages. By implementing these techniques, AI systems can better handle code-switching, which is essential for providing effective communication in a multilingual environment.

Example:

Here's an example demonstrating how to handle code-switching inputs using ChatGPT:

```python
import openai

openai.api_key = "your-api-key"

def chat_with_gpt(prompt):
    response = openai.Completion.create(
        engine="text-davinci-002",
        prompt=prompt,
        max_tokens=50,
        n=1,
        stop=None,
        temperature=0.7,
    )
    message = response.choices[0].text.strip()
    return message

# Example of a code-switching input
input_prompt = "Translate the following English-Spanish mixed sentence to Frenc
h: 'I want to comprar a coche.'"
response = chat_with_gpt(input_prompt)

print(response)
```

This code snippet uses the OpenAI API to send a code-switching input prompt to ChatGPT. The input consists of a mixed English-Spanish sentence, and the prompt instructs ChatGPT to translate it into French. The response from ChatGPT should ideally handle the code-switching and provide a translated sentence in French.

Remember to replace **"your-api-key"** with your actual API key.

4.5.4. Best Practices for Handling Non-Latin Scripts and Different Writing Systems

In this section, we will delve into the intricacies of working with non-Latin scripts and languages that use different writing systems in ChatGPT. Many languages and scripts have unique characteristics and features that require special treatment, such as right-to-left scripts like Arabic and Hebrew, as well as complex scripts like Chinese, Japanese, and Korean. To ensure that ChatGPT can effectively handle these scripts, we will discuss best practices for text normalization, character encoding, and other preprocessing techniques.

Moreover, working with multiple languages and scripts can present unique challenges, such as handling different word orders and sentence structures. To address these challenges, we will provide tips and strategies for overcoming language barriers and ensuring that ChatGPT can provide accurate and helpful responses to users, regardless of the language or writing system they use. This includes testing and validating the performance of ChatGPT across multiple languages and writing systems, as well as conducting user studies and feedback analysis to ensure that the chatbot is performing optimally. With these strategies in mind, you'll be able to use ChatGPT to engage with users from all around the world and provide them with a seamless and personalized experience.

Example:

Here's an example of using Python's **unicodedata** module for text normalization, particularly for handling non-Latin scripts:

```python
import unicodedata

def normalize_text(text):
    # Normalize the text using NFKC normalization
    normalized_text = unicodedata.normalize('NFKC', text)

    # Optionally, remove any non-printable characters
    normalized_text = ''.join(c for c in normalized_text if unicodedata.category
(c) != 'Cc')

    return normalized_text

# Example usage with Arabic text
arabic_text = "السلام عليكم"
normalized_arabic_text = normalize_text(arabic_text)
print(normalized_arabic_text)

# Example usage with Japanese text
japanese_text = "こんにちは"
normalized_japanese_text = normalize_text(japanese_text)
print(normalized_japanese_text)
```

This code snippet demonstrates how to normalize text in different languages and scripts using the NFKC normalization form. It's a helpful preprocessing step for working with non-Latin scripts and languages with different writing systems, such as Arabic and Japanese.

4.6. Conditional Text Generation

In this section, we will explore the fascinating world of conditional text generation, a powerful and highly versatile technique that allows developers to guide the model's output based on specific conditions or rules. Whether you're looking to generate content that follows a certain structure, presents data in a tabular format, or provides different responses based on specific conditions, conditional text generation can help you achieve your goals with impressive accuracy and efficiency.

One of the key advantages of conditional text generation is its ability to handle complex and nuanced data sets with ease. By applying rules and conditions to the model's output, developers can ensure that the resulting text is not only accurate and informative, but also highly relevant and engaging for the end user. From medical diagnoses to financial analysis, conditional text

generation can be applied to a wide range of fields and industries, helping professionals to streamline their workflows and deliver better results in less time.

Of course, like any powerful tool, conditional text generation requires careful planning and execution to achieve optimal results. Developers must carefully consider the specific requirements of their project, as well as the needs and expectations of their target audience, in order to create rules and conditions that produce the desired output. Additionally, it's important to continually test and refine the model's output over time, in order to ensure that it remains accurate and effective even as the data set evolves.

Overall, conditional text generation represents a powerful and exciting development in the field of natural language processing. Whether you're a seasoned developer or just starting out, this technique has the potential to revolutionize the way you approach text generation and analysis, and to unlock new opportunities for innovation and growth in your work. So why not give it a try today, and see what kind of amazing results you can achieve?

4.6.1. Using If-Then-Else Statements in Prompts

When working with ChatGPT, you can make use of if-then-else statements in your prompts to conditionally generate text based on specific requirements. These statements help you to add an additional level of complexity to your input, allowing you to guide the model towards producing outputs that meet your desired criteria.

By incorporating these logical constructs, you can effectively tailor the output to suit your needs. This feature can be especially useful in cases where you want to generate text that is specific to certain scenarios or to include certain information based on user input. By taking advantage of if-then-else statements, you can improve the accuracy of your model's outputs and create more engaging conversations. Overall, the use of these statements can greatly enhance your experience with ChatGPT and help you to achieve the desired results.

Example:

For example, let's say we want to generate a response based on the user's age group:

```
import openai

def generate_response(age):
    prompt = f"If the user is a teenager, say 'You're a teenager!'. If the user
is an adult, say 'You're an adult!'. The user's age is {age}."
    response = openai.Completion.create(
        engine="text-davinci-002",
        prompt=prompt,
        max_tokens=20,
        n=1,
        stop=None,
        temperature=0.8,
    )
    return response.choices[0].text.strip()

print(generate_response(15))
print(generate_response(25))
```

This code snippet demonstrates how to use if-then-else statements in the prompt to generate different responses based on the user's age.

4.6.2. Generating Structured and Tabular Data

ChatGPT is an incredibly versatile tool with a variety of use cases. One such use case is the generation of structured and tabular data. With the right prompt, ChatGPT can output data in a specific format, such as a table or a list.

By utilizing this feature, businesses and organizations can streamline their data gathering and analysis processes, ultimately leading to greater efficiency and productivity. Additionally, ChatGPT's ability to generate data in a structured format can help reduce errors and inconsistencies that may arise when data is manually entered. Overall, ChatGPT's ability to produce structured and tabular data is an incredibly useful feature that can enhance a wide range of industries and applications.

Example:

For example, let's generate a simple table with information about different programming languages:

```python
import openai

prompt = """Create a table with the following columns: Language, Creator, and Ye
ar Released. Include the following programming languages: Python, JavaScript, an
d Ruby.

| Language    | Creator        | Year Released |
|-------------|----------------|---------------|"""

response = openai.Completion.create(
    engine="text-davinci-002",
    prompt=prompt,
    max_tokens=100,
    n=1,
    stop=None,
    temperature=0.8,
)

generated_table = response.choices[0].text.strip()
print(generated_table)
```

This code snippet demonstrates how to guide ChatGPT to generate a table with specific columns and rows. The model will fill in the required information based on the given prompt, outputting a structured table with the requested details.

Remember that the quality of the generated content may vary, and you might need to experiment with different prompt formulations and settings to obtain the desired output.

4.6.3. Advanced Techniques for Conditional Text Generation

To further elaborate on the topic of conditional text generation, here are a few more points to consider:

Advanced conditional logic

You can experiment with more complex conditional logic to create even more intricate and nuanced outputs. For example, you can use nested if-then-else statements to make multiple decisions based on different factors in the input. This can be particularly useful when you need to analyze a wide range of input data and make strategic decisions based on the results.

In addition, you can also consider using more advanced techniques such as decision trees and random forests to further refine your conditional logic. These methods can help you design more complex models that take into account a wide range of variables and factors, allowing you to make more accurate and nuanced predictions.

Another approach to consider is using machine learning algorithms to develop more sophisticated models. With machine learning, you can train your model on large datasets to identify patterns and insights that would be difficult to spot with traditional analytics methods. This can help you create more detailed and comprehensive models that can provide valuable insights and predictions for a wide range of applications.

Overall, there are many different ways to enhance your conditional logic and create more detailed and accurate models. By exploring these advanced techniques and approaches, you can unlock new insights and opportunities for your business or organization.

Example:

Nested conditional logic

```
prompt = (
    "You are an AI language model that helps users decide what to wear based on
the weather. "
    "Today, the weather is {weather}. What should the user wear? "
    "If the weather is sunny, suggest wearing a t-shirt and shorts. "
    "If the weather is rainy, suggest wearing a raincoat and waterproof boots. "
    "If the weather is cold, suggest wearing a jacket and long pants."
)

weather_conditions = ["sunny", "rainy", "cold"]

for condition in weather_conditions:
    response = chatgpt.generate(prompt.format(weather=condition))
    print(f"For {condition} weather: {response}")
```

In this example, we create a prompt that asks the AI to help users decide what to wear based on the weather. The AI's response should be conditional on the weather conditions: sunny, rainy, or cold. We loop through each weather condition and insert it into the prompt before generating a response from ChatGPT.

prompt.format(weather=condition) replaces the placeholder **{weather}** in the prompt with the current weather condition from the **weather_conditions** list. Then, we generate a response for each condition and print it.

Regular expressions

Regular expressions are a powerful tool that can be used to extract or generate specific patterns of text. In scenarios where you need to ensure that outputs follow certain rules or match specific formats, incorporating regex patterns in your prompts can guide the model to produce more accurate and relevant results.

This can be especially useful in a variety of contexts, such as natural language processing, data mining, and web scraping. Additionally, regular expressions can be used to help identify and correct errors in text, and can even be employed to automate certain tasks, such as formatting or data validation.

By taking advantage of the many benefits of regular expressions, you can significantly enhance the quality and efficiency of your work. So why not start exploring the possibilities of regex today?

Example:

```python
import re

prompt = (
    "You are an AI that provides information on various fruits. "
    "Please provide information on the following fruits: Apple, Banana, and Orange."
)

response = chatgpt.generate(prompt)
print("Generated response:", response)

fruit_pattern = re.compile(r"(Apple|Banana|Orange): (.+)")
fruit_info = fruit_pattern.findall(response)

for info in fruit_info:
    print(f"{info[0]}: {info[1]}")
```

In this example, we ask the AI to provide information about three different fruits: Apple, Banana, and Orange. The AI generates a response with information about each fruit.

We then use regular expressions to extract the information about each fruit from the response. The regular expression **fruit_pattern** is designed to match the fruit name followed by a colon and the information provided. **fruit_pattern.findall(response)** returns a list of tuples containing the fruit name and the information. We loop through this list and print the information for each fruit.

Combining with other techniques

Conditional text generation can be combined with other techniques to create even more tailored and dynamic responses. One such technique is the use of user attributes.

By incorporating user attributes such as their name, age, interests, and location into the conversation, the conversational agent can generate responses that are more personalized and relevant to the user. Additionally, system level instructions can also be integrated into the conversation.

These instructions can include information about the user's previous interactions with the system, as well as information about the system's current state and capabilities. By taking these factors into account, the conversational agent can provide more accurate and useful responses. Finally, conversation context can also be used to enhance the agent's responses. By tracking the user's previous messages and the overall flow of the conversation, the agent can generate responses that are more coherent and relevant to the user's needs.

By using these techniques in tandem, you can build advanced conversational agents that adapt to a wide range of user inputs and requirements, ultimately leading to a more satisfying user experience.

Example:

```
user_preference = "Banana"  # This could be collected from the user's profile or
preferences

prompt = (
    f"You are an AI that recommends a fruit based on a user's preference. "
    f"The user's favorite fruit is {user_preference}. "
    "If the user's favorite fruit is Apple, suggest a delicious apple dessert. "
    "If the user's favorite fruit is Banana, suggest a tasty banana dessert. "
    "If the user's favorite fruit is Orange, suggest a refreshing orange desser
t."
)

response = chatgpt.generate(prompt)
print(f"Suggested dessert for {user_preference}: {response}")
```

In this example, we use conditional text generation along with user preferences to recommend a dessert based on the user's favorite fruit. The user's favorite fruit is stored in the **user_preference** variable.

The prompt is designed with conditions for each fruit (Apple, Banana, and Orange), suggesting a dessert based on the user's preference. We insert the user's favorite fruit into the prompt using **prompt.format(user_preference=user_preference)** and generate a response from ChatGPT. The AI recommends a dessert based on the user's favorite fruit, and the result is printed.

Chapter 4 Conclusion

In this chapter, we have explored a range of advanced API features that can be leveraged to build sophisticated and effective applications using ChatGPT. From context and message handling to user attributes and personalization, we have delved into the various techniques that can be employed to create more engaging and context-aware conversational AI experiences.

We have learned how to maintain conversation context and manage user inputs and model responses for more coherent and meaningful interactions. By using a user's unique attributes and preferences, we have seen how we can adapt responses to provide more personalized experiences and deliver more relevant content.

In addition, we have investigated how to use system-level instructions to guide the model's behavior, thereby achieving more targeted and accurate output. Through experimenting with implicit and explicit prompts, we have demonstrated how we can effectively communicate our intentions to the model and obtain desired results.

An important aspect of advanced API features is multi-turn conversation design and dialogue system development. We have discussed the importance of designing effective multi-turn conversations and have introduced techniques for managing conversation flow. Furthermore, we have explored strategies for evaluating and optimizing dialogue systems, ensuring that our conversational AI performs at its best.

Another crucial aspect of advanced API usage is leveraging ChatGPT's multilingual support and translation capabilities. We have seen how ChatGPT can be utilized for language translation and fine-tuning for non-English languages, expanding the reach of our applications to a global audience.

Finally, we have delved into conditional text generation, exploring how to use if-then-else statements in prompts and generate structured and tabular data. We have also covered combining conditional text generation with user attributes and demonstrated the use of regular expressions for advanced text manipulation.

In conclusion, this chapter has provided a comprehensive overview of the advanced features available when working with ChatGPT API. By mastering these techniques, developers can create conversational AI applications that are more engaging, context-aware, and personalized. As we move forward, it is essential to remember that our understanding of these advanced features will continually evolve, and we must stay up-to-date with the latest developments in the field to create the best possible user experiences.

As you continue to build and refine your ChatGPT applications, keep in mind that experimentation and iteration are key. Be prepared to test different strategies and adapt your approach based on user feedback and performance metrics. By doing so, you will ensure that your applications continue to improve and meet the needs of your users.

Chapter 5 - Fine-tuning ChatGPT

ChatGPT is an incredibly powerful and versatile tool that can be used in a variety of ways. However, in order to make it even more effective for your specific needs, it may be necessary to fine-tune its performance. In this chapter, we will explore the process of fine-tuning ChatGPT to better serve your particular use-cases or domains.

To begin with, it is important to prepare your dataset in a way that is suitable for fine-tuning. This may involve cleaning and organizing the data, as well as selecting the most relevant examples. Once you have your dataset prepared, you can begin the process of fine-tuning ChatGPT to better suit your requirements.

During the fine-tuning process, you will need to manage the various settings and parameters that will define the behavior of your customized model. This may involve adjusting the learning rate, selecting the appropriate optimizer, and tweaking various other hyperparameters. It is important to carefully manage this process in order to achieve the best possible results.

Once you have fine-tuned your ChatGPT model, it is important to evaluate its performance to ensure that it is meeting your needs. This may involve testing the model on a variety of different inputs, or comparing its results to those of other models. By carefully managing the fine-tuning process and evaluating the performance of your customized model, you can ensure that ChatGPT is delivering the best possible results for your particular use-cases or domains.

5.1. Preparing Your Dataset

To fine-tune ChatGPT effectively, you will need a high-quality dataset that represents the domain or task you want the model to excel in. In this section, we will explore various strategies for data collection, cleaning, preprocessing, and validation.

One of the most important aspects of creating a high-quality dataset is ensuring that it is representative of the real-world data. This means that you need to collect data from a variety of

sources and ensure that it covers the full range of scenarios that the model will be expected to handle.

Once you have collected the data, you will need to clean and preprocess it to ensure that it is in a format that the model can understand. This may involve removing duplicates, dealing with missing data, or converting the data into a suitable format, such as numerical values.

Finally, you will need to validate the dataset to ensure that it is accurate and reliable. This may involve testing the dataset on a small subset of the data, or comparing it to existing datasets to ensure that it is consistent.

By following these strategies, you can create a high-quality dataset that will allow you to fine-tune ChatGPT effectively and achieve the best possible results.

5.1.1. Data Collection Strategies

Building a dataset for fine-tuning a model is a crucial step in machine learning. To start, you need to collect data from various sources, such as user-generated content, internal databases, or publicly available resources.

When collecting data, it is essential to ensure that the data is representative of the task you want your model to perform. This means that you need to have enough data to cover all possible scenarios that your model may encounter. Another consideration when collecting data is to ensure that the data is of high quality.

This means that the data should be accurate, reliable, and consistent. To achieve this, you may need to clean the data, remove duplicates, and validate the data before using it for fine-tuning your model. Once you have collected and cleaned your data, you can then use it to fine-tune your model, which will improve its accuracy and performance on your specific task.

Here are some data collection strategies:

Web scraping

Web scraping is a useful technique that can help you obtain valuable data from various online sources. One of the most common applications of web scraping is to extract data from websites, forums, or social media platforms.

By doing so, you can gather information that is relevant to your target domain, such as customer feedback, product reviews, or market trends. Additionally, web scraping can be used to monitor

your competitors' activities, track changes in search engine rankings, or identify potential business opportunities. With the right tools and techniques, web scraping can be a powerful tool for data-driven decision making.

Example:

Web scraping using Beautiful Soup and requests libraries in Python:

```python
import requests
from bs4 import BeautifulSoup

url = 'https://example.com'
response = requests.get(url)
soup = BeautifulSoup(response.text, 'html.parser')

# Extract data from a specific HTML element
data = soup.find('div', {'class': 'example-class'})
print(data.text)
```

API data extraction

Access data from services that provide APIs, like news platforms, e-commerce sites, or social media networks. When extracting data, it's important to consider the quality of the data and the reliability of the source.

Additionally, it's important to have a clear understanding of the data that you are trying to extract in order to ensure that you are able to extract the most relevant and useful information. Once the data has been extracted, it can be used for a wide range of purposes, including market research, data analysis, and product development.

By utilizing API data extraction, businesses can gain valuable insights into their customers and competitors, enabling them to make more informed decisions and stay ahead of the competition.

Example:

API data extraction using requests library in Python:

```python
import requests

api_key = 'your_api_key'
endpoint = 'https://api.example.com/data'
params = {'api_key': api_key, 'parameter': 'value'}

response = requests.get(endpoint, params=params)
data = response.json()

# Access a specific field from the JSON data
print(data['field_name'])
```

Internal databases

An important aspect of using internal databases is to ensure that the data is well-organized and easily accessible. It is also essential to have a clear understanding of the data that is being collected, as well as the sources of this information.

One way to leverage internal databases is to use customer support logs, which can provide valuable insights into customer behavior and preferences. Another useful source of information is product descriptions, which can be used to identify key features and benefits of different products. In addition, proprietary information can be used to gain a competitive advantage by providing insights into market trends and customer needs.

When using internal databases, it is important to have a clear plan for how the data will be collected, analyzed, and used to inform business decisions.

Example:

Accessing internal databases using pandas and SQLAlchemy libraries in Python:

```
import pandas as pd
from sqlalchemy import create_engine

engine = create_engine('postgresql://username:password@localhost/dbname')
query = 'SELECT * FROM example_table'

data = pd.read_sql(query, engine)
print(data.head())
```

Open datasets

One of the best ways to get started with data science is to use publicly available datasets. These datasets can be found on various open data repositories, such as Kaggle or Google Dataset Search. By using open datasets, you can gain valuable experience in data manipulation, cleaning, and analysis.

Additionally, you can use these datasets to build your own machine learning models and gain insights into real-world problems. Whether you're interested in healthcare, finance, or social sciences, there's likely an open dataset available that can help you get started. So why not explore the world of open datasets and see what insights you can uncover?

Example:

Loading an open dataset using pandas library in Python:

```
import pandas as pd

url = 'https://raw.githubusercontent.com/datablist/sample-csv-files/master/peopl
e/people-100.csv'
data = pd.read_csv(url)
print(data.head())
```

5.1.2. Data Cleaning and Preprocessing

Once you have collected your data, the next step is to clean and preprocess it. This is a critical step to ensure the quality and suitability of the data for fine-tuning. The process involves several steps.

First, you need to remove any irrelevant data that may be present. This includes data that may not be pertinent to your analysis or data that is not of good quality. For example, if you are analyzing sales data, you may need to remove any data that pertains to returns or refunds.

Second, you need to remove any duplicate data that may be present. Duplicate data can skew your analysis and lead to incorrect conclusions. Therefore, it is important to remove any duplicates before proceeding with the fine-tuning process.

Third, you need to remove any corrupted data that may be present. Corrupted data can also lead to incorrect conclusions and can cause errors in the fine-tuning process. Therefore, it is important to remove any corrupted data before proceeding.

Finally, you need to convert the data into a format that can be ingested by the fine-tuning process. This may involve converting the data into a different file format or using a tool to preprocess the data. It is important to ensure that your data is in the correct format before proceeding with fine-tuning.

Some common preprocessing steps include:

1. Removing HTML tags, URLs, and other irrelevant characters from the text.

   Here an example:

   Removing special characters and digits using regular expressions in Python:

```python
import re

text = 'Example text with special characters!@#4$5%^&*()_+-={}|[]\\\;\',./<>?'
cleaned_text = re.sub(r'[^\w\s]', '', text)
print(cleaned_text)
```

2. **Tokenization**: Tokenization is the process of breaking down a text into individual words or subwords. This is a crucial step in many natural language processing tasks, such as sentiment analysis and machine translation. Tokenization can be done using various techniques, including rule-based methods, statistical methods, and deep learning models. Additionally, tokenization may differ depending on the language and the specific task at hand. Nevertheless, the goal remains the same: to extract meaningful units of language from the text that can be further analyzed and processed.

Here an example:

```
import nltk

nltk.download('punkt')
from nltk.tokenize import word_tokenize

text = 'This is an example sentence.'
tokens = word_tokenize(text)
print(tokens)
```

3. **Lowercasing, stemming, or lemmatization**

Converting text to a standardized form to reduce the dimensionality of the data is an important step in text preprocessing. It can help with tasks such as sentiment analysis, topic modeling, and named entity recognition. Additionally, it can make the data more manageable for machine learning algorithms.

Lowercasing involves converting all text to lowercase, while stemming and lemmatization involve reducing words to their root form. However, it is important to note that these techniques can sometimes result in loss of information, so careful consideration should be taken when deciding whether to use them.

Overall, lowercasing, stemming, and lemmatization are important tools in the text processing toolbox that can help improve the effectiveness of natural language processing applications.

Here an example:

Lowercasing text using Python:

```
text = 'Example Text'
lowercased_text = text.lower()
print(lowercased_text)
```

4. Removing or replacing sensitive information, like personally identifiable information (PII), to maintain data privacy.

Here an example:

Removing stop words using the NLTK library in Python:

```
import nltk

nltk.download('stopwords')
from nltk.corpus import stopwords
from nltk.tokenize import word_tokenize

text = 'This is an example sentence with some stop words.'
stop_words = set(stopwords.words('english'))
tokens = word_tokenize(text)
filtered_tokens = [token for token in tokens if token not in stop_words]

print(filtered_tokens)
```

5.1.3. Dataset Splitting and Validation

Once you have cleaned and preprocessed your data, the next step is to split it into separate sets for training, validation, and testing. This is a crucial step in building any model, as it allows you to train the model on one portion of the data, evaluate its performance on another, and ensure that it generalizes well to unseen data.

To perform this split, there are various techniques you can use, such as simple random sampling or stratified sampling. Simple random sampling involves randomly selecting a subset of the data for each set, while stratified sampling involves ensuring that each set has a similar distribution of classes or labels as the original dataset.

Once you have split your data, it's important to perform some exploratory data analysis on each set to ensure that the distribution of classes or labels is similar across all sets. This will help ensure that your model is not biased towards one particular set and can generalize well to new data.

Overall, the process of splitting your data into separate sets for training, validation, and testing is a crucial step in building any model, and should not be overlooked or rushed. By taking the time to carefully split your data and perform exploratory data analysis, you can ensure that your model is robust and can generalize well to unseen data.

Here is a general guideline for dataset splitting:

Training set

The training set is an essential part of developing a machine learning model. It is typically allocated between 70-80% of the dataset, providing enough data for the model to learn and adjust its weights during the fine-tuning process. During this process, the model is trained on the data, and the weights are updated to minimize the error between the predicted output and the actual output.

By allocating a significant portion of the dataset to the training set, the model can learn more generalizable features and avoid overfitting. Additionally, the training set can be used to evaluate the performance of the model during the training process, enabling the developer to monitor the model's progress and adjust the parameters accordingly.

Example:

Splitting the dataset into training and testing sets using the **train_test_split** function from the **sklearn** library:

```
from sklearn.model_selection import train_test_split

data = ['sample1', 'sample2', 'sample3', 'sample4', 'sample5', 'sample6']
labels = [0, 1, 1, 0, 1, 0]

train_data, test_data, train_labels, test_labels = train_test_split(
    data, labels, test_size=0.33, random_state=42
)

print("Training data:", train_data)
print("Testing data:", test_data)
```

Validation set

Around 10-15% of the dataset is reserved for validation. This is an important step in machine learning model development because it helps to prevent overfitting, which occurs when a model becomes too complex and begins to memorize the training data instead of generalizing to new data.

The validation set is used to evaluate the model's performance during training and to select the best model hyperparameters. By comparing the performance of different models on the validation set, we can identify which hyperparameters and model architectures are most effective for the given task. This process helps to ensure that the final model will perform well on new, unseen data.

Example:

Splitting the dataset into training, validation, and testing sets using the **train_test_split** function from the **sklearn** library:

```
from sklearn.model_selection import train_test_split

data = ['sample1', 'sample2', 'sample3', 'sample4', 'sample5', 'sample6']
labels = [0, 1, 1, 0, 1, 0]

train_data, test_data, train_labels, test_labels = train_test_split(
    data, labels, test_size=0.33, random_state=42
)
train_data, val_data, train_labels, val_labels = train_test_split(
    train_data, train_labels, test_size=0.5, random_state=42
)

print("Training data:", train_data)
print("Validation data:", val_data)
print("Testing data:", test_data)
```

Test set

The remaining 10-15% of the dataset is used for testing. This data provides an unbiased assessment of the model's performance on unseen data. In other words, this is the data that the model has not seen during training, so it serves as a good indicator of how well the model can generalize to new data.

By evaluating the model's performance on the test set, we can gain a better understanding of its strengths and weaknesses and identify areas for improvement. It is important to note that the test set should only be used for evaluation and not for model selection or hyperparameter tuning, as this can lead to overfitting.

Instead, a validation set should be used for these purposes, which is typically a small portion of the training data.

Example:

Using k-fold cross-validation with **cross_val_score** from the **sklearn** library:

```
from sklearn.datasets import load_iris
from sklearn.model_selection import cross_val_score
from sklearn.linear_model import LogisticRegression

iris = load_iris()
X, y = iris.data, iris.target

logreg = LogisticRegression(max_iter=1000)

# Perform 5-fold cross-validation
scores = cross_val_score(logreg, X, y, cv=5)

print("Cross-validation scores:", scores)
```

When splitting your dataset, it is crucial to ensure that the distribution of examples across the sets is representative of the overall data. This is because an uneven distribution may lead to biased results and render your machine learning model less effective.

One way to achieve this is through random sampling, where examples are selected completely at random from the entire dataset. Alternatively, stratified sampling can be used to ensure that each subset contains representative proportions of each class or category present in the overall data.

This can be particularly useful if your data is imbalanced, with certain classes or categories being much more prevalent than others. In either case, it is important to carefully consider the nature of your data and choose a sampling method that is appropriate for your particular use case.

5.1.4. Dataset Augmentation Techniques

Dataset augmentation is a crucial technique in machine learning that involves expanding the existing dataset by creating new samples through various techniques. One such technique involves rotating or flipping existing images to create new ones with different orientations.

Another technique is adding random noise to the dataset, which can help improve the model's ability to handle noisy or distorted input. Furthermore, dataset augmentation can help to balance the distribution of classes in the dataset, which is important when dealing with imbalanced datasets.

By creating new samples, the diversity of the dataset is increased, which in turn can help the model to generalize better and improve its overall performance.

Some common dataset augmentation techniques include:

Text paraphrasing

One approach to generating new text samples is to paraphrase existing ones in the dataset. This can be a manual process, where a human rewrites the text in a different way while retaining the original meaning. Alternatively, advanced NLP models such as T5 or BART can be used to automatically generate paraphrases. By using this approach, new samples can be created with the same underlying message but with different phrasing or wording.

Paraphrasing can be particularly useful in situations where there is a lack of diversity in the original dataset. For example, if a dataset contains a limited number of samples with a particular phrase or sentence structure, paraphrasing can be used to create additional samples with similar meaning. This can help to improve the generalization of the machine learning model trained on the dataset.

Another benefit of paraphrasing is that it can help to reduce overfitting. Overfitting occurs when a machine learning model becomes too specialized to the training data and is unable to generalize to new, unseen data. By creating a more diverse dataset through paraphrasing, the machine learning model is less likely to overfit and can perform better on new data.

However, it is important to note that paraphrasing may not always be appropriate or effective. In some cases, paraphrasing can introduce errors or inaccuracies into the dataset, which can negatively impact the performance of the machine learning model. Additionally, paraphrasing may not be able to capture certain nuances or complexities of the original text, particularly in cases where the text contains cultural references or specialized terminology.

Example:

Text paraphrasing using T5 model (using Hugging Face Transformers library):

```python
from transformers import T5ForConditionalGeneration, T5Tokenizer

tokenizer = T5Tokenizer.from_pretrained("t5-base")
model = T5ForConditionalGeneration.from_pretrained("t5-base")

def paraphrase(text):
    inputs = tokenizer.encode("paraphrase: " + text, return_tensors="pt")
    outputs = model.generate(inputs, max_length=50, num_return_sequences=1)
    paraphrased_text = tokenizer.decode(outputs[0])
    return paraphrased_text

original_text = "ChatGPT is a powerful language model."
paraphrased_text = paraphrase(original_text)
print(paraphrased_text)
```

Data synthesis

Generating entirely new samples based on the patterns in the existing dataset is a crucial step in creating a robust and diverse dataset. In order to accomplish this task, there are several methods that can be deployed.

One of these methods is through the use of generative models, like GPT-3, which can create new samples based on the patterns that it has learned from the existing dataset. Another method is through the use of rule-based techniques, which can be more time-consuming but can create more tailored and specific samples.

Regardless of the method chosen, data synthesis is an important step in creating a dataset that is representative of the population or environment being studied.

Example:

Data synthesis using GPT-3 (assuming you have API access):

```python
import openai

openai.api_key = "your-api-key"

def synthesize_data(prompt):
    response = openai.Completion.create(
        engine="davinci-codex",
        prompt=prompt,
        max_tokens=50,
        n=1,
        stop=None,
        temperature=0.7,
    )
    return response.choices[0].text.strip()

prompt = "Create a new sentence about ChatGPT."
new_sample = synthesize_data(prompt)
print(new_sample)
```

Translation-based augmentation

One potential method to increase the amount of data available for machine learning models is through translation-based augmentation. This involves translating the original text to another language and then back to the original language, which can result in slightly different sentences that still convey the same meaning.

By using this technique, the dataset can be expanded without requiring additional human effort to create new examples. Additionally, this approach can help improve the robustness of the model by exposing it to a wider range of sentence structures and word choices.

However, it is important to note that this method may not be suitable for all languages or text types, and care should be taken to ensure that the resulting sentences are still grammatically correct and maintain the intended meaning.

Example:

Translation-based augmentation (using Hugging Face Transformers library):

```
from transformers import MarianMTModel, MarianTokenizer

def translate_and_back(text, src_lang="en", tgt_lang="fr"):
    model_name = f'Helsinki-NLP/opus-mt-{src_lang}-{tgt_lang}'
    tokenizer = MarianTokenizer.from_pretrained(model_name)
    model = MarianMTModel.from_pretrained(model_name)

    # Translate to target language
    inputs = tokenizer(text, return_tensors="pt")
    translated = model.generate(**inputs)
    tgt_text = tokenizer.decode(translated[0], skip_special_tokens=True)

    # Translate back to source language
    model_name = f'Helsinki-NLP/opus-mt-{tgt_lang}-{src_lang}'
    tokenizer = MarianTokenizer.from_pretrained(model_name)
    model = MarianMTModel.from_pretrained(model_name)

    inputs = tokenizer(tgt_text, return_tensors="pt")
    translated = model.generate(**inputs)
    src_text = tokenizer.decode(translated[0], skip_special_tokens=True)

    return src_text

original_text = "ChatGPT can help in a wide range of tasks."
augmented_text = translate_and_back(original_text)
print(augmented_text)
```

Insertion, deletion, or swapping of words or phrases

One way to create new samples is to make small modifications to the text. This can be achieved by inserting, deleting, or swapping words or phrases. By doing so, we can expand on the original ideas and create a more comprehensive piece of writing.

For instance, we can add more descriptive words to provide a vivid picture of the topic at hand, or we can swap out certain words with synonyms to vary the language and make it more interesting. Through these techniques, we can create a text that is longer and more engaging for the reader.

Text expansion or contraction

Expanding or contracting abbreviations, contractions, or short forms in the dataset to create new samples. Text expansion or contraction is a process in natural language processing that aims to increase or decrease the length of a given text by expanding or contracting abbreviations, contractions, or short forms in the dataset.

The goal of this process is to create new samples that can be used to enhance the performance of machine learning models. Text expansion or contraction can be achieved through various techniques such as rule-based methods, dictionary-based methods, and machine learning-based methods. Rule-based methods involve the use of pre-defined rules to expand or contract abbreviations, contractions, or short forms.

Dictionary-based methods use dictionaries to look up the meanings of abbreviations, contractions, or short forms and expand or contract them accordingly. Machine learning-based methods involve the use of machine learning algorithms to learn the patterns in the dataset and perform text expansion or contraction accordingly.

Example:

For this method, you can use libraries like **contractions** to handle contractions in the English language:

```python
import contractions

text = "ChatGPT isn't just useful; it's essential."
expanded_text = contractions.fix(text)
print(expanded_text)
```

Please keep in mind that choosing the right augmentation techniques is dependent on the unique characteristics of the dataset and the task at hand. It's important to thoroughly evaluate the impact of augmentation on both the model's performance and its ability to generalize during the validation process.

This evaluation should include a careful analysis of how the augmented data impacts the model's accuracy, as well as a thorough comparison of the performance metrics between the augmented and original datasets. In addition, it's essential to consider the potential trade-offs

between the benefits of augmentation and the costs associated with generating and processing the augmented data.

By carefully considering all of these factors, we can ensure that our augmentation strategy effectively improves model performance while minimizing any potential drawbacks.

5.2: Transfer Learning Techniques

Transfer learning is a powerful machine learning technique that has garnered significant attention in recent years. Essentially, the idea behind transfer learning is to take a pre-trained model that has already learned a great deal from a large-scale dataset and then further fine-tune it on a smaller, domain-specific dataset. By doing so, the pre-trained model can leverage its existing knowledge to improve its performance on the domain-specific dataset. Transfer learning can be particularly useful in situations where the available data is limited, as it can help to overcome the challenge of insufficient data.

In this topic, we will delve deeper into the world of transfer learning by exploring various techniques for fine-tuning GPT-4. We will begin by discussing the role of transfer learning and why it has become such an important area of research in machine learning. We will then move on to a discussion of how to choose the right model size and parameters when fine-tuning a pre-trained model like GPT-4. Along the way, we will also explore various training strategies and hyperparameters that can be used to optimize the performance of the model. By the end of this topic, you should have a solid understanding of transfer learning and should be able to apply these techniques to your own machine learning projects.

5.2.1. Understanding Transfer Learning in GPT-4

Fine-tuning is a crucial technique in natural language processing that allows researchers and developers to leverage pre-trained language models like GPT-4 for specific tasks. By doing so, they can take advantage of the enormous amount of text data that these models have been trained on, which enables them to understand and generate natural language text that is both coherent and contextually appropriate.

One of the key benefits of using a pre-trained language model like GPT-4 is that it can help overcome the challenge of insufficient data. In many cases, machine learning models require large amounts of data to be effective, but this data is not always available. Pre-trained models like GPT-4 provide a solution to this problem by allowing researchers and developers to fine-tune the model on smaller, domain-specific datasets.

Fine-tuning GPT-4 involves training the model on a specific task for a smaller number of epochs using a smaller learning rate. During this process, the model adjusts its weights to perform better on the specific task while still retaining the general knowledge it has acquired during pre-training. This approach allows researchers and developers to adapt the model to the particularities of their dataset and task more efficiently.

However, choosing the appropriate model size and parameters for fine-tuning GPT-4 is a crucial step that can significantly impact the model's performance. Selecting the right model size is important because it can impact the model's training time, computational requirements, and performance. Smaller models are faster to train and have lower memory requirements, but they might not perform as well as larger models. On the other hand, larger models can capture more intricate patterns in the data, but they require more computational resources and may be prone to overfitting on small datasets.

In addition to model size, other parameters such as learning rate, batch size, and the number of training epochs should be carefully chosen. These parameters can significantly impact the model's training and convergence, so it's essential to experiment with different values to find the optimal configuration.

Fine-tuning GPT-4 also involves iterating through different hyperparameter configurations to achieve the best performance on the task at hand. Common hyperparameter optimization techniques include grid search, random search, and Bayesian optimization. These techniques can help researchers and developers find the best combination of hyperparameters for their model.

Training strategies such as using learning rate schedules, gradient accumulation, and regularization techniques like weight decay, dropout, and early stopping are also used to improve the model's performance. Monitoring the model's performance on a validation set is crucial to assess the effectiveness of the chosen training strategies and hyperparameter configurations.

Fine-tuning GPT-4 is a powerful technique that allows researchers and developers to adapt pre-trained language models to specific tasks. However, selecting the appropriate model size, parameters, and hyperparameter configurations is critical for achieving optimal performance. Fine-tuning GPT-4 requires careful experimentation and monitoring to ensure that the model is performing well on the task at hand.

Example:

Fine-tuning GPT-4 on a specific task:

```python
import torch
from transformers import GPT4ForSequenceClassification, GPT4Tokenizer, GPT4Confi
g

# Load the pre-trained model and tokenizer
config = GPT4Config.from_pretrained("gpt-4-base")
tokenizer = GPT4Tokenizer.from_pretrained("gpt-4-base")
model = GPT4ForSequenceClassification.from_pretrained("gpt-4-base", config=confi
g)

# Fine-tune the model on your task-specific dataset
# (Assuming you have a DataLoader `dataloader` for your task-specific dataset)

optimizer = torch.optim.AdamW(model.parameters(), lr=1e-5)

for epoch in range(3):  # Number of epochs
    for batch in dataloader:
        inputs, labels = batch
        optimizer.zero_grad()

        outputs = model(**inputs, labels=labels)
        loss = outputs.loss
        loss.backward()
        optimizer.step()
```

5.2.2. Choosing the Right Model Size and Parameters

When fine-tuning GPT-4, it is crucial to carefully consider various factors to achieve the best possible performance. One of the most important factors is the appropriate selection of model size and parameters for your task.

GPT-4 is available in various sizes, ranging from small to large, and each has its own advantages and disadvantages. While smaller models are faster to train and have lower memory requirements, they might not perform as well as larger models. On the other hand, larger models are capable of capturing more complex patterns in the data, but they require more computational resources and may be prone to overfitting on small datasets.

However, the choice of model size is not the only consideration. There are other parameters that are equally important, such as the learning rate, batch size, and the number of training epochs. These parameters play a crucial role in determining the model's training and

convergence. For instance, a higher learning rate can help speed up the training process, but it may also result in unstable convergence. Conversely, a lower learning rate can ensure stable convergence, but it may also make the training process slower.

Similarly, the choice of batch size and the number of training epochs can also significantly impact the model's performance. A larger batch size can help improve the model's convergence and reduce the variance in the training process, but it may also require more memory and computational resources. Similarly, training a model for too few epochs may result in underfitting, while training for too many epochs may result in overfitting.

Given these considerations, it's essential to experiment with different values for these parameters to find the optimal configuration for your task. By carefully selecting the appropriate model size and parameters, you can ensure that your fine-tuned GPT-4 model performs optimally on your specific task.

Example:

Choosing the right model size and parameters:

```
# Using a smaller GPT-4 model
config_small = GPT4Config.from_pretrained("gpt-4-small")
tokenizer_small = GPT4Tokenizer.from_pretrained("gpt-4-small")
model_small = GPT4ForSequenceClassification.from_pretrained("gpt-4-small", confi
g=config_small)

# Using a larger GPT-4 model
config_large = GPT4Config.from_pretrained("gpt-4-large")
tokenizer_large = GPT4Tokenizer.from_pretrained("gpt-4-large")
model_large = GPT4ForSequenceClassification.from_pretrained("gpt-4-large", confi
g=config_large)
```

5.2.3. Training Strategies and Hyperparameter Optimization

Developing an effective fine-tuning strategy involves iterating through different hyperparameter configurations to achieve the best performance on your task. Some common hyperparameter optimization techniques include grid search, random search, and Bayesian optimization. These techniques can help you find the best combination of hyperparameters for your model.

In addition to hyperparameter optimization, you can employ various training strategies to improve the model's performance. For instance, using learning rate schedules (such as cosine annealing or linear warm-up) can help the model adapt its learning rate over time, potentially leading to better convergence. Additionally, using techniques like gradient accumulation can help you train larger models on limited hardware by accumulating gradients from smaller mini-batches before performing a weight update.

Regularization techniques like weight decay, dropout, and early stopping can also be used to prevent overfitting and improve generalization.

Example:

Training strategies and hyperparameter optimization:

```python
# Linear learning rate warm-up
from transformers import get_linear_schedule_with_warmup

total_steps = len(dataloader) * epochs
warmup_steps = int(0.1 * total_steps)  # Warm-up for 10% of total steps

scheduler = get_linear_schedule_with_warmup(optimizer, num_warmup_steps=warmup_s
teps, num_training_steps=total_steps)

for epoch in range(epochs):
    for batch in dataloader:
        inputs, labels = batch
        optimizer.zero_grad()

        outputs = model(**inputs, labels=labels)
        loss = outputs.loss
        loss.backward()
        optimizer.step()
        scheduler.step()  # Update the learning rate
```

When training a model, it is important to keep in mind that the effectiveness of your training strategies and hyperparameter choices can greatly impact the performance of your model. One way to assess the effectiveness of these choices is by monitoring the model's performance on a validation set. By doing so, you can gain insights into how the model is performing and make adjustments as needed.

To optimize your fine-tuning process, it is often necessary to iterate through different configurations and strategies. This can involve adjusting hyperparameters, trying different optimization algorithms, or even changing the structure of the model itself. By experimenting with different approaches, you can gain a better understanding of what works best for your specific task and data.

While training a model may seem like a straightforward process, there are many factors to consider in order to achieve the best possible results. By monitoring the model's performance on a validation set and iterating through different configurations and strategies, you can fine-tune your approach and ultimately achieve success.

5.2.4. Early Stopping and Model Selection

Early stopping is a useful technique that can prevent the issue of overfitting in machine learning models. When we train a model, we want it to generalize well to new data rather than just memorize the training data. However, sometimes a model can become too complex and start to fit the noise in the training data rather than the underlying patterns. In such cases, the model will not perform well on new data and we say that it has overfit.

To avoid overfitting, we can use early stopping. This technique involves monitoring the performance of the model on a validation set during the training process. When the performance on the validation set starts to degrade, we can stop training the model to prevent it from overfitting. By doing this, we can obtain a model that generalizes well to new data.

In addition to early stopping, model selection is another important aspect of training machine learning models. After training many models with different hyperparameters or architectures, we need to choose the best one among them. This is usually done by comparing their performances on the validation set. The model with the best performance on the validation set is selected as the final model.

Therefore, by using both early stopping and model selection, we can obtain a model that generalizes well to new data and avoids the issue of overfitting.

Example:

Here's a code example demonstrating early stopping and model selection:

```python
import copy

# Early stopping and model selection
patience = 3  # Number of epochs to wait before stopping if no improvement
best_model = None
best_val_loss = float("inf")
counter = 0

for epoch in range(epochs):
    # Training loop
    for batch in dataloader:
        inputs, labels = batch
        optimizer.zero_grad()

        outputs = model(**inputs, labels=labels)
        loss = outputs.loss
        loss.backward()
        optimizer.step()

    # Validation loop
    val_loss = 0
    for batch in val_dataloader:
        inputs, labels = batch
        with torch.no_grad():
            outputs = model(**inputs, labels=labels)
            val_loss += outputs.loss.item()

    # Model selection and early stopping
    if val_loss < best_val_loss:
        best_val_loss = val_loss
        best_model = copy.deepcopy(model)
        counter = 0
    else:
        counter += 1
        if counter >= patience:
            break
```

This code example demonstrates how to implement early stopping and model selection during fine-tuning. Be sure to adapt this code to your specific dataset and fine-tuning task.

5.3. Model Evaluation and Testing

In this section, we will discuss various techniques for evaluating and testing fine-tuned ChatGPT models. We will cover quantitative evaluation metrics, qualitative evaluation techniques, and methods for handling overfitting and underfitting. These approaches are essential to ensure that your fine-tuned model performs well and generalizes effectively to unseen data.

Quantitative evaluation metrics are numerical measures that allow us to assess the performance of a fine-tuned ChatGPT model. Common metrics include accuracy, precision, recall, and F1 score. By analyzing these metrics, we can gain insight into the model's strengths and weaknesses.

Qualitative evaluation techniques, on the other hand, involve a more subjective assessment of the model's performance. This can include examining the generated text for coherence, fluency, and relevance to the given prompt. Another technique is to have human evaluators rate the quality of the generated responses.

To ensure that the fine-tuned model generalizes effectively to unseen data, it is important to address overfitting and underfitting. Overfitting occurs when the model is too complex and fits the training data too closely, resulting in poor performance on unseen data. Underfitting, on the other hand, occurs when the model is too simple and cannot capture the complexity of the training data, resulting in poor performance on both training and unseen data. To address these issues, techniques such as regularization, early stopping, and data augmentation can be employed.

By employing these evaluation and testing techniques, you can ensure that your fine-tuned ChatGPT model is performing optimally and can effectively generate high-quality responses for a variety of prompts.

5.3.1. Quantitative Evaluation Metrics

When it comes to assessing the performance of your model for text generation tasks, you want to make sure you're using the right tools to get the best results. This is where quantitative evaluation metrics come in.

These metrics allow you to use numeric scores to measure the effectiveness of your model. Some of the most common metrics used for text generation tasks include BLEU, ROUGE, and Perplexity. Each of these metrics has its own strengths and weaknesses, but by selecting the right one that best aligns with your specific use case, you'll be able to ensure that you're getting the most accurate and reliable results possible.

Additionally, by exploring and experimenting with different evaluation metrics, you may discover new insights into the performance of your model that you hadn't considered before, leading to even more improvements and refinements in the future.

Example:

Here's an example of how to compute BLEU score using the **nltk** library:

```python
from nltk.translate.bleu_score import import sentence_bleu

reference = [["this", "is", "a", "test"]]
candidate = ["this", "is", "a", "test"]

bleu_score = sentence_bleu(reference, candidate)
print("BLEU Score:", bleu_score)
```

5.3.2. Qualitative Evaluation Techniques

Qualitative evaluation techniques are essential tools for assessing the quality of generated text. By analyzing the generated text, researchers can gain valuable insights into the model's ability to produce coherent, contextually appropriate, and engaging responses. One such technique is manual inspection, which involves close scrutiny of the text to identify patterns, errors, and areas for improvement.

Another commonly used technique is user studies, which involve obtaining feedback from human participants about the text. This feedback can help researchers identify areas where the model is performing well and areas where it needs improvement. A third technique is A/B testing, which involves comparing the output of two different models or approaches to see which one performs better.

By using a combination of these techniques, researchers can gain a comprehensive understanding of the strengths and weaknesses of the model and make informed decisions about how to improve it. Overall, qualitative evaluation techniques play a critical role in the development and refinement of natural language generation systems.

Example:

Here's an example of how you might collect user feedback for qualitative evaluation:

```python
generated_responses = ["response1", "response2", "response3"]

for idx, response in enumerate(generated_responses):
    print(f"{idx + 1}: {response}")

user_feedback = input("Which response do you prefer (1, 2, or 3)? ")
```

5.3.3. Handling Overfitting and Underfitting

Overfitting is one of the most common problems in machine learning. It occurs when a model learns the training data too well, leading to poor generalization to unseen data. It is a situation where the model becomes too complex and starts to memorize the training data instead of learning the underlying patterns. This can lead to a very high accuracy on the training data but poor results on the testing data.

Underfitting, on the other hand, occurs when a model doesn't learn the underlying patterns in the data. The model is too simple and cannot capture all the important features in the data. This can lead to poor performance on both training and testing data.

To handle these issues, there are several techniques that can be employed such as early stopping, regularization, or adjusting the model architecture. Early stopping is a technique that can be used to prevent overfitting by stopping the training process when the performance on the validation set does not improve anymore. Regularization is another technique that can be used to reduce overfitting by adding a penalty term to the loss function.

This penalty term discourages the model to learn complex features that might not be useful for the final prediction. Finally, adjusting the model architecture can also help to reduce overfitting or underfitting. This involves changing the number of layers, the number of neurons, or the activation functions to find the best configuration for the particular problem.

Example:

Here's an example of applying weight decay (L2 regularization) during training to reduce overfitting:

```
from transformers import AdamW

optimizer = AdamW(model.parameters(), lr=learning_rate, weight_decay=0.01)
```

5.3.4. Model Monitoring and Continuous Evaluation

After deploying your fine-tuned model, it is critical to continuously monitor its performance, adjust its parameters as needed, and incorporate new data for retraining. It is important to recognize that real-world data is dynamic and may change over time.

The data may present new patterns that were not present in the training data. Regularly evaluating your model helps ensure that it remains relevant and effective, providing an optimal experience to your users and delivering accurate results on a consistent basis.

In addition, it is recommended to compare the performance of the model with other models to ensure that the model is not overfitting or underfitting. By doing so, you can rest assured that your model is well-designed and performs to the best of its abilities.

1. **Monitoring Metrics**: It is highly important to track the performance of your model to ensure optimal results. One way to achieve this is by monitoring metrics such as response time, error rate, and user satisfaction. By doing so, you will be able to identify areas for improvement and make changes accordingly. For example, if you notice a high error rate, you can investigate and refine your model to reduce the frequency of errors. Additionally, monitoring metrics can help you identify potential issues before they become major problems. By keeping track of user satisfaction, you can also identify areas where your model is performing well and areas where it may need improvement. Overall, monitoring metrics is an essential part of ensuring the success of your model and improving its performance over time.

2. **User Feedback**: It is important to collect user feedback to fully understand how well your model is performing in real-world situations. By gathering qualitative information from your users, you can gain valuable insights that can help you identify areas where the model may need improvement or fine-tuning. This can include things like

identifying specific pain points that users are experiencing, understanding how users are interacting with the model, and getting a better sense of the overall user experience. Additionally, collecting user feedback over time can help you track changes and trends in user behavior, allowing you to make adjustments to your model and optimize it for long-term success.

3. **Retraining**: It is important to periodically retrain your machine learning model with new data. This will help ensure that the model remains up-to-date and continues to perform well over time. One way to make this process easier is to automate it using a continuous integration and continuous deployment (CI/CD) pipeline. This pipeline can help you manage the flow of new data into your model, as well as automatically trigger retraining when necessary. By doing so, you can ensure that your machine learning model is always operating at peak performance and delivering the best results possible.

Example:

Here's an example of how you might collect user feedback for monitoring purposes:

```python
import time
from collections import defaultdict

feedback_data = defaultdict(list)

def get_user_feedback(response, user_rating):
    feedback_data["response"].append(response)
    feedback_data["rating"].append(user_rating)
    feedback_data["timestamp"].append(time.time())

generated_responses = ["response1", "response2", "response3"]

for idx, response in enumerate(generated_responses):
    print(f"{idx + 1}: {response}")

user_rating = input("Please rate the response (1 to 5, with 5 being the best): ")

get_user_feedback(generated_responses[int(user_rating) - 1], user_rating)
```

This code snippet demonstrates how to collect user feedback and store it in a dictionary for further analysis. Monitoring this data over time can help you identify potential issues and inform any necessary model updates.

5.4. Customizing Tokenizers and Vocabulary

In this section, we will delve into the significance of tokenizers and vocabulary customization in the context of domain-specific languages. Tokenizers are crucial for processing natural language text, breaking it down into individual words or phrases that can be analyzed in context. By customizing the vocabulary to suit your specific use case, you can improve the accuracy and relevance of your language models.

One important aspect of adapting tokenizers and vocabularies to domain-specific languages is identifying the key concepts and terminology that are unique to that field. This requires a deep understanding of the domain, as well as the ability to recognize and classify different types of language data. Once you have identified the relevant terms and concepts, you can use them to create customized tokenization rules and vocabularies that accurately reflect the nuances of your domain.

Another important consideration when working with domain-specific languages is the need to constantly update and refine your language models. As new concepts and terminology emerge in your field, you must be able to incorporate them into your tokenizers and vocabularies, ensuring that your models remain relevant and effective over time. This requires a flexible and adaptable approach to language processing, as well as a willingness to continually learn and evolve along with your domain.

Overall, the importance of tokenizers and vocabulary customization in the context of domain-specific languages cannot be overstated. By carefully tailoring your language models to suit the unique needs of your domain, you can improve the accuracy and effectiveness of your natural language processing, unlocking new insights and opportunities for innovation and growth.

5.4.1. Adapting Tokenizers for Domain-specific Language

When working with domain-specific language or jargon, it can be challenging to obtain optimal tokenization with the default tokenizer. This is because the default tokenizer may not be designed to handle the specific language used in your domain.

Therefore, it is crucial to adapt the tokenizer to be better suited to the domain-specific jargon. This can be achieved by analyzing the text and identifying the unique characteristics of the language used in the text. Subsequently, the tokenizer can be adjusted to better understand

and handle these unique characteristics, thereby improving the overall quality of the tokenization process.

It is important to note that this process may require some experimentation and fine-tuning to achieve the desired results.

Custom Tokenization Rules

A powerful feature of tokenization is the ability to create custom rules to handle domain-specific terms or expressions that may not be well-represented by the default tokenizer. By creating your own rules, you can ensure that your text is correctly segmented into tokens that are meaningful for your specific use case.

For example, if you are working with medical text, you may need to create rules to correctly tokenize medical terms or abbreviations. Similarly, if you are working with social media data, you may need to create rules to handle hashtags or emoticons.

By leveraging custom tokenization rules, you can improve the accuracy and effectiveness of your text analysis, and ensure that you are capturing all of the relevant information in your data.

Example:

For example, let's say you're working with chemical formulas. You can create a custom tokenizer to split chemical formulas into individual elements:

```python
from transformers import PreTrainedTokenizerFast

class CustomTokenizer(PreTrainedTokenizerFast):
    def __init__(self, *args, **kwargs):
        super().__init__(*args, **kwargs)

    def _tokenize(self, text):
        # Add custom tokenization rules here
        return text.split()

custom_tokenizer = CustomTokenizer.from_pretrained("gpt-4-tokenizer")
tokens = custom_tokenizer.tokenize("H2O CO2 NaCl")
print(tokens)
```

5.4.2. Extending and Modifying Vocabulary

Sometimes, when working with machine learning models, it may be necessary to expand the language and terminology used by the model in order to better tailor it to the specific needs of your domain or application.

This process can involve the introduction of new, domain-specific vocabulary or the modification of existing words and phrases to better capture the nuances of the problem space. By doing so, you can help ensure that your model is better able to understand and categorize data within your specific context, leading to more accurate and effective results.

1. **Extending Vocabulary**: One way to enhance the performance of the model is to incorporate new domain-specific tokens into its vocabulary. Domain-specific tokens are unique terms or symbols that may not be present in the original vocabulary. By introducing such tokens, the model can become more attuned to the specialized language of a particular domain, leading to improved accuracy and relevance in its outputs. In this way, the model can better capture the nuances and subtleties of the domain, making it more effective for a wider range of applications.

2. **Modifying Vocabulary**: One way to improve the model's understanding of your data is to replace existing tokens with domain-specific tokens that are more appropriate for the context. This can help the model to better differentiate between different types of data and improve its accuracy in classification tasks, for example. Additionally, by using more specific and nuanced language, you can provide more detailed and informative descriptions of your data that can be used to generate more accurate and insightful insights. Overall, taking the time to carefully consider the vocabulary used in your data can pay off in the long run by improving the quality and usefulness of the insights that are generated from it.

Example:

Here's an example of how to extend the vocabulary of a tokenizer:

```python
from transformers import GPT2Tokenizer

tokenizer = GPT2Tokenizer.from_pretrained("gpt-4-tokenizer")

# Add new tokens to the tokenizer
new_tokens = ["[DOMAIN_SPECIFIC1]", "[DOMAIN_SPECIFIC2]"]
num_new_tokens = len(new_tokens)
tokenizer.add_tokens(new_tokens)

# Resize the model's embeddings to accommodate the new tokens
model = GPT2LMHeadModel.from_pretrained("gpt-4")
model.resize_token_embeddings(len(tokenizer))

# Test the extended tokenizer
tokens = tokenizer("This is a sentence with [DOMAIN_SPECIFIC1] and [DOMAIN_SPECI
FIC2].", return_tensors="pt")

print(tokens)
```

In this example, we added two new domain-specific tokens to the vocabulary and resized the model's embeddings to accommodate these new tokens. This allows the model to better handle domain-specific content in the input text.

5.4.3. Handling Out-of-vocabulary (OOV) Tokens

In some cases, such as when dealing with informal language or jargon, you may encounter words or tokens that are not present in the model's vocabulary. These out-of-vocabulary (OOV) tokens can potentially impact the model's performance, and it is important to develop strategies to handle them.

One such strategy is to use techniques such as subword segmentation to break down complex words into smaller, more manageable units. Another approach is to use techniques such as transfer learning, where a pre-trained model is fine-tuned on a smaller dataset that includes the specific vocabulary of interest.

Additionally, it may be beneficial to incorporate human-in-the-loop processes, such as manual annotation, to help the model learn and adapt to new vocabulary. Overall, while OOV tokens can pose a challenge, there are various techniques and strategies available to mitigate their impact and improve model performance.

Here are some strategies to handle OOV tokens:

Subword Tokenization

In order to avoid out-of-vocabulary (OOV) words, which can negatively impact the performance of machine learning models, it is recommended to utilize subword tokenization methods such as Byte-Pair Encoding (BPE) or WordPiece. These methods break down words into smaller subwords that are more likely to be present in the model's vocabulary.

By doing this, the model is able to better understand the meaning of the text and produce more accurate results. Additionally, subword tokenization can also help with the problem of rare words, which can be difficult for models to learn due to their infrequency in the training data.

Therefore, it is important to consider subword tokenization as a useful technique for improving the performance of machine learning models.

Train on New Vocabulary

In order to improve the language model's performance on out-of-vocabulary (OOV) words, it is recommended to fine-tune the model on a dataset that specifically includes these types of tokens.

By incorporating the new vocabulary into the model, it can learn to recognize and respond to a wider range of words and phrases, ultimately improving its overall accuracy and effectiveness in various natural language processing tasks. This approach is particularly useful when dealing with specialized domains or emerging trends in language usage, where the model may not have been previously exposed to certain types of words or expressions.

With fine-tuning, the model can continually adapt and evolve to keep up with the changing linguistic landscape, ensuring its continued relevance and usefulness in a rapidly evolving field.

Character-level Tokenization

A common way to tokenize text is to break it down into words. However, this can be problematic when dealing with Out of Vocabulary (OOV) tokens. One solution to this problem is to tokenize text at the character level, which can help handle OOV tokens by breaking them down into individual characters. This approach has been shown to be effective in a variety of natural language processing tasks, such as machine translation and speech recognition.

By taking this approach, the tokenizer can handle previously unseen words by breaking them down into their constituent characters, allowing the model to better understand the meaning of the text. Overall, character-level tokenization is a useful technique that can help improve the performance of natural language processing models.

Example:

Here's a code example demonstrating how to handle OOV tokens using the Hugging Face Transformers library with the subword tokenization approach:

```python
from transformers import GPT2Tokenizer

# Initialize the GPT-2 tokenizer
tokenizer = GPT2Tokenizer.from_pretrained("gpt2")

# Example text with OOV word
text = "I love playing with my pet quokka."

# Tokenize the text using GPT-2 tokenizer
tokens = tokenizer.tokenize(text)
print("Original tokens:", tokens)

# The word 'quokka' is not in the GPT-2 vocabulary and is split into subword tok
ens
# ['I', ' love', ' playing', ' with', ' my', ' pet', ' qu', 'ok', 'ka', '.']

# If you need to replace OOV subword tokens with a specific token (e.g., [UNK]),
you can do so as follows:
oov_token = "[UNK]"

tokens_with_oov = []
for token in tokens:
    if token.startswith("Ġ"):
        if token[1:] not in tokenizer.vocab:
            tokens_with_oov.append(oov_token)
        else:
            tokens_with_oov.append(token)
    elif token not in tokenizer.vocab:
        tokens_with_oov.append(oov_token)
    else:
        tokens_with_oov.append(token)

print("Tokens with OOV handling:", tokens_with_oov)
# ['I', ' love', ' playing', ' with', ' my', ' pet', '[UNK]', '[UNK]', '[UNK]',
'.']
```

This example shows how to tokenize a text containing an OOV word ('quokka') using the GPT-2 tokenizer. The tokenizer breaks 'quokka' into subword tokens. If you prefer to replace the OOV subword tokens with a specific token (e.g., [UNK]), you can iterate through the tokens and make the replacement as demonstrated.

While the GPT-4 tokenizer already uses subword tokenization, it's essential to be aware of these strategies when dealing with OOV tokens, as they can help improve the model's performance and understanding of domain-specific language.

Overall, customizing tokenizers and vocabulary can greatly enhance the performance of ChatGPT in domain-specific tasks. Adapting tokenizers for domain-specific languages, extending and modifying vocabulary, and handling OOV tokens are key techniques to ensure that your fine-tuned model can handle the unique challenges of your specific use case.

5.4.4. Handling Special Tokens and Custom Formatting

This sub-topic can cover the usage of special tokens in the tokenizer for specific purposes, such as formatting or indicating the beginning and end of sentences or paragraphs. For example, special tokens can be used to denote the start and end of quotations, or to indicate the beginning and end of a block of code.

Additionally, this sub-topic can discuss the customization of the tokenizer to handle unique formatting requirements or domain-specific needs. For instance, in the medical domain, a tokenizer may need to handle complex medical terms and abbreviations that are not commonly used in other fields. Similarly, in the legal domain, a tokenizer may need to recognize and handle specific legal terms and phrases.

Overall, by customizing the tokenizer to suit specific needs, one can improve the accuracy and performance of natural language processing tasks. For example:

Adding special tokens to the tokenizer vocabulary

In order to improve the performance of your tokenizer for specific tasks, it is sometimes necessary to include special tokens in the vocabulary. These tokens, such as [CLS] and [SEP], can be used to indicate the beginning and end of a sentence or sequence, or to mark certain words or phrases for special treatment. By adding these tokens to the tokenizer's vocabulary, you can ensure that they are recognized during tokenization and that your models are able to take advantage of their presence.

For example, if you are working on a task that requires sentence classification, you might use the [CLS] token to indicate the beginning of each sentence in your input data. This will allow your model to treat each sentence as a separate unit and make more accurate predictions. Similarly, if you are working with text that contains special formatting, you can create custom tokens to represent these formatting elements and add them to your tokenizer's vocabulary. This will ensure that your models are able to recognize the formatting and incorporate it into their predictions.

In general, adding special tokens to your tokenizer's vocabulary is a powerful way to customize its behavior and improve the performance of your models. However, it is important to use these tokens judiciously and to carefully evaluate their impact on your results.

Example:

Adding special tokens to the tokenizer vocabulary:

```
from transformers import GPT2Tokenizer

tokenizer = GPT2Tokenizer.from_pretrained("gpt2")

special_tokens = ["[CLS]", "[SEP]"]
tokenizer.add_special_tokens({"additional_special_tokens": special_tokens})

# Now you can use the tokenizer with the added special tokens
input_text = "[CLS] This is an example sentence. [SEP]"
encoded_input = tokenizer.encode(input_text, return_tensors="pt")
```

Custom formatting

When dealing with text data, there are times when you need the tokenizer to handle custom formatting. This can include recognizing and preserving certain tags or symbols within the text. By customizing the tokenizer, you can make it more suitable for your specific use case.

For example, you may need to preserve HTML tags or Markdown syntax, or perhaps you need to identify and extract specific entities from the text, such as dates, phone numbers, or email addresses. Whatever your requirements may be, customizing the tokenizer can help you achieve your goals more effectively and efficiently.

Example:

```
# Example: Preserving custom tags in the text
from transformers import PreTrainedTokenizerFast

tokenizer = PreTrainedTokenizerFast(tokenizer_file="path/to/your/tokenizer.json")

def custom_tokenizer(text):
    # Replace custom tags with special tokens
    text = text.replace("<custom>", "[CUSTOM]").replace("</custom>", "[/CUSTOM]")
    return tokenizer(text)

input_text = "This is a <custom>custom tag</custom> example."
encoded_input = custom_tokenizer(input_text)
```

Fine-tuning the tokenizer for specific tasks

Depending on the task at hand, you might need to adjust the tokenizer to handle specific input structures, such as question-answering, summarization, or translation tasks. This means that you can tweak the tokenizer to better handle the type of data you're working with, making the overall model more effective.

For example, in a question-answering task, you might need to ensure that the tokenizer can properly segment the text into questions and answers, while in a summarization task, you might need to adjust the tokenizer to recognize important keywords and phrases that should be included in the summary.

Similarly, in a translation task, you may need to customize the tokenizer to handle multiple languages and ensure that it can properly segment the input text into individual phrases or sentences in order to generate accurate translations. By taking the time to fine-tune the tokenizer for your specific task, you can optimize your model's performance and ensure that it delivers the most accurate and effective results possible.

Example:

Fine-tuning the tokenizer for specific tasks:

```
# Example: Customizing the tokenizer for a question-answering task
from transformers import GPT2Tokenizer

tokenizer = GPT2Tokenizer.from_pretrained("gpt2")

question = "What is the capital of France?"
context = "The capital of France is Paris."

input_text = f"[QUESTION] {question} [CONTEXT] {context}"
encoded_input = tokenizer.encode(input_text, return_tensors="pt")
```

5.5. Advanced Fine-tuning Techniques

As you continue to fine-tune ChatGPT, you may encounter situations where you need to apply advanced techniques to improve your model's performance. In this section, we'll discuss some advanced fine-tuning techniques that can help enhance your model's capabilities.

One of the techniques you can use to improve your model's performance is transfer learning. Transfer learning allows you to leverage the training data and pre-trained weights of an existing model to improve the performance of your own model. By using transfer learning, you can significantly reduce the amount of training data required for your model and achieve better results with less effort.

Another technique you can use is data augmentation. Data augmentation involves generating new training data from your existing data by applying various transformations such as rotation, translation, and scaling. By using data augmentation, you can increase the diversity of your training data and improve your model's ability to generalize to new examples.

Finally, you can also consider using ensemble learning to improve your model's performance. Ensemble learning involves combining the predictions of multiple models to produce a final prediction. By using ensemble learning, you can reduce the risk of overfitting and improve your model's accuracy and robustness.

In summary, these advanced fine-tuning techniques can help you improve your model's performance and achieve better results with less effort.

5.5.1. Curriculum Learning and Progressive Training

Curriculum learning is a technique that has been widely used in machine learning to train models on a sequence of tasks that gradually increase in difficulty. The aim is to help the model learn more efficiently and effectively, inspired by how humans learn.

This approach has been shown to be particularly useful when training large models like GPT-4, which require a lot of data and computing power. By breaking down the learning process into smaller, more manageable tasks, the model can build a solid foundation before moving on to more complex challenges.

Another benefit of progressive training is that it can help prevent overfitting, a common problem in machine learning where the model becomes too specialized to the training data and performs poorly on new data. By gradually increasing the difficulty of the tasks, the model is forced to generalize its knowledge and become more robust.

In summary, curriculum learning is an effective technique for training machine learning models, especially large ones like GPT-4. By breaking down the learning process into smaller, more manageable tasks, the model can learn more efficiently and effectively, while also avoiding overfitting and becoming more robust.

Example:

```python
# This is a conceptual example
tasks = [easy_task, medium_task, hard_task]

for task in tasks:
    # Fine-tune the model on the current task
    model.train(task.train_dataloader)
    # Evaluate the model on the current task
    model.evaluate(task.val_dataloader)
```

5.5.2. Few-shot Learning and Prompt Engineering

Few-shot learning is a powerful technique that has gained significant traction in recent years. This approach allows a model to learn new tasks with minimal training data, which is particularly

relevant for GPT-4. The model's large knowledge base can be leveraged to learn new tasks quickly and efficiently, which makes it a highly sought-after technique in machine learning.

However, the process of few-shot learning is not always straightforward. Prompt engineering plays a crucial role in guiding the model's behavior during few-shot learning. It involves designing effective prompts that help the model to learn and adapt to new tasks. This requires careful consideration of the task at hand, as well as the model's capabilities and limitations. By designing effective prompts, we can improve the accuracy and efficiency of the few-shot learning process, and enable the model to learn new tasks more effectively than ever before.

Example:

```
# This is a conceptual example
prompts = ["Translate the following English text to French: {text}",
           "Please convert the following English sentence into French: {text}",
           "English to French translation: {text}"]

for prompt in prompts:
    input_text = prompt.format(text="The weather is nice today.")
    # Generate the model's response
    response = model.generate(input_text)
```

5.5.3. Multi-task Learning and Task-specific Adaptation

Multi-task learning is a powerful approach that allows a single model to be trained on multiple tasks simultaneously. This can be useful in various contexts, such as natural language processing, where different tasks such as language modeling, named entity recognition, and sentiment analysis can be learned together. By sharing the model's parameters across tasks, multi-task learning can improve the model's generalization capabilities, enabling it to perform better on new data.

Another technique that can be used in conjunction with multi-task learning is task-specific adaptation, which involves fine-tuning the model on a specific task after initial multi-task training. This can be useful when the model's performance on a particular task is not satisfactory, as it allows the model's parameters to be adjusted to better fit that task. Task-specific adaptation can also help prevent overfitting on the training set, as the model is fine-tuned on a smaller set of task-specific examples. By combining multi-task learning with task-

specific adaptation, we can create more robust and accurate models that perform well across a variety of tasks.

Example:

```
# This is a conceptual example
tasks = [task1, task2, task3]

# Train the model on multiple tasks simultaneously
model.train_multi_tasks(tasks)

# Fine-tune the model on a specific task
target_task = task2
model.train(target_task.train_dataloader)

# Evaluate the model on the target task
model.evaluate(target_task.val_dataloader)
```

5.5.4. Adversarial Training and Robustness

Adversarial training is a powerful technique that can help improve the robustness of your model. By training the model on adversarial examples, which are inputs that have been intentionally modified to deceive the model, you can enhance its ability to handle challenging situations and improve its overall performance.

It is worth noting that adversarial examples can take many different forms and can be created in a variety of ways. Some examples include adding small amounts of noise to an image, changing the color of certain pixels, or modifying the text of a sentence. By incorporating adversarial training into your model, you can ensure that it is better prepared to handle these types of inputs and produce accurate predictions.

Overall, adversarial training is an incredibly useful technique that can greatly enhance the performance of your model. By taking the time to incorporate this technique into your training process, you can ensure that your model is better equipped to handle a wide range of inputs and produce accurate predictions in even the most challenging situations.

Example:

```python
# This is a conceptual example
import torch
import torch.optim as optim

# Define the loss function
loss_fn = torch.nn.CrossEntropyLoss()

# Define the optimizer
optimizer = optim.Adam(model.parameters(), lr=1e-4)

for epoch in range(epochs):
    for inputs, targets in train_dataloader:
        # Create adversarial examples
        inputs_adv = create_adversarial_examples(inputs, targets, model, loss_f
n)

        # Zero the gradients
        optimizer.zero_grad()

        # Compute model predictions on adversarial examples
        outputs_adv = model(inputs_adv)

        # Calculate the loss
        loss = loss_fn(outputs_adv, targets)

        # Perform backpropagation
        loss.backward()

        # Update the model's weights
        optimizer.step()
```

Incorporating adversarial training can make ChatGPT more resistant to adversarial attacks, ensuring that it remains effective even when faced with deceptive inputs. This can be particularly important for applications where security and reliability are paramount.

Chapter 5 Conclusion

In conclusion, the process of fine-tuning ChatGPT is a crucial step in adapting the model to specific tasks, domains, or applications. This chapter has provided an in-depth exploration of various aspects related to fine-tuning, from dataset preparation and transfer learning techniques to model evaluation, testing, and advanced fine-tuning approaches.

We began by discussing the importance of preparing your dataset, which involves data collection strategies, data cleaning and preprocessing, dataset splitting and validation, and dataset augmentation. A well-prepared dataset serves as the foundation for effective fine-tuning, ensuring that the model can learn relevant patterns and perform well on the task at hand.

Next, we explored transfer learning techniques, delving into the specifics of GPT-4, choosing the right model size and parameters, and training strategies with hyperparameter optimization. Understanding these techniques allows developers to better adapt the pre-trained GPT-4 model to their specific use case, optimizing its performance and relevance to the task.

Model evaluation and testing are crucial for understanding the effectiveness of the fine-tuned model. We discussed quantitative evaluation metrics, qualitative evaluation techniques, and handling overfitting and underfitting. By employing a combination of evaluation methods, developers can gain a comprehensive understanding of the model's performance and make informed decisions about further fine-tuning or deployment.

Customizing tokenizers and vocabulary is an essential aspect of adapting ChatGPT to domain-specific languages or extending its capabilities. We examined adapting tokenizers for domain-specific language, extending and modifying vocabulary, and handling out-of-vocabulary tokens. These customization techniques enable developers to further enhance the model's performance in specialized contexts.

Finally, we delved into advanced fine-tuning techniques, covering curriculum learning and progressive training, few-shot learning and prompt engineering, multi-task learning and task-specific adaptation, and adversarial training for robustness. These advanced techniques offer additional avenues for improving model performance, enabling developers to create state-of-the-art language models tailored to their specific needs.

In summary, fine-tuning ChatGPT is an involved but rewarding process that enables developers to harness the power of GPT-4 for various tasks and applications. By understanding and applying the concepts discussed in this chapter, developers can create highly effective, domain-specific language models that cater to their unique requirements. The key to success lies in

carefully preparing datasets, selecting appropriate fine-tuning techniques, evaluating model performance, and iterating on the fine-tuning process as needed to achieve the desired results.

Chapter 6 - Adapting ChatGPT for Specific Industries

In this chapter, we will explore how ChatGPT can be adapted for various industries and the specific challenges and opportunities each domain presents. While ChatGPT is a versatile and powerful language model, the requirements and nuances of individual industries necessitate fine-tuning and customization to ensure optimal performance and usefulness.

We will discuss several industries, starting with healthcare and medical applications, and provide insights into how ChatGPT can be utilized effectively in each context. As we examine these industry-specific adaptations, we will provide code examples and best practices to help guide developers in adapting ChatGPT to suit their specific industry needs.

6.1. Healthcare and Medical Applications

Adapting ChatGPT for healthcare and medical applications offers numerous potential benefits. One such benefit is the ability to assist with medical diagnosis by using the vast data that ChatGPT has gathered. This can help medical professionals in making more informed decisions. In addition, ChatGPT can also provide treatment recommendations based on the patient's symptoms and medical history.

Another potential benefit of using ChatGPT for healthcare is drug discovery. The technology can be used to analyze large amounts of data and identify patterns that could lead to the development of new drugs or therapies.

Patient support is yet another area where ChatGPT can be useful. By providing personalized recommendations and support, the technology can help patients better manage their health and achieve their health goals.

However, these applications also come with unique challenges. One of the most important challenges is the need for high levels of accuracy. In a healthcare setting, accuracy is critical as it can impact patient outcomes. Additionally, strict adherence to regulatory requirements is also essential. Healthcare regulations are designed to protect patients and ensure that medical professionals are providing the best possible care.

Finally, sensitivity to patient privacy concerns is crucial when developing ChatGPT for healthcare applications. Patient privacy must be protected at all times, and the technology must be designed to ensure that sensitive patient information is kept confidential and secure.

To adapt ChatGPT for healthcare and medical applications, developers should consider the following steps:

1. **Data collection and preparation**

    The process of gathering domain-specific data related to medical knowledge is critical in the development of machine learning models. To ensure the accuracy, reliability, and up-to-date nature of the data, it is important to carefully select sources such as medical textbooks, research articles, and clinical guidelines.

    In addition to these sources, it may be beneficial to incorporate anonymized patient records or case studies to expose the model to real-world scenarios. However, it is important to strictly adhere to data privacy regulations when doing so. It is also worth noting that the process of preparing the data for use in machine learning models is equally important.

    This may involve cleaning and preprocessing the data, ensuring that it is formatted correctly, and selecting the appropriate features for use in the model. Therefore, it is important to allocate sufficient time and resources towards data collection and preparation in order to build robust and effective machine learning models for medical applications.

2. **Fine-tuning the model**

    In order to optimize ChatGPT for healthcare-specific tasks, one important step is fine-tuning the model on a dataset that is specific to this domain. This will ensure that the model is able to accurately diagnose patients, provide treatment recommendations, and offer necessary support.

    It is crucial, however, to be cautious when using patient-generated data for fine-tuning, as this data could introduce biases or inaccuracies that could undermine the

performance of the model. Therefore, it may be necessary to carefully curate the dataset used for fine-tuning, selecting only high-quality, reliable data that is free from any potential biases or inaccuracies.

3. **Evaluation and testing**

The importance of rigorously evaluating the performance of the fine-tuned model cannot be overstated. To ensure the model is as accurate and effective as possible, it is crucial to utilize both quantitative and qualitative evaluation techniques. In medical applications, it is especially important to collaborate closely with domain experts to ensure the model's output aligns with current medical knowledge and best practices.

This can involve working with doctors, nurses, and other healthcare professionals to obtain feedback and insights on the model's performance and results. Additionally, it may be beneficial to conduct further research on the specific medical conditions or situations the model is designed to address, in order to refine and improve its accuracy and efficacy. By taking these steps, we can ensure that the fine-tuned model is not only effective, but also reliable and trustworthy for use in real-world medical settings.

4. **Ensuring compliance and privacy**

It is imperative to implement strict data handling and privacy measures in order to maintain the trust of our users and comply with regulations such as HIPAA and GDPR. In order to do this, we will need to take several measures to ensure the confidentiality, integrity, and availability of our data.

One of the most important steps we will take is to encrypt sensitive data, such as personally identifiable information (PII) and financial data, both in transit and at rest. This will prevent unauthorized access and ensure that our data remains private and secure.

In addition to encryption, we will implement proper data storage and access control mechanisms, such as secure databases and role-based access control (RBAC) systems. This will ensure that only authorized personnel have access to sensitive data, and that it is stored securely and appropriately.

Finally, we will ensure that our users have transparency about how their data is being used, and we will provide them with the ability to control their own data. This includes providing clear and concise privacy policies that explain how we collect, use, and share data, as well as giving users the option to opt out of certain data collection and sharing practices. By taking these steps, we can ensure that our users' data is kept safe and

secure, while also complying with the relevant regulations and maintaining their trust in our organization.

5. **Post-processing and content filtering**

    In order to ensure the accuracy and adherence to medical guidelines, it is essential to apply various post-processing techniques and content filters to the model's output. One way to achieve this is by collaborating with medical professionals to identify potential areas of concern and implement safeguards to mitigate risks.

    For instance, one could work with healthcare providers to identify common errors or concerns in the data and adjust the model's output accordingly. Additionally, one could implement various safeguards such as automated alerts or notifications to alert healthcare providers of potential issues. Ultimately, the goal is to ensure that the model's output is accurate and reliable, which will help to improve patient outcomes and overall healthcare quality.

6.1.1 Practical Example

Let's consider a scenario where we adapt ChatGPT to assist with symptom analysis and provide potential medical conditions that might be related to the reported symptoms. Please note that this is just an example for illustration purposes and should not be used for real medical diagnosis without proper evaluation and collaboration with healthcare professionals.

1. **Data collection and preparation:**

    Assume we have collected domain-specific data related to medical knowledge in a file called **medical_data.txt**. This file contains information from medical textbooks, research articles, and clinical guidelines.

2. **Fine-tuning the model:**

    We will use the OpenAI API to fine-tune ChatGPT on the healthcare-specific dataset. First, we need to preprocess and tokenize our **medical_data.txt** dataset before training.

```python
import openai

openai.api_key = "your_openai_api_key"

# Load medical data and preprocess
with open("medical_data.txt", "r") as f:
    medical_data = f.read()

# Tokenize medical data
tokens = openai.Tokenizer.tokenize(medical_data)

# Perform fine-tuning (assuming you have a base model checkpoint)
# This is a simplified example; actual fine-tuning requires more steps and confi
guration
openai.FineTuner.train(
    model_checkpoint="path/to/base_model",
    tokens=tokens,
    output_dir="path/to/output_dir",
    num_train_epochs=3,
)
```

3. **Evaluation and testing**:

   After fine-tuning, evaluate the performance of the fine-tuned model using both quantitative and qualitative evaluation techniques. Collaborate with domain experts to ensure the model's output aligns with current medical knowledge and best practices.

4. **Ensuring compliance and privacy**:

   Make sure to follow all necessary privacy and compliance guidelines for your region, including data storage, encryption, and access control.

5. **Post-processing and content filtering**:

   Here's a sample code snippet for querying the fine-tuned ChatGPT model to analyze symptoms and provide potential medical conditions:

```python
import openai

openai.api_key = "your_openai_api_key"

def analyze_symptoms(symptoms):
    prompt = f"Given the following symptoms: {symptoms}, what are the potential
medical conditions that might be related?"

    response = openai.Completion.create(
        engine="your_fine_tuned_engine",
        prompt=prompt,
        max_tokens=100,
        n=1,
        stop=None,
        temperature=0.8,
    )

    # Apply post-processing or content filtering if necessary
    result = response.choices[0].text.strip()

    return result

symptoms = "fever, headache, and muscle aches"
conditions = analyze_symptoms(symptoms)
print(conditions)
```

In this example, the **analyze_symptoms** function queries the fine-tuned ChatGPT model to provide potential medical conditions related to the given symptoms. The model's response is post-processed and filtered as necessary.

6.2. Legal and Regulatory Compliance

Adapting ChatGPT for legal and regulatory compliance use cases can significantly enhance the capabilities of organizations and professionals in the field. The AI model can provide accurate and relevant information that can be used by professionals in a variety of tasks.

For example, the AI model can assist in contract analysis by reviewing contracts and identifying key terms and clauses, which can help organizations to identify potential risks and

opportunities. The AI model can also help in tasks related to risk assessment, by analyzing data and identifying patterns that can help organizations to identify potential risks and opportunities.

Additionally, the AI model can assist in regulatory research by analyzing and organizing large amounts of data, making it easier for professionals to find and understand relevant laws and regulations. However, it's important to ensure that the AI model is fine-tuned and configured to adhere to legal and regulatory guidelines, including privacy laws and regulations, to avoid legal and ethical issues.

6.2.1. Data Collection and Preparation

Creating a legal and regulatory compliance AI model may seem daunting, but it is a necessary process for any organization that wants to stay compliant and avoid legal complications. Before building the model, it is important to start by collecting and preparing relevant data. This includes legal documents, regulatory guidelines, statutes, case laws, and other sources of legal information.

Once you have collected the data, it is important to prioritize reputable sources and ensure that the data collection process is compliant with data privacy and copyright laws. This means that you must obtain permission to use the data and ensure that the data is properly anonymized and secured.

After collecting the data, the next step is to preprocess the data in order to extract relevant features and ensure that the data is in a format that the AI model can understand. This may involve cleaning the data, removing duplicates, and transforming the data into a standardized format.

Once the data has been collected and preprocessed, the next step is to train the AI model. This involves selecting an appropriate algorithm, choosing the right hyperparameters, and splitting the data into training, validation, and test sets.

It is important to evaluate the performance of the AI model and ensure that it is meeting the desired levels of accuracy and recall. This may involve fine-tuning the model, improving the quality of the data, or retraining the model with additional data.

By following these steps, you can create a legal and regulatory compliance AI model that is accurate, efficient, and compliant with all relevant laws and regulations.

6.2.2. Fine-tuning the Model

To fine-tune ChatGPT using the prepared legal dataset, we must take several steps. First, we need to ensure that the training process follows appropriate guidelines. This includes anonymizing sensitive data and removing personally identifiable information (PII) to protect the privacy of individuals involved in legal cases.

Once we have taken these necessary steps, we can begin training the model iteratively. This process involves regular evaluations and refinements to improve the model's understanding of legal concepts and regulatory requirements.

In addition to the technical aspects of the training process, we must also consider the broader implications of using ChatGPT in the legal field. For example, we need to ensure that the model is not biased in any way and that it does not reinforce existing power imbalances. It is also important to consider the ethical implications of using AI in the legal field and to develop guidelines that promote responsible use of this technology.

6.2.3. Evaluation and Testing

To ensure that the AI model generates responses that are accurate, relevant, and conform to legal standards, it is crucial to involve legal professionals in the evaluation and testing process. Legal professionals can provide valuable insights into the legal implications of the model's responses and ensure that they do not violate any laws or regulations.

In addition to involving legal professionals, it is important to use both quantitative and qualitative evaluation techniques to measure the performance of the model. Quantitative evaluation techniques, such as precision and recall, can provide a numerical measure of the model's accuracy. Qualitative evaluation techniques, such as user surveys and expert evaluations, can provide a more nuanced understanding of the model's performance and identify areas for improvement.

By employing a combination of legal expertise and rigorous evaluation techniques, organizations can ensure that their AI models are not only accurate and relevant, but also compliant with legal standards and ethical considerations.

6.2.4. Ensuring Compliance and Confidentiality

Ensuring compliance with data protection laws and maintaining confidentiality are crucial when working with legal and regulatory data. However, it is not enough to simply implement strong access controls, encryption, and secure data storage mechanisms to safeguard sensitive

information. In addition to these necessary measures, it is important to establish policies and procedures for data handling, data retention and destruction, and incident response. These policies and procedures should be regularly reviewed and updated to ensure that they are aligned with any changes in data privacy regulations.

Furthermore, staying up-to-date with changes in data privacy regulations is not a one-time task. It requires continuous monitoring and assessment of the AI model and its impact on data privacy. This includes identifying any potential privacy risks and addressing them through the implementation of additional safeguards or modifications to the AI model. It is also important to engage with legal and regulatory experts to ensure that the AI model remains compliant with any new or updated regulations.

While implementing strong access controls, encryption, and secure data storage mechanisms is a critical step in safeguarding sensitive information, it is only the beginning. Establishing policies and procedures for data handling, retention, and destruction, along with continuous monitoring and assessment of the AI model and engagement with legal and regulatory experts, are all necessary components of maintaining compliance with data protection laws and ensuring the confidentiality of legal and regulatory data.

6.2.5. Post-processing and Content Filtering

After fine-tuning ChatGPT for legal and regulatory compliance, it is important to implement post-processing techniques and content filters to further refine the model's output. This can be done in several ways. One approach is to filter out irrelevant content that may not be helpful to the user.

This can help ensure that the responses generated by the model are relevant and useful. Another approach is to ensure accurate references to legal provisions. By doing this, you can make sure that the responses generated by the model are legally sound and reliable. Furthermore, it is important to validate the generated responses with legal professionals.

This can help ensure that the responses are accurate and reliable. By taking these steps, you can create a ChatGPT model that is both compliant with legal and regulatory requirements, and provides users with accurate and reliable information.

Example:

Here's a sample code snippet for querying a fine-tuned ChatGPT model for legal advice on a specific topic:

```python
import openai

openai.api_key = "your_openai_api_key"

def get_legal_advice(topic):
    prompt = f"Provide legal advice on the following topic: {topic}"

    response = openai.Completion.create(
        engine="your_fine_tuned_engine",
        prompt=prompt,
        max_tokens=150,
        n=1,
        stop=None,
        temperature=0.7,
    )

    # Apply post-processing or content filtering if necessary
    result = response.choices[0].text.strip()

    return result

topic = "intellectual property rights for software"
advice = get_legal_advice(topic)
print(advice)
```

In this example, the **get_legal_advice** function queries the fine-tuned ChatGPT model to provide legal advice on a given topic. The response is then post-processed and filtered as needed.

6.3. Customer Support and CRM Systems

Integrating ChatGPT into customer support and customer relationship management (CRM) systems can help businesses offer efficient and personalized support experiences to their customers. By training the AI model on customer interactions, FAQs, and product information, ChatGPT can provide instant support, resolve common issues, and answer customer queries.

In addition to these benefits, ChatGPT can also help businesses save time and money by reducing the need for human customer support agents. This can be especially useful during peak customer service hours or during unexpected spikes in customer inquiries. By automating

certain aspects of customer support, businesses can ensure that their customers receive timely and accurate responses without having to hire additional staff.

Furthermore, ChatGPT can also provide valuable insights into customer behavior and preferences. By analyzing customer interactions and feedback, businesses can gain a deeper understanding of their customers' needs and preferences, and use this information to improve their products and services. For example, if a large number of customers are asking the same question about a particular product, a business can use this information to update their product documentation or improve the product itself.

Overall, integrating ChatGPT into customer support and CRM systems can provide businesses with a range of benefits, including more efficient support, cost savings, and valuable customer insights.

6.3.1. Data Collection and Preparation

To collect data relevant to customer support interactions, it is important to gather transcripts of live chats, email exchanges, support tickets, and product documentation. Once you have collected this data, it is crucial to ensure that it is properly cleaned, anonymized, and preprocessed.

This is important for several reasons. First, cleaning the data helps to remove any errors or inconsistencies that could lead to inaccurate analysis. Second, anonymizing the data helps to protect the privacy of customers and ensure compliance with data privacy regulations. Finally, preprocessing the data can help to identify patterns and trends that can be used to improve the customer support experience.

6.3.2. Fine-tuning the Model

To optimize and improve the performance of ChatGPT, you can utilize the customer support dataset that has been prepared. Incorporating this dataset will allow the AI model to become more familiar with industry-specific terminology, enabling it to better understand and resolve common customer issues.

Furthermore, it will also be able to provide more relevant and accurate information about different products and services, which will ultimately lead to a better overall customer experience. By utilizing this approach, you can significantly enhance the capabilities of ChatGPT and ensure that it remains a valuable tool for your business.

6.3.3. Integration with CRM Systems

To implement the fine-tuned ChatGPT model, first, we must ensure that our existing CRM systems are fully compatible with the model. This can be achieved by integrating the API of the model with the APIs of the CRM system. We should also consider how to best use the data structures of both the model and the CRM system, to ensure seamless communication between the two.

In order to provide real-time support through various communication channels, we can explore different methods. For example, we can use live chat or email to communicate with customers and respond to their queries. Social media is also a viable communication channel, and we can leverage it to provide customer support as well.

Additionally, we can use the data generated through these communication channels to improve the performance of the ChatGPT model. By analyzing the types of queries customers have and the responses that are most effective, we can fine-tune the model further to provide better support. This would result in a more powerful and efficient AI system that can provide better customer service and support.

6.3.4. Personalization and Context-Awareness

To enhance the customer support experience, we propose the implementation of personalized AI-generated responses. By utilizing customer data available in the CRM system, we can tailor the responses to the specific needs and preferences of the customer. With this approach, we can ensure that every interaction with the customer is unique and engaging, leading to better customer satisfaction and loyalty.

Moreover, we suggest the implementation of context-awareness to maintain conversation history and provide accurate, relevant support. By keeping track of the customer's previous interactions, we can understand the context of their current inquiry and provide solutions that are tailored to their specific needs. This feature will not only streamline the support process but also improve the overall customer experience.

6.3.5. Evaluation and Monitoring

To ensure the highest level of customer satisfaction, it is essential to continuously monitor and evaluate the performance of the ChatGPT model in the customer support context. This can be achieved through a variety of means, such as gathering user feedback, tracking resolution rates, and measuring customer satisfaction.

By doing so, areas for improvement can be identified and addressed, leading to a better overall experience for all parties involved. Additionally, it is important to consider external factors that may impact the performance of the model, such as changes in customer behavior or the introduction of new products or services. By taking a proactive approach to monitoring and evaluation, businesses can stay ahead of the curve and ensure that their customer support remains top-notch even as the landscape continues to evolve.

Example:

Here's a sample code snippet for integrating a fine-tuned ChatGPT model into a customer support chatbot:

```python
import openai

openai.api_key = "your_openai_api_key"

def handle_customer_query(customer_id, query, conversation_history):
    customer_data = get_customer_data_from_crm(customer_id)  # Retrieve customer
data from CRM system
    prompt = f"{conversation_history}\n\nCustomer: {query}\nSupportBot:"

    response = openai.Completion.create(
        engine="your_fine_tuned_engine",
        prompt=prompt,
        max_tokens=150,
        n=1,
        stop=None,
        temperature=0.7,
    )

    # Personalize and post-process the response
    result = personalize_response(customer_data, response.choices[0].text.strip
())

    return result

def personalize_response(customer_data, response):
    # Implement personalization logic based on customer_data
    # For example, replace placeholders with actual customer details
    personalized_response = response.format(**customer_data)
    return personalized_response

def get_customer_data_from_crm(customer_id):
    # Retrieve customer data from the CRM system
    # Dummy data is used here for demonstration purposes
    return {
        "first_name": "John",
        "last_name": "Doe",
        "product_name": "Gizmo 3000",
    }

customer_id = 12345
query = "How can I reset my Gizmo 3000?"
conversation_history = ""

answer = handle_customer_query(customer_id, query, conversation_history)
print(answer)
```

In this example, the **handle_customer_query** function takes a customer ID, a query, and the conversation history as input. It retrieves customer data from the CRM system and generates a personalized response using the fine-tuned ChatGPT model.

6.4. Content Generation and SEO

ChatGPT can be an incredibly powerful tool for content generation and SEO. With its ability to learn and analyze a vast array of content types and topics, it can generate unique, high-quality content that is both engaging and relevant to the target audience. This tool can provide businesses with a competitive edge in the digital world by helping them create content that not only adheres to SEO best practices but also resonates with their target market. In addition, ChatGPT can help businesses save time and resources in content creation. Instead of spending countless hours brainstorming, researching, and writing content, businesses can rely on ChatGPT to do the heavy lifting for them. This frees up time for businesses to focus on other important tasks such as customer engagement or product development. Overall, ChatGPT is a game-changer for businesses looking to improve their online presence and drive organic traffic to their websites. By leveraging the power of this tool, businesses can create high-quality, relevant content that resonates with their target audience and boosts their search engine rankings.

6.4.1. Data Collection and Preparation

To gather a diverse dataset of high-quality content, there are several methods that can be employed. One such method is to scour the web for blog posts, articles, and web pages that are relevant to the industry or topic of interest. It is important to ensure that the content is of high quality, as this will have a significant impact on the effectiveness of the model.

In addition to collecting content, it is also important to gather data that can be used to fine-tune the model for SEO-aware content generation. This includes conducting keyword research to identify the most relevant and popular search terms for the industry or topic of interest. It is also important to collect metadata, such as title tags and meta descriptions, to ensure that the generated content is optimized for search engines.

When gathering data, it is important to keep in mind that the more diverse the dataset, the better. By incorporating content from a variety of sources and perspectives, the model will be able to generate more nuanced and sophisticated content that is tailored to the needs and interests of the target audience.

6.4.2. Fine-tuning the Model

To fine-tune ChatGPT, you can use the prepared content dataset as well as SEO-focused data to provide the AI model with more information to learn from. By doing so, the model will be able to recognize industry-specific terminology and generate more relevant content. Additionally, optimizing for target keywords and phrases will help improve the model's performance in search engines and attract more users to your platform.

Furthermore, you could also consider utilizing user feedback to improve the model's accuracy and relevance, as well as leveraging social media data to gain insights into popular topics and trends.

6.4.3. Content Generation

One way to leverage the fine-tuned ChatGPT model is to create compelling blog posts that delve into complex topics. This will allow readers to gain a deeper understanding of the subject matter and potentially attract more organic traffic to your website. Additionally, you can use the model to generate informative articles that highlight the benefits and features of your products or services. These articles can be published on third-party websites, further increasing your brand's visibility.

Another effective use of the ChatGPT model is to craft engaging social media posts that resonate with your target audience. By incorporating relevant keywords and hashtags, you can increase the reach of your posts and drive more traffic to your website. Finally, you can use the model to create persuasive product descriptions that communicate the unique selling points of your offerings. These descriptions can help potential customers make informed purchase decisions and ultimately boost your sales.

In addition to these content types, you can also use the ChatGPT model to generate other types of materials, such as whitepapers, case studies, and e-books. By diversifying your content strategy, you can attract a wider audience and establish yourself as a thought leader in your industry. Remember to always incorporate SEO best practices like keyword targeting, readability, and proper formatting to maximize the impact of your content and improve your search engine rankings.

6.4.4. Metadata and SEO Optimization

In addition to generating the main content, ChatGPT can assist in creating metadata, such as titles, descriptions, and keywords. By providing relevant metadata, you can improve your content's visibility on search engines and increase click-through rates.

This can ultimately lead to more traffic and conversions for your website. Furthermore, optimized metadata can help search engines better understand the content's relevance and increase the chances of your content appearing in relevant search results. With ChatGPT's assistance in creating metadata, you can ensure that your content is optimized for search engines and effectively reaches your target audience.

6.4.5. Evaluation and Monitoring

To ensure that the ChatGPT model is consistently generating high-quality content and driving traffic to your website, it's important to continuously evaluate its performance. This can be done by monitoring a variety of metrics, including search engine rankings, organic traffic, and user engagement.

In addition, consider conducting A/B tests to compare the performance of different versions of the model and identify areas for improvement. It may also be helpful to analyze user feedback and comments to gain insights into what aspects of the content are resonating with your audience and what areas could be improved upon.

By taking a comprehensive approach to evaluating the ChatGPT model's performance, you can make informed decisions about how to optimize its output and drive even greater success for your business.

Example:

Here's a sample code snippet for generating SEO-optimized content using a fine-tuned ChatGPT model:

```python
import openai

openai.api_key = "your_openai_api_key"

def generate_seo_optimized_content(target_keyword, content_type):
    prompt = f"Write a {content_type} about '{target_keyword}' optimized for search engines."

    response = openai.Completion.create(
        engine="your_fine_tuned_engine",
        prompt=prompt,
        max_tokens=1024,
        n=1,
        stop=None,
        temperature=0.7,
    )

    return response.choices[0].text.strip()

target_keyword = "sustainable gardening"
content_type = "blog post"

generated_content = generate_seo_optimized_content(target_keyword, content_type)
print(generated_content)
```

In this example, the **generate_seo_optimized_content** function takes a target keyword and a content type as input. It generates an SEO-optimized content piece using the fine-tuned ChatGPT model by providing a prompt that specifies the requirements.

6.5. Finance and Investment Analysis

ChatGPT can be a valuable tool for finance and investment analysis. With its ability to generate insightful reports, forecasts, and summaries, it can help users make informed decisions about investments and financial planning.

For example, the model can be fine-tuned with financial data and domain-specific knowledge to provide even more accurate and comprehensive analysis. Additionally, ChatGPT can assist with risk assessment and management, identifying potential market trends, and providing real-time

updates on financial news and events. With all of these features, ChatGPT is a powerful asset for anyone looking to improve their financial knowledge and decision-making abilities.

6.5.1. Data Collection and Preparation

To gather a comprehensive dataset containing financial data, it is recommended that you look into a variety of sources. For example, you could consider collecting stock prices, financial reports, and economic indicators from multiple sources, including government agencies, financial institutions, and market data providers.

Additionally, it is important to collect domain-specific knowledge to help fine-tune the model for the finance domain. This could include expert analysis from finance professionals, investment strategies from successful investors, and insights from academic research. By collecting a diverse range of data and knowledge, you will be better equipped to build a robust and accurate financial model.

6.5.2. Fine-tuning the Model

One way to improve the effectiveness of ChatGPT is by fine-tuning it with the collected financial dataset and domain-specific knowledge. By incorporating this additional data, the AI model will be able to generate more comprehensive and detailed financial analysis, forecasts, and summaries.

This can be particularly useful for businesses looking to gain a competitive edge in the financial industry. In addition, the improved accuracy and insights provided by ChatGPT could potentially lead to better decision-making and more successful outcomes for individuals and organizations alike.

Therefore, it is highly recommended to invest the time and resources necessary to fine-tune ChatGPT in order to maximize its potential and reap the benefits it can offer.

6.5.3. Generating Financial Reports and Summaries

The use of ChatGPT model to create financial reports, earnings summaries, and investment analyses is a highly efficient and reliable way to gather and present financial data. With its ability to be guided to provide detailed information, trends, and data visualization based on specific user requirements, the model ensures that all key financial metrics and indicators are included in the report.

Furthermore, the model can help in identifying potential investment opportunities and risks by analyzing market trends and comparing the financial performance of different companies. By utilizing the ChatGPT model, financial analysts and investors can make informed decisions and gain a competitive edge in the financial market.

6.5.4. Financial Forecasting

One way to potentially improve the quality of investment decision-making is by leveraging the advanced capabilities of the ChatGPT model. This cutting-edge technology is specifically designed to analyze large amounts of financial data in order to generate detailed and highly accurate financial forecasts.

By utilizing this technology, it may be possible to identify key trends and patterns in market behavior that might not be immediately apparent to the naked eye. Armed with this information, investors can make more informed decisions about how to allocate their resources and manage their risk exposure.

Additionally, the ChatGPT model can be used to conduct scenario analysis, which can help investors prepare for potential future market developments and adjust their strategies accordingly. Overall, the ChatGPT model represents a powerful tool for anyone looking to gain a deeper understanding of the financial landscape and make more effective investment decisions.

6.5.5. Evaluation and Monitoring

To continuously evaluate the performance of the ChatGPT model in the context of finance and investment analysis, it is important to establish a robust set of metrics and benchmarks. These metrics should take into account factors such as accuracy, relevance, and timeliness of generated content.

In addition, it is important to monitor the model's performance over time to identify any trends or patterns that may emerge. This will allow for timely adjustments to be made to the model to ensure it stays up-to-date with evolving market conditions.

Furthermore, it may be beneficial to conduct regular testing of the model, using real-world scenarios and data, to assess its ability to generate accurate and relevant content in a variety of market conditions. This will help to identify any areas for improvement and inform future development of the model.

Overall, by implementing a robust evaluation and monitoring process, the ChatGPT model can be continuously improved to provide valuable insights and analysis for finance and investment professionals.

Example:

Here's a sample code snippet for generating a financial summary using a fine-tuned ChatGPT model:

```python
import openai

openai.api_key = "your_openai_api_key"

def generate_financial_summary(company_name, financial_quarter):
    prompt = f"Write a financial summary for {company_name} for {financial_quarter}."

    response = openai.Completion.create(
        engine="your_fine_tuned_engine",
        prompt=prompt,
        max_tokens=1024,
        n=1,
        stop=None,
        temperature=0.7,
    )

    return response.choices[0].text.strip()

company_name = "Apple Inc."
financial_quarter = "Q3 2023"

financial_summary = generate_financial_summary(company_name, financial_quarter)
print(financial_summary)
```

In this example, the **generate_financial_summary** function takes a company name and a financial quarter as input. It generates a financial summary using the fine-tuned ChatGPT model by providing a prompt that specifies the requirements.

6.6. E-commerce and Personalized Recommendations

ChatGPT can be an extremely valuable tool for e-commerce businesses. By leveraging machine learning algorithms, ChatGPT can generate highly personalized recommendations for customers based on their browsing history, preferences, and other relevant data. This can help businesses not only to improve customer satisfaction but also to increase sales by cross-selling and up-selling relevant products.

Fine-tuning ChatGPT for e-commerce applications can involve training the algorithm on specific product categories, incorporating new data sources such as social media activity or customer reviews, and optimizing the recommendation engine for different stages of the customer journey. By investing in ChatGPT and its customization for e-commerce, businesses can gain a significant competitive advantage in the online marketplace.

6.6.1. Data Collection and Preparation

To gather a comprehensive dataset, we recommend that you collect not only customer behavior data such as browsing history, purchase history, and product preferences, but also demographic data such as age, gender, and location.

It is also important to collect information on the products themselves, including their specifications, features, and any additional details that may be relevant. Additionally, we suggest gathering customer reviews and feedback, as this can provide valuable insights into the strengths and weaknesses of the products, as well as potential areas for improvement.

By combining all of these data points, you can gain a more holistic understanding of your customers and their needs, which can help to inform future product development and marketing efforts.

6.6.2. Fine-tuning the Model

To further improve ChatGPT's performance, we will conduct a comprehensive analysis of the e-commerce dataset that we have collected. This includes a detailed examination of customer behavior data and product information. By doing so, we can gain a deeper understanding of the factors that drive customer decision-making processes.

With this knowledge, we can develop a more sophisticated AI model that is capable of generating highly personalized product recommendations and other relevant content for each individual customer. In addition to this, we will also explore other ways in which we can leverage

the data to enhance ChatGPT's capabilities, such as identifying emerging trends and patterns in customer behavior that can inform our marketing strategies and product development efforts.

Overall, these efforts will not only improve ChatGPT's performance, but also enable us to better serve our customers and stay ahead of the competition in the fast-paced e-commerce industry.

6.6.3. Generating Personalized Recommendations

One way to enhance the shopping experience for customers is to use the fine-tuned ChatGPT model. This model is able to analyze customer preferences and browsing history to create personalized product recommendations.

By implementing such a system, businesses can ensure that their customers are receiving tailored suggestions, leading to a higher likelihood of customer satisfaction and repeat business. In addition, the ChatGPT model can be guided to provide diverse recommendations, taking into account a wider range of products that the customer may not have otherwise considered.

This provides a unique shopping experience that can foster trust and loyalty between the customer and the business. Overall, the use of the ChatGPT model is an effective way to improve the shopping experience for customers and increase sales for businesses.

6.6.4. Product Descriptions and Reviews

One way to enhance the shopping experience of customers is by utilizing the ChatGPT model that has been fine-tuned to generate engaging product descriptions as well as summaries of customer reviews. By providing customers with a detailed and comprehensive analysis of the products, they will be able to make informed decisions, which will ultimately lead to a greater level of satisfaction.

Furthermore, this approach can help to increase brand loyalty and retain customers in the long run. In addition, the use of this model can also help to improve the efficiency of the sales process by reducing the need for human intervention and automating certain aspects of the customer service experience.

6.6.5. Evaluation and Monitoring

It is highly recommended to establish a systematic and periodic evaluation of the ChatGPT model's performance in the context of e-commerce and personalized recommendations. This

evaluation should aim to monitor the quality and relevance of the generated content, identify its strengths and weaknesses, and identify areas for improvement.

In addition to this evaluation, it is also important to stay up-to-date with evolving customer preferences and market trends to ensure that the ChatGPT model remains effective and useful in providing relevant and valuable recommendations to the users.

Therefore, it is recommended to conduct regular market research and customer surveys to identify emerging trends and preferences, and to integrate this information into the ChatGPT model's training and development process.

By doing so, we can ensure that the ChatGPT model continues to meet the needs and expectations of its users and remains a valuable tool in the field of e-commerce and personalized recommendations.

Example:

Here's a sample code snippet for generating personalized product recommendations using a fine-tuned ChatGPT model:

```python
import openai

openai.api_key = "your_openai_api_key"

def generate_product_recommendations(user_profile, user_browsing_history):
    prompt = f"Based on the following user profile: {user_profile} and browsing
history: {user_browsing_history}, recommend 3 products for the user."

    response = openai.Completion.create(
        engine="your_fine_tuned_engine",
        prompt=prompt,
        max_tokens=1024,
        n=1,
        stop=None,
        temperature=0.7,
    )

    return response.choices[0].text.strip()

user_profile = "25-year-old male, interested in technology and fitness"
user_browsing_history = "smartphones, fitness trackers, wireless headphones"

product_recommendations = generate_product_recommendations(user_profile, user_br
owsing_history)
print(product_recommendations)
```

In this example, the **generate_product_recommendations** function takes a user profile and browsing history as input. It generates personalized product recommendations using the fine-tuned ChatGPT model by providing a prompt that specifies the requirements.

6.7. Education and Personalized Learning

ChatGPT has immense potential in the education sector, enabling the development of personalized learning experiences for students. By fine-tuning ChatGPT for educational applications, it can assist with content generation, answer questions, and provide tailored learning resources based on students' needs and preferences.

Moreover, ChatGPT can also be used to develop intelligent tutoring systems that can help students learn more effectively. These systems can provide feedback to students in real-time, allowing them to adjust their learning strategies as needed. Additionally, ChatGPT can be used to create virtual learning assistants that can help students with their homework, provide additional learning resources, and offer guidance on study habits.

In addition to these educational applications, ChatGPT can also be used in a variety of other industries. For example, it can be used in customer service to help customers find the information they need more quickly and easily. It can also be used in healthcare to provide patients with personalized health advice and support.

Overall, ChatGPT has the potential to revolutionize the way we learn and work. Its ability to generate content, answer questions, and provide personalized learning resources make it an invaluable tool for educators and students alike. As more industries begin to adopt ChatGPT, we can expect to see even more innovative applications emerge in the future.

6.7.1. Data Collection and Preparation

To gather a comprehensive dataset containing educational materials, including textbooks, articles, and online resources, it's essential to conduct thorough research. It's also necessary to collect information about student profiles, learning styles, and preferences to effectively tailor educational resources to meet their needs.

One way to do this is to conduct surveys and interviews with students to gather as much information as possible. Additionally, reaching out to experts in the field and collaborating with educational institutions can provide valuable insights and data to make the dataset as comprehensive as possible. By taking these steps, we can ensure that the dataset we gather is not only extensive but also highly relevant to its intended audience.

6.7.2. Fine-tuning the Model

One approach to fine-tuning ChatGPT using the collected education dataset is to employ neural network architectures. These architectures can be specifically designed to focus on subject-specific content, learning strategies, and student profiles. By doing so, the AI model can generate personalized learning materials that cater to the individual needs of students.

The neural network can also be trained to effectively address students' questions by analyzing their responses and providing feedback that is tailored to their learning style. In this way, the AI model can become a powerful tool for enhancing student learning outcomes and promoting academic success.

6.7.3. Generating Personalized Learning Content

Our platform is powered by the fine-tuned ChatGPT model. With this model, we can create customized learning materials that are specifically designed to cater to the learning needs and preferences of each individual student. Our platform offers a wide range of materials, including but not limited to study guides, lesson plans, and summaries of complex topics. These materials are curated by our team of experts and are designed to provide students with a comprehensive understanding of the subject matter.

Our platform allows for interactive learning, which enables students to engage with the material in a meaningful way and retain the information more effectively. We believe that personalized learning is the key to unlocking a student's full potential, and our platform is designed to help students achieve their academic goals by providing them with the tools they need to succeed.

6.7.4. Question-Answering and Tutoring

One great way to take advantage of the fine-tuned ChatGPT model is to use it as a tool for answering students' questions and providing them with helpful tutoring assistance on a wide range of subjects.

As an AI-powered model, ChatGPT has the ability to explain complex concepts in a way that is both clear and easy to understand. Whether you are struggling with a difficult math problem or need help understanding the intricacies of a complex scientific theory, ChatGPT can provide the guidance you need to succeed.

With its advanced natural language processing capabilities and vast knowledge base, ChatGPT is an invaluable resource for students of all ages and backgrounds. So why not give it a try today and see just how much it can help you achieve your academic goals?

6.7.5. Evaluation and Monitoring

To ensure the efficacy of the ChatGPT model in the realm of education and personalized learning, it is crucial to consistently and systematically evaluate its performance. This can be achieved through ongoing monitoring of the quality and relevance of the content generated by the model.

By doing so, any areas for improvement can be identified and addressed, ensuring that the model remains up-to-date and relevant with the ever-evolving educational standards and trends. It may be beneficial to analyze the impact of the ChatGPT model on student learning outcomes, taking into consideration factors such as engagement, comprehension, and retention.

By gaining insight into the model's impact on student outcomes, adjustments can be made to further refine and optimize the model for education and personalized learning purposes. Overall, it is essential to prioritize ongoing evaluation and improvement of the ChatGPT model in order to maximize its potential as a valuable tool for enhancing educational experiences for students.

Example:

Here's a sample code snippet for generating personalized learning content using a fine-tuned ChatGPT model:

```python
import openai

openai.api_key = "your_openai_api_key"

def generate_learning_content(student_profile, topic):
    prompt = f"Create a personalized summary of the topic '{topic}' for a studen
t with the following profile: {student_profile}."

    response = openai.Completion.create(
        engine="your_fine_tuned_engine",
        prompt=prompt,
        max_tokens=1024,
        n=1,
        stop=None,
        temperature=0.7,
    )

    return response.choices[0].text.strip()

student_profile = "16-year-old high school student, visual learner"
topic = "Photosynthesis"

learning_content = generate_learning_content(student_profile, topic)
print(learning_content)
```

In this example, the **generate_learning_content** function takes a student profile and a topic as input. It generates personalized learning content using the fine-tuned ChatGPT model by providing a prompt that specifies the requirements.

6.8. Gaming and Interactive Storytelling

ChatGPT is a fantastic tool that can be leveraged for a wide range of applications, from gaming to interactive storytelling. It is particularly useful for generating engaging and immersive narratives, dialogues, and creative content in real-time.

By fine-tuning ChatGPT for gaming and storytelling applications, developers can create truly immersive gaming experiences that transport players to new worlds and introduce them to unique characters. Moreover, ChatGPT can be used to develop virtual characters that can

interact with users in a natural and intuitive way, making the overall experience more engaging and memorable.

With ChatGPT, developers can create interactive stories that are rich in detail and dynamic in nature, providing users with a more personalized and memorable experience. Overall, ChatGPT's potential is vast, and it can be a game-changer for anyone looking to develop innovative and engaging content.

6.8.1. Data Collection and Preparation

One potential strategy to ensure a more diverse training set for the model is to collect a broad range of data sets containing game scripts, dialogues, and interactive story narratives. This can include genres such as adventure, action, puzzle, and role-playing games, as well as different styles of storytelling, such as linear or branching narratives.

It may be beneficial to collect data from different sources, such as indie game developers, AAA game studios, and even fan fiction communities. By incorporating a diverse range of data sets, the model will be better equipped to handle a wider variety of inputs and generate more creative and engaging outputs.

6.8.2. Fine-tuning the Model

To optimize ChatGPT for gaming and interactive storytelling applications, we can use a dataset of gaming scenarios, character dialogues, and story events to train the model. By doing so, we can enable the model to generate content that is more relevant to these specific applications.

This will not only improve the overall quality of the generated content but also enhance the user experience by providing more engaging and interactive content. We can also explore the possibility of including other types of datasets, such as virtual reality environments or augmented reality experiences, to further expand the model's capabilities and improve its performance in various applications.

6.8.3. Generating Dynamic Game Content

One potential application of the fine-tuned ChatGPT model is to generate game content that is tailored to the player's choices and actions. This could include dynamically adapting quests, challenges, and storylines to create a truly personalized gaming experience.

By leveraging the power of natural language processing, developers could create a game in which the player's decisions have a tangible impact on the world and story around them. This

could lead to a more immersive and engaging experience for players, as they feel that their choices truly matter and have consequences in the game.

This approach could enable game developers to create more content in less time, as the model could generate new and unique content based on the player's actions, rather than relying solely on pre-written dialogue and scenarios. Overall, incorporating the ChatGPT model into game development has the potential to revolutionize the way games are created and experienced, leading to more dynamic, immersive, and personalized gaming experiences.

6.8.4. Creating Virtual Characters

One way to enhance the overall gaming experience is by leveraging the capabilities of the fine-tuned ChatGPT model. With this, virtual characters can be created with unique personalities, backstories, and dialogues that can engage players in a more immersive way. Imagine having a game where the characters have their own distinct quirks and mannerisms, making the gameplay more exciting and enjoyable.

By using this technology, game developers can take the gaming experience to the next level and provide players with a more engaging and unforgettable experience that they will surely love.

6.8.5. Evaluation and Monitoring

It is important to regularly evaluate the performance of the ChatGPT model in the context of gaming and interactive storytelling. This can be achieved through various methods such as monitoring the quality and relevance of the generated content, identifying areas for improvement, and ensuring that the model stays up-to-date with the latest gaming trends and narrative techniques.

In order to monitor the quality and relevance of the generated content, it is necessary to create a set of metrics that can be used to evaluate the model's performance. These metrics should include measures of both the technical accuracy of the model and the overall user experience. For example, technical accuracy metrics may include measures of the model's ability to accurately predict user responses, while user experience metrics may include measures of the model's ability to generate engaging and immersive content.

Identifying areas for improvement is also an important aspect of evaluating the ChatGPT model's performance. This can be achieved through various methods such as conducting user surveys or analyzing user feedback. By identifying areas for improvement, developers can work to enhance the model's capabilities and improve the overall user experience.

Finally, it is crucial to ensure that the ChatGPT model stays up-to-date with the latest gaming trends and narrative techniques. This can be achieved through ongoing research and development, as well as collaboration with experts in the gaming and interactive storytelling industries. By staying up-to-date with the latest trends and techniques, the ChatGPT model can continue to provide users with high-quality and engaging content.

Example:

Here's a sample code snippet for generating a game quest using a fine-tuned ChatGPT model:

```python
import openai

openai.api_key = "your_openai_api_key"

def generate_game_quest(player_profile, game_genre):
    prompt = f"Create an engaging game quest for a player with the following pro
file: {player_profile} in a {game_genre} game."

    response = openai.Completion.create(
        engine="your_fine_tuned_engine",
        prompt=prompt,
        max_tokens=512,
        n=1,
        stop=None,
        temperature=0.7,
    )

    return response.choices[0].text.strip()

player_profile = "casual gamer, enjoys exploration and story-driven games"
game_genre = "fantasy RPG"

quest = generate_game_quest(player_profile, game_genre)
print(quest)
```

In this example, the **generate_game_quest** function takes a player profile and game genre as input. It generates a game quest using the fine-tuned ChatGPT model by providing a prompt that specifies the requirements.

Chapter 6 Conclusion

In conclusion, Chapter 6, "Adapting ChatGPT for Specific Industries," has demonstrated the wide-ranging applicability of ChatGPT across various domains, showcasing its versatility and potential for customization. As we have seen throughout this chapter, ChatGPT can be fine-tuned to cater to specific industry needs, making it a valuable tool for developers and organizations in various sectors.

We began with an exploration of healthcare and medical applications, where ChatGPT can be utilized to enhance medical research, assist in diagnostics, and provide personalized health recommendations. By fine-tuning ChatGPT on domain-specific medical datasets and carefully designing prompts, developers can create AI-driven applications that can help healthcare professionals make better-informed decisions and improve patient outcomes.

Next, we discussed the role of ChatGPT in legal and regulatory compliance, where it can be used to analyze and summarize legal documents, perform contract reviews, and assist with compliance tasks. By training ChatGPT on legal texts, developers can create AI assistants that can help lawyers and other legal professionals save time and reduce the risk of human errors.

In the customer support and CRM systems domain, we examined how ChatGPT can be employed to automate customer service tasks, create personalized customer interactions, and enhance CRM workflows. Fine-tuning ChatGPT on customer support data can help organizations streamline their support processes, reduce response times, and improve overall customer satisfaction.

We also explored the potential of ChatGPT for content generation and SEO, where it can be used to generate high-quality, engaging content for various purposes such as blog posts, social media updates, and SEO-friendly articles. Fine-tuning the model on domain-specific content enables marketers and content creators to generate creative and optimized content that drives traffic and engagement.

In the finance and investment analysis segment, we highlighted how ChatGPT can assist with financial forecasting, risk assessment, and sentiment analysis. By training the model on financial datasets, developers can create AI-driven tools that support investors and financial professionals in making better-informed decisions.

For e-commerce and personalized recommendations, we discussed the use of ChatGPT to generate product descriptions, marketing content, and personalized recommendations based on user data. Fine-tuning the model on e-commerce data can help businesses boost sales, increase customer retention, and enhance user experience.

In the education and personalized learning sector, we explored how ChatGPT can be employed for creating tailored learning experiences, generating educational content, and providing feedback on student work. Fine-tuning the model on educational data can support teachers and educators in delivering personalized learning experiences and improving student outcomes.

Finally, we investigated the application of ChatGPT in gaming and interactive storytelling, where it can be used to generate dynamic game content, create virtual characters, and design immersive storylines. Fine-tuning the model on gaming and storytelling data can help game developers create engaging, personalized, and dynamic gaming experiences.

Throughout this chapter, we have provided numerous examples and code snippets to demonstrate the application of ChatGPT across various industries. As we have seen, fine-tuning ChatGPT for specific industries can result in highly effective AI-driven solutions that cater to the unique needs and challenges of each sector, unlocking new possibilities for innovation and efficiency.

Chapter 7 - Ensuring Responsible AI Usage

As AI systems like ChatGPT continue to play an increasingly important role in various industries, it is critical to address the ethical and responsible usage of these systems. The widespread adoption of AI has brought about many benefits, but also poses new challenges that require careful consideration. One of the key challenges is mitigating biases, which can lead to unfair and discriminatory outcomes. This involves not only identifying and correcting biases in the data used to train AI systems, but also ensuring that the algorithms and models used are transparent and fair.

Another important consideration is privacy and security. AI systems often rely on large amounts of personal data, which must be safeguarded to prevent unauthorized access and protect individual privacy. This means implementing strong security measures and adhering to data protection regulations.

It is important to address the potential for misuse of AI systems. This includes identifying and preventing malicious uses of the technology, as well as ensuring that the benefits of AI are distributed fairly and equitably across society.

Promoting transparency and accountability is crucial for ensuring that AI systems are used in an ethical and responsible manner. This involves making the decision-making processes of AI systems transparent, so that individuals and organizations can understand how the technology is being used. It also involves establishing clear lines of responsibility and accountability for the development and deployment of AI systems.

In summary, while the benefits of AI are clear, its widespread adoption requires careful consideration of the ethical and responsible usage of these systems. By addressing challenges such as mitigating biases, ensuring privacy and security, preventing system misuse, and promoting transparency and accountability, we can ensure that AI is used in a manner that upholds ethical standards and mitigates potential harm.

7.1. Mitigating Biases in AI

As the use of AI systems increases, so does the possibility of bias in decision making. Bias can result in unfair, discriminatory, or erroneous outcomes that negatively affect individuals and society as a whole. Therefore, it is crucial to identify and mitigate biases in AI systems to ensure responsible usage.

There are several types of biases that can occur in AI systems, including selection bias, confirmation bias, and algorithmic bias. Selection bias occurs when the data used to train the AI system is not representative of the entire population. Confirmation bias occurs when the system is designed to confirm pre-existing beliefs or assumptions, leading to biased decisions. Algorithmic bias occurs when the algorithm used to make decisions is inherently biased.

To mitigate these biases, it is necessary to develop techniques that can detect and reduce them. For example, one way to detect selection bias is to analyze the dataset and check if it is representative of the entire population. Another way to reduce algorithmic bias is to use a diverse range of data to train the AI system.

Continuous monitoring of the AI system's performance is also essential to ensure fairness and accuracy. This can involve regular testing and retraining of the system to ensure it is making unbiased decisions.

In the following sections, we will provide code examples for detecting and mitigating biases in AI systems, helping to ensure responsible and ethical usage of AI technology.

7.1.1. Types of Bias in AI Systems

Artificial Intelligence (AI) systems have become increasingly prevalent in today's world, with applications in various fields, such as healthcare, finance, and transportation. However, despite their many benefits, AI systems are not without their challenges. One of the most significant issues facing AI systems is that they are prone to biases. These biases can stem from various sources, such as the training data used to create the AI system, the model architecture, or even the unconscious biases of the human developers who created the system.

Furthermore, these biases can have far-reaching consequences. For example, a biased AI system used in healthcare could lead to incorrect diagnoses or inadequate treatment for certain groups of people. Similarly, a biased AI system used in finance could lead to unfair lending practices or investment decisions that disadvantage certain groups of people.

As such, it is crucial to address and mitigate these biases in AI systems. This can involve measures such as ensuring diverse representation in the development team, using diverse and representative training data, and regularly auditing AI systems for biases. By taking these steps, we can help ensure that AI systems are not only accurate and effective but also fair and equitable for all.

Some common types of biases include:

Representation Bias

Representation bias is a problem that arises when the dataset used to train an algorithm does not accurately reflect the characteristics of the target population, leading to skewed predictions and outcomes. This type of bias can be introduced in many ways, such as through sampling bias, where the training data is not representative of the target population, or through selection bias, where certain types of data are overrepresented in the dataset.

Representation bias is a particularly pressing concern in fields such as healthcare, where the consequences of biased predictions can be severe and even life-threatening. Therefore, it is important to carefully consider the representativeness of training data when developing algorithms and to use techniques such as oversampling or undersampling to address any imbalances in the data.

Label Bias

Arises when the labels assigned to training examples are biased, causing the model to learn incorrect associations. One way this bias can occur is when the data being used to train the model is not representative of the broader population. It is important to ensure that the training data is diverse and reflects the full range of potential inputs that the model may encounter in the real world. Another possible source of label bias is the way that the labels themselves are assigned.

For example, a human annotator may have their own biases or preconceptions that influence the labeling process, leading to incorrect associations being learned by the model. To mitigate these risks, it is important to have multiple annotators review the data and to establish clear guidelines for how the labels should be assigned.

Measurement Bias

Results from errors in measuring the input features, which can lead to incorrect predictions. Measurement bias can occur in a variety of ways, such as when the data collection tool is not

calibrated correctly, when the data collector has a personal bias that affects the measurements, or when there are errors in the data entry process.

Measurement bias can be influenced by the environment in which the data is collected, such as lighting or sound levels. In order to mitigate measurement bias, it is important to carefully design the data collection process and to use reliable and validated measurement tools. Furthermore, ongoing monitoring and evaluation of the data collection process can help to identify and address any issues with measurement bias that may arise.

Algorithmic Bias

This is a phenomenon that is becoming increasingly relevant in modern society. It occurs when the model architecture or algorithm itself introduces bias into the system, leading to inaccurate or unfair results.

This can happen for a variety of reasons, including the quality of the data used to train the model, the assumptions made by the model creator, or even the cultural or societal biases that are inherent in the dataset. As such, it is important for those who work with algorithms to be aware of the potential for bias and take steps to mitigate its impact.

One way to do this is to ensure that the data used to train the model is diverse and representative of the population it is meant to serve. Additionally, it may be necessary to adjust the algorithm itself or to use multiple algorithms in combination to create a more balanced and accurate result.

Example:

While it's not possible to provide specific code examples for each type of bias, as they depend on the context and data, we can demonstrate how to detect potential representation bias in a dataset using Python and pandas library.

```python
import pandas as pd

# Load the dataset
data = pd.read_csv('your_dataset.csv')

# Check for representation bias by examining the distribution of a sensitive att
ribute, e.g., gender
gender_counts = data['gender'].value_counts(normalize=True)

print("Gender distribution in the dataset:")
print(gender_counts)
```

This code snippet calculates the distribution of a sensitive attribute (gender in this case) in the dataset. If the distribution is significantly skewed, it may indicate the presence of representation bias.

7.1.2. Techniques for Bias Detection and Reduction

Several techniques can be employed to detect and reduce biases in AI systems:

Diversify Training Data

One of the keys to reducing representation bias in machine learning models is to ensure that the training data accurately represents the target population. One way to do this is by collecting more diverse data.

For example, if the model is being trained to recognize faces, it may be necessary to collect data from a wider range of skin tones, ages, and genders to avoid over-representation of a particular group. Another approach is to re-sample the dataset to obtain a more balanced distribution.

This can involve removing some of the over-represented data points or adding more data points from under-represented groups. Overall, by diversifying the training data, machine learning models can become more accurate and fairer to all members of the target population.

Fairness Metrics

AI systems have the potential to perpetuate biases and discrimination. In order to measure and quantify these biases, various fairness metrics have been developed. Demographic parity, for example, is a measure of equal representation of different groups in a given dataset.

Equal opportunity measures whether the same opportunities are available to all individuals, regardless of their background. Equalized odds, on the other hand, measures whether the rate of positive outcomes is the same for all groups. By using these metrics, we can better understand how AI systems may be perpetuating biases and work towards creating more fair and equitable systems.

Bias Mitigation Algorithms

Techniques like re-sampling, re-weighting, and adversarial training can be applied during the training process to mitigate biases. When it comes to re-sampling, there are different strategies that can be used, such as over-sampling and under-sampling. Over-sampling involves increasing the number of instances of the minority class, while under-sampling involves reducing the number of instances of the majority class.

Another technique, re-weighting, involves assigning different weights to different instances during training to reduce the bias towards the majority class. Adversarial training, on the other hand, involves training a model to be robust against adversarial attacks that can be used to exploit biases in the data. By using a combination of these techniques, it is possible to develop algorithms that are more fair and unbiased.

Post-hoc Analysis

Once the training of the model is complete, it is important to conduct a thorough analysis of its predictions to identify any potential biases that may be present. This analysis can be done through a series of techniques such as calibration or threshold adjustment. These techniques can help to correct any biases that may be present in the model's predictions, ensuring that the model is making accurate and unbiased predictions.

It is important to note that this analysis should be done regularly to ensure that the model is continuing to make accurate and unbiased predictions over time. Additionally, it is important to consider the impact that any changes made to the model may have on its predictions and to carefully monitor the model's performance after any changes are made.

Continuous Monitoring

It is essential to keep an eye on the model's performance over time. This will help to identify any emerging biases or discrepancies in its predictions, which can be addressed before they cause significant issues.

To achieve continuous monitoring, regular reviews and updates are required. This includes checking the accuracy of the data, ensuring that the model is still relevant and up-to-date, and making any necessary adjustments to the model as new information becomes available. Additionally, it is essential to communicate the results of the monitoring process to stakeholders to ensure that they are aware of any potential risks or issues that may arise.

Example:

Here's an example of how to apply the re-sampling technique to mitigate representation bias in a dataset using Python and the imbalanced-learn library.

```python
import pandas as pd
from imblearn.over_sampling import SMOTE
from sklearn.model_selection import train_test_split

# Load the dataset
data = pd.read_csv('your_dataset.csv')

# Separate features (X) and target (y)
X = data.drop('target', axis=1)
y = data['target']

# Split the data into train and test sets
X_train, X_test, y_train, y_test = train_test_split(X, y, test_size=0.2, random_state=42)

# Apply SMOTE to balance the dataset
smote = SMOTE(sampling_strategy='auto', random_state=42)
X_train_resampled, y_train_resampled = smote.fit_resample(X_train, y_train)

# Now you can train your model with the resampled dataset
```

This code snippet demonstrates the use of Synthetic Minority Over-sampling Technique (SMOTE) to balance an imbalanced dataset. The resampled dataset can then be used to train the AI system, reducing the impact of representation bias on the model's predictions.

7.1.3. Fairness Metrics for AI Systems

Fairness metrics are a critical tool for assessing the performance of AI systems with respect to different demographic groups or protected attributes. These metrics provide a quantitative measure of fairness, which is essential for developers to understand the potential biases in their models and take appropriate measures to mitigate them.

One of the key benefits of using fairness metrics is that they allow developers to identify and rectify potential biases in AI systems. For example, if an AI system is found to be systematically underperforming for a particular demographic group, developers can investigate the root cause of this bias and take corrective action.

Moreover, fairness metrics can also help to promote transparency and accountability in AI systems. By providing a quantitative measure of fairness, developers can demonstrate to stakeholders that their systems are designed to treat all users fairly, regardless of their demographic characteristics or protected attributes.

In sum, fairness metrics are an essential tool for ensuring that AI systems are fair and unbiased. By quantifying fairness, developers can identify potential biases and take appropriate measures to mitigate them, thereby promoting transparency, accountability, and trust in AI systems.

Some common fairness metrics include:

Demographic Parity

This metric checks whether the positive outcomes are distributed equally across all demographic groups. It measures the difference in the probability of positive outcomes between different groups. To elaborate further, demographic parity is a crucial aspect of fairness in machine learning models. It is important to ensure that the benefits of the model are shared equally among different groups of people.

The metric of demographic parity provides a framework for assessing this aspect of fairness. By analyzing the probability of positive outcomes across different groups, we can determine whether the model is biased towards one group or another. Moreover, we can use the insights gained from this analysis to make improvements to the model and ensure that it is fair for everyone.

Equalized Odds

This metric checks whether the true positive rates (sensitivity) and false positive rates (1-specificity) are the same across all demographic groups. It ensures that the AI system has the same performance for each group, regardless of the base rate. In other words, it seeks to eliminate any potential biases that may be present in the system's decision-making process. By ensuring that the true positive rates and false positive rates are the same across all groups, it helps to ensure a fair and just outcome for everyone involved.

This is particularly important in situations where the stakes are high, such as in healthcare or criminal justice, where AI systems are increasingly being used to make important decisions. By using the equalized odds metric, we can help to ensure that these systems are making decisions that are fair and unbiased, and that they are not inadvertently discriminating against any particular group.

Equal Opportunity

This metric is similar to equalized odds but focuses only on the true positive rates. It ensures that an AI system has the same sensitivity for all demographic groups. One way to interpret this metric is to consider the notion of fairness. In other words, when an algorithm is used to make decisions about people, it is important that it does not discriminate against any particular group. For example, it would be unfair if an AI system was more likely to approve loan applications from one ethnic group over another. This is why the equal opportunity metric is a crucial tool in ensuring that AI systems are fair and unbiased. By using this metric, we can detect and correct any discrepancies in the true positive rates, and ensure that the algorithm is treating all demographic groups equally.

Example:

Below is a code example that calculates demographic parity using scikit-learn and NumPy:

```python
import numpy as np
from sklearn.metrics import confusion_matrix

def demographic_parity(y_true, y_pred, protected_attribute):
    """
    Calculate demographic parity for a binary classification task.

    Parameters:
    y_true: np.array, ground truth labels (binary)
    y_pred: np.array, predicted labels (binary)
    protected_attribute: np.array, binary attribute to check for fairness (e.g.,
gender)

    Returns:
    demographic_parity_difference: float, difference in the probability of posit
ive outcomes between the two groups
    """

    group_1_indices = np.where(protected_attribute == 1)[0]
    group_2_indices = np.where(protected_attribute == 0)[0]

    group_1_outcome_rate = np.mean(y_pred[group_1_indices])
    group_2_outcome_rate = np.mean(y_pred[group_2_indices])

    demographic_parity_difference = abs(group_1_outcome_rate - group_2_outcome_r
ate)
    return demographic_parity_difference

# Example usage:
y_true = np.array([1, 0, 1, 1, 0, 1, 0, 0])
y_pred = np.array([1, 1, 1, 0, 0, 1, 0, 0])
protected_attribute = np.array([1, 1, 0, 1, 0, 0, 1, 0])  # 1: Group 1, 0: Group
2

dp_difference = demographic_parity(y_true, y_pred, protected_attribute)
print(f"Demographic Parity Difference: {dp_difference:.2f}")
```

This code defines a function, **demographic_parity**, that takes the ground truth labels, predicted labels, and a protected attribute (e.g., gender, race) as inputs. It calculates the positive outcome rates for each group based on the protected attribute and returns the absolute difference between these rates.

7.1.4. Bias Mitigation Algorithms

Bias mitigation algorithms are a set of techniques used to reduce biases in AI systems. These techniques can be implemented at different stages of the AI process, including pre-processing, in-processing, and post-processing. Pre-processing techniques involve modifying the data before it is used to train the AI system. Some popular pre-processing techniques include data augmentation and re-sampling, which can adjust the distribution of the training data to ensure that different demographic groups are represented in a balanced way.

In-processing techniques, on the other hand, alter the training process itself. For example, some algorithms may adjust the weights assigned to different features in the data to reduce bias. Others may introduce constraints or penalties to discourage the AI system from making biased predictions.

Finally, post-processing techniques adjust the model predictions after training. This can involve adjusting the decision threshold used to classify data points, or using techniques such as calibration to ensure that the model's predicted probabilities accurately reflect the likelihood of each class.

Overall, bias mitigation algorithms are an important tool for ensuring that AI systems are fair and unbiased. By using a combination of pre-processing, in-processing, and post-processing techniques, developers can help to reduce the impact of biases and ensure that their AI systems are effective for all users, regardless of their demographic background.

Example:

Here's a code example illustrating re-sampling using the imbalanced-learn library:

```python
import numpy as np
from imblearn.over_sampling import SMOTE
from sklearn.datasets import make_classification
from sklearn.model_selection import train_test_split
from sklearn.svm import SVC
from sklearn.metrics import classification_report

# Create an imbalanced dataset
X, y = make_classification(n_classes=2, class_sep=2, weights=[0.1, 0.9],
                           n_informative=3, n_redundant=1, flip_y=0,
                           n_features=20, n_clusters_per_class=1,
                           n_samples=1000, random_state=10)

# Split the dataset into training and testing sets
X_train, X_test, y_train, y_test = train_test_split(X, y, test_size=0.5, random_
state=42)

# Train a support vector machine classifier on the imbalanced dataset
clf = SVC(kernel='linear', C=1, random_state=42)
clf.fit(X_train, y_train)
y_pred = clf.predict(X_test)

# Evaluate the classifier's performance on the imbalanced dataset
print("Imbalanced dataset classification report:")
print(classification_report(y_test, y_pred))

# Apply Synthetic Minority Over-sampling Technique (SMOTE) for re-sampling
smote = SMOTE(random_state=42)
X_resampled, y_resampled = smote.fit_resample(X_train, y_train)

# Train the support vector machine classifier on the resampled dataset
clf.fit(X_resampled, y_resampled)
y_pred_resampled = clf.predict(X_test)

# Evaluate the classifier's performance on the resampled dataset
print("Resampled dataset classification report:")
print(classification_report(y_test, y_pred_resampled))
```

In this code example, we create an imbalanced dataset and train a support vector machine classifier. We then apply the Synthetic Minority Over-sampling Technique (SMOTE) to re-sample the dataset and train another classifier on the resampled data. Finally, we compare the

performance of the classifiers on the imbalanced and resampled datasets using classification reports. The re-sampling technique aims to improve the classifier's performance on the minority class by generating synthetic samples.

7.2. Privacy and Security Considerations

As AI systems continue to gain widespread use, the importance of privacy and security concerns associated with these systems grows more acute. Ensuring that these systems are secure and protect users' privacy is of paramount importance.

In order to safeguard personal data, companies must take special steps to protect privacy. One important technique used to protect privacy is anonymization. This involves removing or encrypting identifying information from data sets, which can be an effective way to protect users' identities. However, it is important to note that anonymization is not foolproof and can be circumvented by those with sufficient expertise.

To anonymization, other best practices must be implemented to ensure the secure deployment and storage of data. This can involve using secure databases and networks, as well as implementing access controls and other security measures. Companies must also take care to comply with relevant regulations and standards related to data privacy and security.

Overall, it is clear that as AI systems become more widespread, the need for privacy and security measures will only increase. It is essential that companies take these concerns seriously and take all necessary steps to ensure that their systems are secure and protect users' privacy.

7.2.1. Data Privacy and Anonymization Techniques

Data privacy is an essential aspect of AI systems that handle user data. It is crucial because it helps protect sensitive information from unauthorized access or misuse. With the increasing amount of data being collected, it is becoming more and more important to ensure that personal information is kept confidential.

One way to do this is through anonymization techniques, which can be used to remove personally identifiable information (PII) from datasets before processing. By doing so, privacy risks can be reduced, and individuals can feel more secure about their personal data. Additionally, it is important to note that privacy is not only a legal obligation but also an ethical responsibility for companies that handle user data. Therefore, it is crucial to implement proper data privacy measures to ensure that user data is protected and handled responsibly.

Data masking

Data masking is a technique used to protect sensitive information by replacing it with fictitious or scrambled data that still retains the basic structure of the original information. This method is commonly used to safeguard data elements such as credit card numbers, social security numbers, and other personally identifiable information.

By replacing sensitive data with a fictional counterpart, data masking ensures that the original sensitive information remains concealed, while still allowing for the use of the data in non-sensitive contexts. This technique is often used in conjunction with other data security measures to provide a multi-layered approach to data protection.

Example:

```python
import pandas as pd
import random
import string

def random_string(length):
    return ''.join(random.choice(string.ascii_letters) for _ in range(length))

def mask_names(names, length=5):
    return [random_string(length) for _ in range(len(names))]

data = pd.DataFrame({
    'Name': ['Alice', 'Bob', 'Charlie'],
    'Age': [25, 32, 22]
})

data['Name'] = mask_names(data['Name'])
print(data)
```

k-Anonymity

This method groups data records together so that each group contains at least k records, ensuring that each individual's data is indistinguishable from at least k-1 others. The idea behind k-Anonymity is to protect individuals' privacy and sensitive information from data mining and analysis tools.

By using this method, we can reduce the risk of re-identification attacks, where an individual's identity can be revealed by combining and analyzing different datasets. Moreover, k-Anonymity can be used in various fields, such as healthcare and finance, where data privacy is of utmost importance and data sharing or analysis can be challenging due to legal or ethical concerns.

Example:

```python
# Note: This example is conceptual and not a complete implementation of k-anonym
ity
def k_anonymize(data, k, sensitive_columns):
    for column in sensitive_columns:
        data[column] = data.groupby(data[column]).transform(lambda x: x if len
(x) >= k else None)
    return data

data = pd.DataFrame({
    'Name': ['Alice', 'Bob', 'Charlie', 'David', 'Eve'],
    'Age': [25, 32, 22, 25, 32]
})

k_anonymized_data = k_anonymize(data, k=2, sensitive_columns=['Age'])
print(k_anonymized_data)
```

7.2.2. Secure Deployment and Data Storage

When deploying AI systems, it is crucial to ensure the security of the infrastructure and data storage. This can be achieved through a variety of methods, such as implementing strong encryption algorithms, utilizing multi-factor authentication, and conducting regular security audits. In addition, it is important to consider the potential risks associated with the deployment of AI systems, including the possibility of data breaches, unauthorized access, and system failures.

To mitigate these risks, it is recommended to create a comprehensive security plan that addresses each potential vulnerability and outlines the steps required to prevent and respond to security incidents. Furthermore, it is important to stay up-to-date with the latest security trends and technologies in order to adapt to changing threats and ensure the ongoing protection of your AI infrastructure and data. Overall, taking a proactive approach to AI security is essential for ensuring the long-term success and viability of your AI systems.

Best practices include:

- **Encryption**: Use encryption for data at rest and in transit to protect sensitive information from unauthorized access. Encryption is an important security measure that helps to prevent unauthorized users from accessing sensitive information. In order to ensure that your data is kept secure, it is important to use strong encryption methods that are difficult to crack. This can include using advanced encryption algorithms, such as AES or RSA, and ensuring that your keys are kept secure. Additionally, it is important to regularly review and update your encryption methods to ensure that they are still effective and up-to-date with the latest security standards.

- **Access control**: It is important to implement strong access control policies to ensure that the AI system and data are protected from unauthorized access. Limiting access to authorized users only is a key step in achieving this goal. One way to accomplish this is by using multi-factor authentication, which requires users to provide additional forms of identification beyond a password. Additionally, implementing role-based access control can help ensure that users only have access to the data and functions that are necessary for their job duties. Another important consideration is to regularly review access permissions to ensure that they are still appropriate and up-to-date.

- **Regular security audits**: Security is a critical concern when it comes to AI infrastructure. That's why it's important to conduct regular security audits to identify potential vulnerabilities. These audits can help you stay ahead of threats and ensure that your infrastructure is secure. During a security audit, you can assess your infrastructure's current security posture, identify any weaknesses or vulnerabilities, and take steps to address them promptly. By conducting regular security audits, you can stay on top of potential security risks and keep your AI infrastructure secure.

- **Secure software development**: It is important to follow secure software development practices to minimize the risk of vulnerabilities in your artificial intelligence (AI) application. One such practice is input validation, which ensures that the data entered by users is properly formatted and meets certain criteria. Another practice is output encoding, which helps prevent attacks that attempt to inject malicious code into the output of your application. Proper error handling is also critical in ensuring the security of your AI application, as it helps prevent attackers from exploiting vulnerabilities in your code. By following these best practices, you can help ensure that your AI application is as secure as possible.

- **Monitoring**: Set up monitoring and logging mechanisms to detect potential security threats and respond to them in a timely manner. This will involve designing, implementing, and maintaining a comprehensive monitoring system that can detect any suspicious activity on the network. The monitoring system should be able to track all network traffic, including data packets, and should be able to detect any unauthorized access attempts or other suspicious behavior. Additionally, the system should be able to generate alerts or notifications when potential security threats are detected, so that the security team can respond quickly and take appropriate action. In

order to ensure the system is effective, regular testing and evaluation should be conducted to identify any weaknesses or areas for improvement. Overall, having a robust monitoring system in place is essential for maintaining the security and integrity of the network and protecting against potential threats.

Example:

While it is difficult to provide comprehensive code examples for each aspect of secure deployment and data storage, we can provide a few snippets demonstrating the encryption of data at rest using Python.

Here's an example of how to encrypt and decrypt data using the cryptography library in Python:

```python
from cryptography.fernet import Fernet

# Generate a key for encryption and decryption
key = Fernet.generate_key()
cipher_suite = Fernet(key)

# Encrypt data
data = b"Sensitive information"
encrypted_data = cipher_suite.encrypt(data)
print("Encrypted data:", encrypted_data)

# Decrypt data
decrypted_data = cipher_suite.decrypt(encrypted_data)
print("Decrypted data:", decrypted_data)
```

For secure data storage, you can use cloud storage providers like Amazon S3, Google Cloud Storage, or Azure Blob Storage, which offer encryption, access control, and other security features. Here's an example of how to store data securely on Amazon S3 using the boto3 library:

```python
import boto3

# Set up the S3 client
s3 = boto3.client('s3')

# Encrypt data using server-side encryption with an AWS Key Management Service
(KMS) managed key
bucket_name = 'your-bucket-name'
file_name = 'your-file-name'
data = b'Sensitive information'

s3.put_object(
    Bucket=bucket_name,
    Key=file_name,
    Body=data,
    ServerSideEncryption='aws:kms'
)

# Retrieve the encrypted data from S3
response = s3.get_object(Bucket=bucket_name, Key=file_name)

# The encryption is transparent, so you can access the decrypted data directly
print("Retrieved data:", response['Body'].read())
```

These examples showcase encryption and secure data storage in AWS S3. However, remember that security is a continuous process that requires attention to multiple aspects, including access control, monitoring, and regular security audits.

7.2.3. User Authentication and Access Control

User authentication and access control are critical aspects of ensuring responsible AI usage. By implementing proper access control, you can manage which users have the right to access and interact with your AI system. This is important because it ensures that only authorized users with a legitimate need for access are allowed to interact with the system.

This helps to prevent unauthorized access and misuse of the system, which can lead to data breaches and other security incidents. In addition, proper access control can also help to protect the privacy and confidentiality of sensitive information by limiting access to only those who are

authorized to view it. By implementing these measures, you can help to ensure the responsible and secure use of your AI system.

Here's a simple example using Flask, a Python web framework, to demonstrate user authentication and access control with the help of the Flask-Login library:

1. First, install Flask and Flask-Login:

```
pip install Flask Flask-Login
```

2. Create a simple Flask application with user authentication:

```python
from flask import Flask, render_template, redirect, url_for
from flask_login import LoginManager, UserMixin, login_user, login_required, log
out_user

app = Flask(__name__)
app.secret_key = 'your-secret-key'
login_manager = LoginManager(app)

class User(UserMixin):
    def __init__(self, id):
        self.id = id

# In a real-world application, use a database for user management
users = {'user@example.com': {'password': 'password123'}}

@login_manager.user_loader
def load_user(user_id):
    return User(user_id)

@app.route('/login', methods=['GET', 'POST'])
def login():
    if request.method == 'POST':
        email = request.form['email']
        password = request.form['password']
        if email in users and users[email]['password'] == password:
            user = User(email)
            login_user(user)
            return redirect(url_for('protected'))
        else:
            return "Invalid credentials"
    else:
        return render_template('login.html')

@app.route('/logout')
@login_required
def logout():
    logout_user()
    return redirect(url_for('index'))

@app.route('/')
def index():
    return "This is a public page."

@app.route('/protected')
@login_required
def protected():
    return "This is a protected page, accessible only to authenticated users."

if __name__ == '__main__':
    app.run()
```

3. Create a simple login.html template in a "templates" folder:

```html
<!doctype html>
<html>
    <head><title>Login</title></head>
    <body>
        <form method="post">
            <input type="email" name="email" placeholder="Email" required>
            <input type="password" name="password" placeholder="Password" requir
ed>
            <button type="submit">Login</button>
        </form>
    </body>
</html>
```

This code demonstrates a basic user authentication system with Flask and Flask-Login. The example is simplified for demonstration purposes and should not be used as-is in production. In real-world applications, you should store user information in a database and secure the passwords using hashing and salting techniques.

7.2.4. Monitoring and Auditing AI System Usage

Monitoring and auditing AI system usage are essential to ensure responsible AI usage. By keeping track of user interactions with your AI system, you can identify unauthorized access, detect potential abuse, and maintain a transparent history of system usage.

Furthermore, monitoring AI system usage can help in identifying patterns of usage and usage trends. This information can be used to improve the AI system, and to optimize its performance based on user behavior. For example, if the AI system is being used heavily for a particular task, then the system can be optimized to improve performance for that task.

Additionally, auditing AI system usage can help in identifying areas where the system can be improved. For example, if the system is experiencing a high rate of errors or is not performing as expected, auditing can help in identifying the root cause of the problem.

Finally, monitoring and auditing AI system usage can help in ensuring compliance with regulations and ethical standards. By maintaining a record of system usage, you can demonstrate that your AI system is being used in a responsible and ethical manner, which can be important in gaining the trust of stakeholders and the wider public.

Example:

Here's an example of how to implement simple logging and monitoring in a Python application using the standard library's **logging** module:

1. First, import the **logging** module and set up basic configuration:

```
import logging

logging.basicConfig(filename='ai_system.log', level=logging.INFO, format='%(asct
ime)s - %(levelname)s - %(message)s')
```

This sets up a logging system that records log messages with a level of INFO or higher in a file called 'ai_system.log'. The log messages will include a timestamp, the log level, and the log message.

2. Add log messages in your code, for example:

```
def authenticate_user(user_credentials):
    # Validate user credentials
    if validate_user_credentials(user_credentials):
        logging.info(f'User {user_credentials["username"]} authenticated success
fully.')
        return True
    else:
        logging.warning(f'User {user_credentials["username"]} failed authenticat
ion.')
        return False

def execute_ai_task(user, task_parameters):
    if user.is_authenticated:
        result = perform_ai_task(task_parameters)
        logging.info(f'User {user.username} executed AI task with parameters {ta
sk_parameters}.')
        return result
    else:
        logging.warning(f'Unauthorized user {user.username} attempted to execute
AI task.')
        return None
```

In this example, the **authenticate_user** and **execute_ai_task** functions log events related to user authentication and AI task execution. The logs can be used to monitor system usage and detect suspicious activities.

This demonstrates a basic logging and monitoring setup. In real-world applications, consider using more advanced logging libraries or monitoring services to enhance your logging capabilities and facilitate system auditing.

7.3. Ethical Guidelines and Best Practices

Ethical guidelines and best practices for AI development are of paramount importance to ensure that the responsible usage of AI technologies, such as ChatGPT, is maintained. AI technologies have the potential to revolutionize society, and with that comes a great responsibility.

By adhering to ethical principles and industry standards, organizations can mitigate the potential risks associated with AI deployment and contribute positively to society. Moreover, it is important to recognize that AI technologies are constantly evolving, as such, organizations need to stay up-to-date with the latest developments in the field.

For instance, machine learning algorithms are becoming increasingly sophisticated, and it is essential that organizations keep abreast of these developments to ensure that their AI systems are optimized. It is important that organizations have a clear understanding of the potential implications of AI deployment on society, as well as the ethical considerations that need to be taken into account.

By taking a proactive approach to AI development and deployment, organizations can ensure that they are creating AI systems that are both effective and ethical.

7.3.1. Principles for Ethical AI Development

To ensure that AI systems are developed ethically, several organizations have proposed guiding principles. While there is no universally accepted set of principles, some commonly agreed-upon themes include:

1. **Transparency**: It is important to ensure that the AI system's decision-making process is transparent and comprehensible to users and other stakeholders. To achieve this, it is necessary to provide an explanation of how the system works, what data it uses, and how it arrives at its conclusions. Additionally, it is important to establish clear guidelines for how the system will be used and how users can access and interpret the

information it provides. By taking these steps, we can build trust and confidence in the system, and ensure that it is used effectively and responsibly.

2. **Fairness**: One of the most important considerations when developing AI systems is fairness. It is crucial that AI systems minimize biases and do not discriminate against any group. In order to ensure fairness, several measures can be taken. For example, AI systems can be trained using diverse datasets that represent different groups, and the data can be carefully analyzed to detect and correct any biases. Additionally, it is important to involve a diverse group of people in the development process to ensure that different perspectives are taken into account. Finally, it is important to continually monitor AI systems for biases and make adjustments as needed to ensure that they remain fair and impartial.

3. **Privacy**: As the world becomes more digitized, the issue of privacy has become increasingly important. Users want to be assured that their personal data is being protected and used responsibly. Companies must take this issue seriously and put in place measures to protect users' privacy. This includes implementing strong security protocols, being transparent about data collection and use, and giving users control over their data. Ultimately, it is the responsibility of companies to respect users' privacy and safeguard their personal data.

4. **Accountability**: In order to ensure that the AI system is able to be audited, it is important to establish a clear chain of responsibility for the outcomes that the system generates. By doing so, it is possible to understand who is accountable for the actions of the system and to ensure that any issues or errors can be identified and addressed in a timely manner. Additionally, by establishing a clear chain of responsibility, it is possible to ensure that all stakeholders are aware of their role in the system and are able to make informed decisions about its use. This can help to build trust in the system and ensure that it is used in a way that is ethical and responsible.

5. **Safety**: It is of utmost importance that AI systems are designed with robustness and security in mind to prevent unintended consequences and malicious use. This means that the system should be tested under various conditions to ensure that it functions properly, and that it is protected against cyber attacks that may compromise its integrity. In addition, it is important to consider the social and ethical implications of AI technologies, such as their impact on privacy, fairness, and accountability. For example, it may be necessary to establish guidelines for the collection, handling, and use of data, or to implement mechanisms for explaining the decisions made by AI systems. Ultimately, the goal should be to create AI systems that are not only safe and reliable, but also transparent and accountable to the public.

To fully embrace these ethical principles in your AI development process, it is essential to not only adopt them into your organization's culture and practices but also ensure that they are fully integrated and implemented as part of your day-to-day operations. One way to do this is by creating policies and guidelines that are tailored to your specific needs and goals. These

policies should outline the ethical principles that your organization will follow in all aspects of AI development, from data collection to algorithm design and testing.

In addition to policies and guidelines, it is important to provide ongoing training to all members of your organization who are involved in AI development. This can include training on ethical principles, as well as technical training on the development and implementation of AI systems. By providing ongoing training, you can ensure that your team members are up-to-date on the latest best practices and technologies, and that they are equipped with the knowledge and skills needed to develop AI systems that are both effective and ethical.

Finally, conducting regular reviews of your AI systems is crucial for ensuring that they continue to meet ethical standards and align with your organization's goals. These reviews should be conducted by a team of experts who are well-versed in the principles of AI ethics, and should include a thorough analysis of the data and algorithms used in your systems. By conducting regular reviews, you can identify and address any ethical issues that may arise, and ensure that your systems are always operating in a manner that is consistent with your organization's values and goals.

7.3.2. Industry Standards and Compliance

In addition to ethical principles, organizations must also comply with industry standards and regulations related to AI development. These standards and regulations are put in place to ensure that AI is developed in a responsible and safe way that benefits society as a whole. In order to achieve this, organizations should work to stay up to date with the latest developments in AI regulation and compliance.

This may involve collaborating with industry associations and government bodies to develop best practices and guidelines for AI development. Depending on the jurisdiction and sector, different standards and regulations may apply, and it is the responsibility of organizations to be aware of these and to take steps to comply with them.

Failure to comply with AI regulation and compliance requirements can have serious consequences for organizations, including legal liability, reputational damage, and loss of consumer trust. Therefore, organizations should take a proactive approach to AI regulation and compliance, and integrate these considerations into their overall AI development strategy. Some examples include:

1. The General Data Protection Regulation (GDPR) is a crucial regulation in the European Union that aims to protect the privacy of individuals. It is a comprehensive data protection framework that applies to all organizations processing personal data, including AI systems. The GDPR also establishes important provisions related to the

processing of sensitive data, such as health or biometric data, and the rights of individuals, including the right to access their data and the right to have their data erased. In addition, the GDPR has a significant extraterritorial effect, which means that it can apply to organizations located outside the EU if they process data of EU residents. Overall, the GDPR is a vital piece of legislation that aims to ensure that personal data is protected and used in a responsible and transparent manner.

2. **Health Insurance Portability and Accountability Act (HIPAA):** The Health Insurance Portability and Accountability Act (HIPAA) is a US regulation that has been in place since 1996. Its purpose is to protect the privacy and security of health information. One of the areas it covers is the use of artificial intelligence (AI) systems in healthcare. AI systems have become increasingly prevalent in recent years due to their ability to analyze large amounts of data quickly and accurately. However, as with any technology, there are concerns about the potential misuse of AI systems, particularly when it comes to sensitive personal information such as health data. By including regulations around the use of AI systems in healthcare, HIPAA aims to ensure that patients' privacy and security are protected even as technology advances.

3. **Payment Card Industry Data Security Standard (PCI DSS):** The Payment Card Industry Data Security Standard (PCI DSS) is a global standard that applies to organizations handling payment card data, including AI systems involved in payment processing. The standard was developed to ensure the security of payment card information and to minimize the risk of data breaches. PCI DSS includes a set of requirements that organizations must follow to protect payment card data, such as implementing strong access controls, encrypting cardholder data, and regularly monitoring and testing security systems. Compliance with the PCI DSS standard is essential for organizations that handle payment card data, as non-compliance can result in fines, legal action, and reputational damage.

To ensure compliance with industry standards and regulations, it is essential to:

- Stay informed about relevant regulations in your jurisdiction and sector.
- Implement appropriate technical and organizational measures to ensure compliance.
- Regularly audit and assess your AI systems and practices for compliance.

7.3.3. Involving Stakeholders and Ensuring Accountability

In this topic, we will discuss the importance of involving various stakeholders in the AI development process and how to ensure accountability when deploying AI systems like ChatGPT. It's essential to have a diverse range of perspectives when developing AI systems to avoid bias and ensure that ethical considerations are accounted for. AI systems like ChatGPT can have a significant impact on society, and it's crucial to involve stakeholders like

policymakers, domain experts, and end-users in the development process. By doing so, we can ensure that AI systems are developed with the best interests of society in mind.

When deploying AI systems like ChatGPT, it's important to ensure accountability to avoid unintended consequences. One way to do this is by having clear guidelines and standards for AI development and deployment. These guidelines should include considerations like data privacy, transparency, and accountability. Additionally, it's essential to have mechanisms in place to monitor and evaluate the impact of AI systems after deployment. By doing so, we can ensure that AI systems like ChatGPT are being used in ways that are beneficial to society as a whole.

Engaging Stakeholders:

1. Collaboration with domain experts, end-users, and other relevant stakeholders is essential in identifying potential risks and benefits of AI systems in different contexts. This includes reaching out to experts in the field who can offer insight into the nuances of AI technology, as well as soliciting feedback from the end-users who will ultimately interact with these systems. It is also important to engage with stakeholders who may be impacted by the implementation of AI systems, such as policymakers and regulatory bodies, to ensure that the technology is being utilized in an ethical and responsible way. By working together with a variety of perspectives and experiences, a more comprehensive understanding of the potential implications of AI systems can be achieved, leading to better decision-making and ultimately better outcomes for all involved.

2. One important aspect of ensuring the success of AI systems is to establish feedback loops with users. These feedback loops allow for continuous improvement and refinement of the system, reducing the risk of errors and addressing concerns. For example, you could collect feedback from users on the functionality and accuracy of the system, and use this feedback to make adjustments and improvements. Additionally, you could also use feedback to identify any potential biases in the system and work to address them. Establishing these feedback loops is a crucial step in creating AI systems that are effective, reliable, and trusted by users.

3. One important aspect to consider when working on AI projects is to foster an environment that encourages open communication and collaboration among team members. This can include not only data scientists and engineers, but also other professionals such as project managers, technical writers, and user experience designers. By promoting a culture of transparency and inclusivity, team members can feel more comfortable sharing their ideas and insights, leading to a more creative and innovative work environment. Additionally, encouraging collaboration can help mitigate any potential conflicts or misunderstandings that may arise during the course of a project, leading to more efficient and successful outcomes.

Ensuring Accountability:

1. One important aspect of AI development and deployment is to clearly define roles and responsibilities within the organization. This can be done by setting up a team dedicated to AI development and deployment, with each member having a specific role and responsibility. For example, there could be a team lead who oversees the entire project, a data scientist who is responsible for data collection and analysis, a software engineer who develops the AI model, and a deployment specialist who ensures the model is properly integrated into the organization's existing systems and processes. By having a clear understanding of each team member's role and responsibility, the organization can ensure that the AI development and deployment process runs smoothly and efficiently.

2. To ensure the proper functioning of AI systems, it is important to implement monitoring and auditing mechanisms. These mechanisms can help track the system's performance, detect any potential issues, and ensure that the system is operating in compliance with ethical guidelines and regulations.

One way to implement these mechanisms is to establish a system of regular checks and evaluations. This may involve reviewing the system's performance data on a regular basis to identify any patterns or anomalies that may indicate issues with the system's performance. Additionally, it may be useful to conduct occasional audits to evaluate the system's compliance with ethical guidelines and regulations.

Another way to enhance the monitoring and auditing of AI systems is to establish clear reporting mechanisms. This may involve creating standard reports that are regularly generated and reviewed by relevant stakeholders. Additionally, it may be useful to establish a hotline or other reporting mechanism that allows users to report any concerns or issues related to the system's performance or compliance.

Overall, implementing monitoring and auditing mechanisms is a critical step in ensuring the effective and responsible use of AI systems. By monitoring the system's performance and ensuring its compliance with ethical guidelines and regulations, organizations can help mitigate potential risks and ensure that they are using these powerful technologies in a responsible and ethical manner.

3. In order to foster a culture of responsibility and ethical behavior among AI practitioners within the organization, it is important to first define what that means and what it looks like in practice. This may involve creating a code of conduct that outlines specific behaviors and expectations for AI practitioners, as well as providing regular training and development opportunities to ensure that everyone is up-to-date on the latest thinking and best practices in the field. It may be helpful to establish clear channels of

communication and accountability, so that people feel comfortable reporting any concerns or issues that arise, and so that everyone knows exactly what is expected of them in terms of ethical conduct and decision-making. Finally, it is important to recognize and reward those who demonstrate a strong commitment to responsible and ethical behavior, both to encourage others to follow their lead and to ensure that these values are deeply ingrained in the organization's culture and DNA.

These points emphasize the importance of communication, collaboration, and accountability during the development and deployment of AI systems. By considering these aspects, organizations can build more responsible, transparent, and ethically aligned AI solutions.

7.3.4. Transparency and Explainability

Here, we will discuss the importance of transparency and explainability in AI systems like ChatGPT and how to promote these qualities in the development and deployment process. One way to promote transparency is to implement a logging system that tracks the decisions made by the AI model during inference.

Another way is to provide users with access to the training data and model architecture used to create the AI system. Explainability can be improved by developing models that provide human-understandable justifications for their decisions. This can be achieved through techniques like attention mechanisms and decision trees.

Creating documentation that explains the process of developing and deploying the AI system can also increase explainability. By prioritizing transparency and explainability in the development and deployment process, we can ensure that AI systems like ChatGPT are trustworthy and can be used effectively and ethically.

Achieving Transparency:

1. One important aspect in developing AI models is to provide a clear documentation of the process, data sources, training methodologies, and assumptions made during the creation of such models. This can help ensure transparency and accountability in the development of AI models.

   It can also help other researchers and practitioners to replicate the process, improve upon the methodology, and avoid making similar mistakes in the future. In order to provide a detailed documentation, it is recommended to include information such as the data collection process, data pre-processing techniques, feature selection methods, model architectures, hyperparameters tuning, and evaluation metrics used to assess the performance of the model.

Furthermore, it is important to also discuss any limitations or potential biases in the data and methodology used, as well as any ethical considerations that were taken into account during the development process. By providing a comprehensive documentation, it can help to ensure the reliability and validity of the AI models that are being developed and deployed.

2. It is important to effectively communicate the limitations and potential biases of AI systems to users, stakeholders, and decision-makers. This can include discussing the inherent limitations of the technology, such as the inability of AI to understand certain nuances and contexts, as well as the potential for biases to be introduced into the system based on the data used to train it.

   It may be necessary to address the ethical implications of using AI in certain contexts, particularly in areas where the decisions made by the system can have a significant impact on individuals or society as a whole. By having a thorough understanding of the limitations and potential biases of AI systems, users, stakeholders, and decision-makers can make more informed decisions about the appropriate use of these technologies and ensure that they are used in a responsible and ethical manner.

3. It is important to openly share information about the AI system's objectives. This includes identifying the specific use cases that the system is intended for, as well as potential risks associated with its use. By providing detailed information about the system's intended use cases and potential risks, stakeholders can better understand how the system should be used and what precautions should be taken to mitigate any potential negative impact.

   Providing detailed information about the system's objectives can help to build trust with stakeholders, which is critical for the successful adoption and implementation of AI systems. Furthermore, by being transparent about the AI system's objectives, we can encourage greater collaboration and innovation in the development of AI technologies, ultimately leading to more effective and beneficial systems.

Promoting Explainability:

1. To gain more transparency into the decision-making process of an AI system, it is important to utilize explainable AI techniques. One such technique is feature importance, which can help identify which features of the input data are most important in making a decision. Another technique is local interpretable model-agnostic explanations (LIME), which provides an understanding of how the AI system is making decisions on a local level. Lastly, Shapley values can be used to explain the contribution of each feature towards the final decision. Employing these techniques

can provide a deeper understanding of how an AI system is functioning and how decisions are being made. Furthermore, this knowledge can be used to improve the system's performance or identify potential biases in the decision-making process.

2. One important aspect of developing AI systems is creating user interfaces and visualizations that can help users understand how the system works. These interfaces and visualizations can provide users with a more intuitive understanding of the system's behavior and reasoning. For example, a user interface could show the system's decision-making process, allowing users to see how the system arrives at its conclusions. Similarly, a visualization could show the data being used by the system, giving users a better understanding of the inputs that are feeding into the AI algorithms. By providing these types of interfaces and visualizations, developers can help users to better understand and trust the AI systems they are interacting with.

3. It is critical to ensure that the AI system's recommendations or predictions are clearly explained, especially in sensitive or high-stakes domains. This can help build trust in the system and ensure that users understand the reasoning behind the recommendations. To achieve this, it may be useful to provide detailed documentation or user-friendly interfaces that explain the system's inner workings. Additionally, it may be necessary to involve domain experts, who can provide additional context and ensure that the system's recommendations align with best practices and ethical standards. Overall, clear explanation and transparency should be a top priority when designing and implementing AI systems in sensitive or high-stakes domains.

7.4. User Consent and Transparency

In this topic, we will explore the importance of user consent and transparency when using AI systems like ChatGPT. Ensuring that users are aware of the capabilities and limitations of AI applications and obtaining their informed consent is essential for responsible AI usage.

One of the key reasons why obtaining user consent and providing transparency is so important is because AI systems like ChatGPT can have a significant impact on users' lives. For example, these systems can be used to make decisions that affect users' access to resources, opportunities, and services. This means that if users do not understand how AI systems work and what they are being used for, they may not be able to make informed decisions about their lives.

Another reason why user consent and transparency are so important is that AI systems like ChatGPT are not perfect. These systems are designed to make decisions based on patterns and data, but they can also make mistakes or produce biased results. When users are not aware of the limitations of AI systems, they may mistakenly assume that the decisions made by these systems are always accurate and unbiased. This can lead to a false sense of security and potentially harmful outcomes.

In order to address these challenges, it is important for AI developers and companies to prioritize user consent and transparency. This means providing clear and accessible information about how AI systems work, what data is being used, and how decisions are being made. It also means giving users the ability to opt out or provide feedback on the use of AI systems. By doing so, we can ensure that AI is used responsibly and ethically to improve users' lives.

7.4.1. Informed Consent in AI Applications

Informed consent is a crucial step in the development and implementation of AI applications that involves obtaining permission from users before collecting, processing, or using their data. This process is important as it ensures that users are aware of the ways in which their data is being used and have the opportunity to make informed decisions about whether or not to share their data.

To obtain informed consent, it is essential to provide users with clear, accurate, and relevant information about the AI system's purpose, data usage, and potential risks. This information can be presented in a variety of ways, such as through user-friendly interfaces and plain language explanations. Additionally, it is important to ensure that users understand the implications of their consent, including the potential risks and benefits associated with sharing their data.

Overall, the process of obtaining informed consent is a critical component of responsible AI development and implementation. By ensuring that users are informed and have the opportunity to make informed decisions about their data, we can promote transparency, trust, and accountability in AI applications.

Here are some best practices for obtaining informed consent in AI applications:

1. The AI system must be carefully explained to ensure that users understand why it is being used, what data is being collected, and how it will be used. In addition to these basic details, it is important to provide more information about the potential benefits and risks associated with the system. For example, will the AI system help users to make more informed decisions or to complete tasks more efficiently? Will it improve overall system performance or reduce the likelihood of errors? On the other hand, what risks are associated with the system, such as data breaches, privacy concerns, or potential biases in data collection? By providing detailed information about the purpose and scope of the AI system, users will be better equipped to make informed decisions about its use and to feel more confident in their interactions with it.
2. When developing an AI system, it's important to consider the privacy of the users. As such, it's essential to provide users with a clear and easy-to-understand privacy policy that outlines the system's data collection and usage practices. This policy should be

easily accessible to users and should provide comprehensive information about the types of data collected, how it is used, and who it is shared with. The policy should clearly state the measures taken to protect user data and how users can opt-out of the data collection process if desired. By providing users with a detailed privacy policy, you can build trust with your users and ensure that their privacy is protected while using your AI system.

3. As data becomes an increasingly valuable commodity, it is important for companies to be transparent about their data collection practices. One way to do this is to offer users the option to opt-in or opt-out of data collection and AI-driven features. In addition to this, companies could also provide more detailed information about how user data is collected, stored and used. By doing so, users can make informed decisions about their data privacy and feel more in control of their personal information. This can help build trust between users and companies, leading to stronger relationships and increased customer loyalty.

4. In order to comply with best practices in data privacy, it is important to ensure that users are given sufficient control over their personal data. One way to achieve this is by implementing mechanisms that allow users to access, edit, and delete their data. This can include providing users with a dashboard where they can view their data, allowing them to make changes to their profile information, and giving them the ability to delete their data if they choose to do so. Additionally, it is important to ensure that users are able to revoke their consent to the collection and processing of their data at any time. This can be accomplished by providing users with a clear and easy-to-use mechanism for revoking consent, such as a simple opt-out button or an email address where users can request that their data be deleted.

7.4.2. Communicating AI Capabilities and Limitations

Effectively communicating the capabilities and limitations of AI systems is crucial for setting realistic user expectations and fostering trust. In addition to this, it is important to highlight the various ways in which AI systems can be used in different industries, from healthcare to finance.

By doing so, we can better understand the impact that AI can have on society as a whole. Moreover, it is imperative that we remain cognizant of the ethical considerations surrounding AI, such as privacy concerns and potential biases.

By addressing these issues head-on, we can work towards creating AI systems that are both effective and ethical, ultimately benefiting society as a whole.To ensure transparency in AI applications, consider the following guidelines:

1. It is important to inform users when they are interacting with an artificial intelligence system. One way to achieve this is by providing a clear and concise message that states

the system is AI-powered and not human-generated. Additionally, it is recommended to differentiate AI-generated content from human-generated content by using a unique visual or verbal identifier. This will help users better understand the source of the information they are receiving and prevent any confusion or misinterpretation. By following these best practices, users can feel more confident and informed when interacting with AI systems, which can ultimately lead to greater trust in the technology and better overall user experience.

2. AI-driven recommendations, predictions, or decisions can be confusing for users who may not understand how the AI system works. To help them better understand the rationale behind the recommendations, predictions, or decisions, it is important to provide clear and concise explanations. These explanations can provide users with the necessary context to make informed decisions based on the AI system's output. Additionally, providing explanations can help to build trust in the AI system, as users will have a better understanding of how it arrived at its recommendations, predictions, or decisions. This can be especially important in situations where the AI system's output may have significant consequences, such as in healthcare or finance.

3. It is important to clearly state the limitations, biases, and potential errors of the AI system to ensure that users have a full understanding of its capabilities. By acknowledging these limitations, users can appropriately interpret and use the system's outputs. It is also important to provide guidance on how to use the system effectively, including any best practices or recommendations. Additionally, it may be helpful to provide examples of how the system has been used successfully in the past, or how it can be used to address specific challenges or opportunities. By providing more detail and context, users can more fully understand the value and potential of the AI system.

7.4.3. Algorithmic Accountability and Auditing

Another important aspect of responsible AI usage is algorithmic accountability, which refers to the need for AI systems to be transparent, explainable, and auditable. Ensuring algorithmic accountability can help identify and address biases, maintain user trust, and comply with legal and regulatory requirements.

In order to achieve this accountability, it is important to have clear documentation of the algorithms used, including information on how they were designed, tested, and validated. It may be necessary to have a system in place for continuous monitoring and evaluation of the algorithms' performance and impact.

This can involve regular audits, user feedback, and analysis of the system's outputs. By implementing these measures, organizations can not only promote ethical and responsible AI usage, but also gain a competitive advantage by demonstrating their commitment to

transparency and accountability. Here are some guidelines for achieving algorithmic accountability:

1. In order to ensure that AI models are trustworthy and ethical, it is important to develop clear and comprehensive documentation. This documentation should include not only the objectives of the model, but also a description of the training data used to create it and the features it takes into account. Additionally, it is important to provide transparency into the decision-making processes that the model employs when making predictions or classifications. By doing so, stakeholders can better understand how the model works and can ensure that it is being used in a responsible and ethical manner.
2. When implementing AI techniques, it is crucial to consider the importance of explainability. By integrating explainable AI techniques, we can gain valuable insights into the inner workings of complex models. These methods can facilitate human understanding and provide a clear path towards building more transparent and trustworthy AI systems. Additionally, explainability can improve model performance and reduce bias, making AI more accessible and fair for everyone. Therefore, it is essential to prioritize the implementation of explainable AI techniques to ensure the success and ethical use of AI in various industries.
3. To ensure the proper functioning of AI systems, it is crucial to carry out regular and comprehensive audits. These audits should aim to evaluate not only the performance of the models, but also their fairness and any potential biases that may exist. In doing so, we can identify areas for improvement and work towards creating more accurate and reliable AI models that can better serve our needs. Additionally, these audits can help to identify any unintended consequences of AI systems and provide insights into how to mitigate them. As such, conducting regular audits of AI systems is not only necessary, but also beneficial for the continued development and improvement of this technology.
4. It is important to seek input from a diverse group of external stakeholders to ensure that AI systems are being developed in a responsible and ethical manner. In addition to ethicists, regulators, and industry experts, it may be beneficial to involve representatives from civil society organizations and advocacy groups. By involving a wide range of perspectives, the development of AI systems can be guided by a more comprehensive understanding of ethical and legal standards. This can help to ensure that AI systems are not only effective, but also uphold important values such as privacy, fairness, and accountability.

7.4.4. User Control and Customization

Giving users control over their interactions with AI systems and the ability to customize their experiences can contribute to more responsible and transparent AI usage. This can be achieved

by providing users with a range of options to choose from, such as different levels of automation or personalization settings.

By doing so, users can feel more confident in their interactions with the AI, knowing that they have some say in how it operates. Additionally, allowing users to influence the behavior and output of AI applications can improve trust, satisfaction, and overall user experience.

This can be done by providing feedback mechanisms for users to report issues or provide suggestions for improvement. By having a more active role in shaping the AI's behavior, users can develop a sense of ownership and investment in the technology, leading to a more positive and rewarding experience. Here are some suggestions for providing user control and customization:

1. One way to improve user experience is to allow users to customize the level of detail, tone, and style of AI-generated content. By offering options to adjust these aspects, users can better align the content with their preferences and needs. For instance, users who are looking for a more casual or conversational tone can opt for a less formal style of writing, while those who require more technical details can choose a higher level of detail. Additionally, users can also choose the tone of the content, such as upbeat, informative, or persuasive, depending on their needs and preferences. By providing such customization options, AI-generated content can be tailored to suit a wider range of users, thereby improving the overall user experience.

2. A key feature of AI systems is their ability to adapt and improve over time. To enable this, it is important to provide mechanisms that allow users to easily provide feedback on the results or recommendations generated by the system. This feedback can then be used to refine and improve the algorithms that drive the AI, resulting in more accurate and helpful results for all users. By actively soliciting and incorporating user feedback, AI systems can become more tailored to the needs and preferences of their users, ultimately leading to a better user experience and greater satisfaction with the technology.

3. One important aspect of user data and privacy is giving users control over their information. A way to achieve this is by allowing them to opt-out of certain AI features or data collection practices that they may not be comfortable with. This will not only give users peace of mind, but also show that your company values transparency and respects their privacy. Additionally, it may be helpful to provide clear and concise explanations of how user data is being used and stored, as well as the measures being taken to protect it. By taking these steps, you can build trust with your users and establish a positive reputation for your brand.

4. It is of utmost importance to provide adequate information to the users about the level of control and customization available in the AI system. Not only does this help the users better understand their experiences, but it also helps them to make informed

decisions. By providing detailed information on the level of influence that users have over their experiences, it encourages them to take more ownership and responsibility for their interactions with the AI system. This, in turn, can lead to a more positive user experience and greater satisfaction with the product overall. Therefore, it is highly recommended that the communication of the extent of user control and customization available in the AI system is done in a clear and comprehensive manner.

7.5. AI Governance and Accountability

As AI systems continue to advance and become more integrated into our daily lives, it is increasingly important to establish comprehensive governance structures and mechanisms to ensure accountability. This includes not only setting up policies, guidelines, and monitoring practices, but also creating a comprehensive framework that takes into account the unique needs and concerns of various stakeholders, including users, developers, and regulators.

To ensuring responsible and ethical design and deployment of AI systems, governance structures must also address issues related to data privacy, security, and ownership. This includes establishing clear guidelines for data collection, storage, and usage, as well as implementing appropriate safeguards to protect against cyber threats and other potential risks.

Moreover, governance structures must be flexible and adaptable, able to respond to changing circumstances and emerging technologies. This requires ongoing monitoring and evaluation of AI systems, as well as regular updates to policies and guidelines to reflect changing needs and priorities. Ultimately, effective governance of AI systems is essential to ensuring that they are developed and deployed in ways that benefit society while minimizing potential risks and negative impacts.

7.5.1. Establishing AI Governance Frameworks

An AI governance framework is a comprehensive set of policies, guidelines, and practices that organizations can implement to ensure the responsible management of their AI systems. This framework should be designed to address various aspects, including but not limited to ethical considerations, compliance, privacy, security, and risk management.

In the case of ethical considerations, an AI governance framework should provide guidance on the ethical implications of AI systems, such as their impact on society, fairness, accountability, transparency, and explainability. It should also establish a clear ethical code of conduct that aligns with the organization's values and mission.

Regarding compliance, an AI governance framework should ensure that all AI systems comply with relevant laws and regulations. This includes data protection laws, intellectual property laws, and consumer protection laws, among others.

Privacy is also an essential aspect that an AI governance framework should address. It should establish clear policies and procedures for the collection, storage, and processing of personal data, ensuring that all data is protected and used in compliance with applicable laws and regulations.

Security is another crucial aspect that an AI governance framework should cover. It should ensure that AI systems are designed and implemented with robust security measures to prevent unauthorized access, data breaches, and other cybersecurity threats.

Risk management should be a fundamental component of an AI governance framework. It should provide guidance on identifying and mitigating risks associated with AI systems, such as biases, errors, and unintended consequences. The framework should also establish a clear process for reporting and addressing any incidents or issues that may arise in the course of using AI systems.

Here are some steps to create an AI governance framework:

1. To ensure responsible and ethical use of AI, it is important for organizations to establish clear principles and guidelines for AI development and deployment. These principles should be grounded in the organization's values and should take into account the potential impact of AI on society, including issues such as privacy, bias, and transparency. Additionally, the guidelines should provide specific recommendations for the development and deployment of AI systems, such as ensuring that data is representative and unbiased, and that the system is transparent and understandable to its users. By establishing clear AI principles and ethical guidelines, organizations can help to ensure that AI is developed and deployed in a responsible and ethical manner that benefits society as a whole.

2. To effectively identify relevant regulations, industry standards, and best practices for responsible AI usage in the organization's domain, it is important to conduct a comprehensive review of all available resources. This can include researching legislative frameworks and guidelines that govern AI usage, analyzing industry-specific standards and protocols for ethical AI development, and consulting with subject matter experts in the field.

   Once these resources have been reviewed, it is important to assess the organization's current practices and policies related to AI usage, and compare them against the identified regulations and standards. This can involve conducting a gap analysis to

identify areas where the organization may need to improve its practices or develop new policies to ensure responsible AI usage.

It is important to consider the potential ethical implications of AI usage, particularly in areas such as data privacy and bias. Organizations should strive to develop AI applications that are transparent, accountable, and fair, and that take into account the potential impact on all stakeholders.

Taking a proactive approach to identifying and implementing responsible AI practices can help organizations to build trust with stakeholders, reduce risk, and promote the long-term sustainability of their AI initiatives.

3. One important step towards effective AI governance is to establish clear roles and responsibilities within the organization. This will help ensure that the right people are making decisions and overseeing the use of AI technologies. Additionally, clear roles and responsibilities can help promote transparency and accountability, which are critical for building trust in AI systems.

   To achieve this, organizations may need to create new positions or modify existing ones. For example, they may need to appoint an AI governance officer or establish a dedicated AI governance team. These individuals or teams would be responsible for developing and implementing policies, identifying and managing risks, and ensuring compliance with relevant regulations and ethical principles.

   To clear roles and responsibilities, effective AI governance also requires ongoing education and training for employees. This can help ensure that everyone in the organization understands the risks and benefits of AI technologies, as well as their roles and responsibilities in using them.

   Establishing clear roles and responsibilities for AI governance is an essential step towards building a trustworthy and responsible AI system.

4. To ensure the proper handling of data, it is important for companies to develop robust policies and guidelines that cover various aspects of data management. In addition to policies and guidelines for data handling, it is also important to establish procedures for ensuring user privacy and security of information.

   This may include implementing firewalls, encryption protocols, and user authentication systems to prevent unauthorized access to sensitive data. Furthermore, user consent is a critical component of any data management strategy, and companies should have clear policies in place for obtaining and managing user consent. These policies should

be regularly reviewed and updated to reflect the changing needs of the organization and the evolving regulatory environment.

5. In order to ensure that AI systems operate effectively, it is essential to implement proper processes for monitoring, auditing, and risk management. This involves creating a framework for evaluating the performance of the system, as well as identifying and tracking any potential risks or issues that may arise.

    For example, one approach to monitoring could involve regularly testing the system against various scenarios to identify any areas of weakness or vulnerability. In addition, an audit trail should be established to track system activity and detect any unusual or suspicious behavior.

Finally, a risk management plan should be developed to address any potential threats or challenges that may arise, including developing contingency plans and implementing appropriate controls to mitigate risk. By implementing these processes, organizations can ensure that their AI systems operate in a reliable and secure manner, while minimizing the risk of errors or other issues.

7.5.2. Monitoring AI Systems and Maintaining Accountability

Ensuring accountability in AI systems is a complex and ongoing process that involves continuous monitoring and evaluation of their performance, behavior, and impact. To achieve this goal, it is necessary to establish clear guidelines and standards for measuring the effectiveness and ethical implications of these systems.

Regular testing and assessment of AI algorithms and models is crucial to identify and address any potential biases or errors that may arise. Moreover, it is important to involve diverse stakeholders, including experts in AI ethics, legal and regulatory authorities, and affected communities, in the monitoring and evaluation process to ensure transparency and accountability.

Ultimately, a comprehensive and collaborative approach to accountability in AI systems is essential to promote trust, fairness, and safety in their development and deployment. Some strategies for monitoring AI systems and maintaining accountability include:

1. One potential area for further development in this project is the implementation of AI system monitoring tools. These tools could track a variety of performance metrics, such as processing speed and accuracy, to ensure that the AI system is functioning at optimal levels. Additionally, monitoring user interactions with the system could provide valuable insights into how users are interacting with the system and where

improvements could be made. Finally, implementing monitoring tools that detect potential biases in the system could help ensure that the AI system is fair and equitable for all users. By incorporating these monitoring tools into the project, we can not only improve the overall performance of the AI system, but also ensure that it is being used in a responsible and ethical manner.

2. One way to ensure that AI systems stay compliant with ethical guidelines, policies, and regulations is to conduct regular audits and reviews. This involves evaluating the system's performance and assessing any potential risks it may pose. Additionally, it may be helpful to establish a system of checks and balances to monitor the AI's decision-making processes. These checks can help ensure that the AI is making decisions that align with ethical principles and do not negatively impact individuals or society as a whole. Another important consideration is transparency - ensuring that stakeholders are aware of how the AI system is making decisions and that they have access to information about its operation. By implementing these measures, we can help ensure that AI systems are operating ethically and in the best interests of society.

3. One of the key elements in the development of AI systems is the establishment of feedback loops that allow users to report concerns, issues, or biases. Such feedback is critical in enabling the continuous improvement and adjustment of AI systems, ensuring that they are as effective and efficient as possible. Additionally, feedback loops help to build trust in AI systems by ensuring that users feel heard and their concerns are taken seriously. By listening and responding to user feedback, developers can improve the accuracy, reliability, and fairness of AI systems, making them more useful and accessible to a wider range of users. In short, feedback loops are an essential part of the ongoing development and refinement of AI systems, and must be carefully designed and implemented to ensure that they are effective, user-friendly, and beneficial to all involved.

4. One of the important steps in the development of AI systems is to ensure that their performance, behavior, and impact are transparently communicated to all relevant stakeholders. This includes not only users and regulators but also the general public, who are increasingly concerned about the ethical implications of advanced AI technologies.

To achieve this goal, it is essential to develop a robust reporting mechanism that can provide clear and comprehensive information about the AI system's performance and behavior. This mechanism should include detailed metrics and benchmarks that can be used to evaluate the system's accuracy, efficiency, and reliability, as well as its potential impact on human lives and society as a whole.

Moreover, the reporting mechanism should be designed to be user-friendly and accessible to non-experts as well as experts. This can be achieved through the use of visual aids, such as graphs and charts, and plain language explanations that avoid technical jargon.

By implementing a transparent reporting mechanism, AI developers and practitioners can build trust and confidence among stakeholders, and ensure that their systems are used in a responsible and ethical manner.

It is crucial to keep these considerations in mind when developing and deploying AI systems. Integrating these practices into the AI development lifecycle can help ensure that AI systems are designed and operated responsibly and transparently.

7.5.3. Incident Response and Remediation

As AI systems become more and more prevalent in various industries and applications, it is imperative to have a well-defined plan in place for addressing incidents that may arise. These incidents can include unintended biases, privacy breaches, or other harmful consequences that can lead to a loss of trust in the system and its developers. Developing a comprehensive incident response and remediation plan can help organizations effectively manage such situations and minimize their impact.

To begin with, it is important to identify potential incidents and assess their likelihood and potential impact. This can involve reviewing different scenarios and evaluating the potential risks and consequences of each one. Once potential incidents have been identified, it is necessary to establish a clear protocol for reporting and responding to them. This protocol should include steps such as notifying relevant stakeholders, gathering necessary information, and determining the appropriate course of action.

In addition, it is important to regularly review and update the incident response and remediation plan as new risks and challenges arise. This can involve conducting regular assessments of the system and its applications, as well as staying up-to-date on industry best practices and emerging technologies. By taking a proactive approach to incident response and remediation, organizations can demonstrate their commitment to ethical and responsible AI development and build trust with their stakeholders.

Develop a clear and comprehensive incident response plan

It is of utmost importance to have a well-defined incident response plan in place when dealing with AI systems. This can be achieved by outlining the steps to be taken in detail when an issue is identified.

These steps should include the roles and responsibilities of each team member, communication channels to be used, and the escalation process that should be followed in case the issue cannot be resolved by the team. It is recommended that the incident response plan is tested regularly to ensure its effectiveness and efficiency. This will not only enable a more effective response to

any issues that may arise but also ensure that the system remains secure and reliable at all times.

Establish a dedicated team

One of the most important steps in preparing for AI-related incidents is to establish a dedicated team of experts from various disciplines. This team should have a diverse set of skills and expertise, including in AI, ethics, legal, and security. By bringing together individuals from different backgrounds, the team can approach incidents from various angles and perspectives, which can lead to more effective and efficient solutions.

The dedicated team should be responsible for evaluating the situation and understanding the scope of the incident. This includes identifying the root cause and determining the potential impact on the organization. Once the situation has been assessed, the team can then implement corrective actions to prevent similar incidents from occurring in the future.

To responding to incidents, the dedicated team should also be responsible for proactive measures, such as developing policies and procedures for AI-related incidents. This can involve conducting risk assessments, identifying potential vulnerabilities, and implementing controls to mitigate the risk of incidents.

Establishing a dedicated team is essential for effective incident management and proactive risk mitigation in the realm of AI. By bringing together a diverse set of experts and implementing comprehensive policies and procedures, organizations can better prepare for and respond to AI-related incidents.

Implement monitoring and alerting systems

One effective way to safeguard against incidents is to use monitoring tools and alerting systems. These tools can provide valuable insights into system performance and detect potential issues before they become critical problems.

To do this, organizations can leverage a wide variety of monitoring tools. For example, they may use automated scripts to check system performance at regular intervals. They may also use specialized software to monitor network traffic and look for unusual activity.

Once potential issues have been detected, organizations can use alerting systems to notify key personnel and take appropriate action. This can help to prevent incidents from escalating and causing significant harm.

Implementing effective monitoring and alerting systems is a crucial step in ensuring the security and stability of any organization's IT infrastructure.

Conduct root cause analysis

In order to truly understand the factors contributing to a problem, it is essential to conduct a thorough root cause analysis. This involves a comprehensive investigation of all relevant factors, including environmental, personnel, and technical factors, in order to uncover the root cause of the issue at hand.

Once the root cause has been identified, corrective measures can be implemented to prevent similar incidents from occurring in the future. This could include changes to processes or procedures, additional training for personnel, or even modifications to equipment or infrastructure.

By conducting a root cause analysis, organizations can not only improve their incident response capabilities, but also identify and address underlying issues that may be impacting their overall operations.

Document lessons learned

After resolving an incident, it is important to take the time to document the lessons learned before moving on. These lessons can be shared with relevant stakeholders to help improve the organization's AI governance framework and make it more robust in the long run.

Documenting the lessons learned can also serve as a reference in case a similar incident occurs in the future, helping the organization to respond more quickly and effectively. Additionally, the process of documenting the lessons learned provides an opportunity to reflect on the incident and identify areas for improvement.

By taking the time to document the lessons learned, the organization can not only learn from its mistakes, but also continuously improve and evolve its AI governance practices.

7.6. Fairness, Accessibility, and Inclusivity

AI systems have the potential to completely revolutionize industries and transform people's lives for the better. It is truly remarkable how much potential there is for AI to make a positive impact on society. However, it is crucial that these systems are designed and developed with fairness, accessibility, and inclusivity in mind. When AI systems are truly accessible and serve diverse populations, they can truly shine and make an even larger impact.

By ensuring AI systems are accessible to users with varying abilities, we can harness the full potential of AI while minimizing negative impacts and disparities. This is a truly exciting time for AI, and we have the opportunity to shape the future by ensuring that AI systems are designed with inclusivity in mind.

7.6.1. Ensuring AI Systems Serve Diverse Populations

To create AI systems that are fair and serve a wide range of users, it is crucial to account for diversity in both data and design. One way to do this is to collect data from a variety of sources, including different geographic locations, socioeconomic backgrounds, and cultural groups.

It is important to consider the potential biases of the designers and developers working on the AI system and to actively work to mitigate any biases through training and education. By taking these steps, we can ensure that AI systems are truly serving the needs of all users, regardless of their background or identity.

A few important considerations include:

Diverse data sources

One way to address biases in an AI system is by gathering data from a wide range of sources to ensure that the training data is representative of the target population. This can include sources such as online databases, surveys, social media, and other publicly available information. Additionally, organizations can collect data from their own employees, customers, and partners to ensure that the AI system reflects the diversity of their stakeholders.

By incorporating diverse data sources, organizations can not only reduce the risk of biases but also improve the accuracy and effectiveness of the AI system. This is because a more diverse dataset can capture a wider range of perspectives and experiences, leading to a more comprehensive understanding of the target population. Furthermore, a diverse dataset can help identify and address potential blind spots or gaps in the AI system's understanding of the data.

Leveraging diverse data sources is a crucial step in building a fair and effective AI system. Organizations should prioritize gathering data from a wide range of sources to ensure that the AI system is inclusive and reflective of the diversity of its stakeholders.

Demographic representation

It is crucial to have a fair representation of various demographic groups in the data used to train AI systems because biased data can lead to unintended consequences.

For example, if an AI system is trained on data that is mostly composed of a single demographic group, the system may struggle to generalize to other groups. Additionally, if the data used to train an AI system is biased towards a particular group, the system may make unfair or discriminatory decisions that adversely affect other groups.

Therefore, it is essential to ensure that the data used to train AI systems includes adequate representation of various demographic groups, such as different age groups, genders, and ethnicities. This not only helps to prevent biased decision-making but also ensures that the AI system is more inclusive and equitable.

Testing for fairness

One of the key challenges in AI is ensuring that the models we build and the data we use to train them don't result in biased outcomes. To address this concern, it's important to test AI systems across various demographic groups to measure and evaluate their fairness.

This can help us identify any disparities that might exist and make necessary adjustments to the model or data to ensure that everyone is treated equally. By doing so, we can create more inclusive and equitable systems that benefit all members of society, regardless of their background or identity.

7.6.2. Promoting Inclusive Design and Development

Inclusive design and development are crucial in ensuring that AI systems can be used by as many people as possible, regardless of their abilities or disabilities. To achieve this goal, it is important to consider the diverse needs of users, such as people with visual, auditory, or motor impairments.

For example, designers can create accessible interfaces that are easy to navigate using assistive technologies like screen readers or voice recognition software. Additionally, developers can incorporate features like closed captioning and audio descriptions to make content more accessible to people with hearing or visual impairments.

By implementing inclusive design and development practices, we can help ensure that AI systems are truly accessible to everyone. This can be achieved by:

Accessibility guidelines

It is crucial to follow established accessibility guidelines, such as the Web Content Accessibility Guidelines (WCAG), when designing user interfaces for AI applications. These guidelines ensure that individuals with disabilities can use your application with ease, and that your application is inclusive and equitable.

Consider incorporating features such as alternative text for images, descriptive link text, and keyboard accessibility. Additionally, it is important to test your application with individuals who have disabilities to ensure that your application truly meets their needs. By following accessibility guidelines, you can create a better user experience for all individuals who use your application.

Inclusive user testing

It is important to conduct user testing with diverse groups of users, including people with disabilities, to ensure that AI systems are usable and accessible to all. This involves not only identifying users with different abilities, but also considering their different perspectives and experiences.

Conducting user testing with a diverse group of users can reveal a range of issues that may not be apparent when testing with a homogenous group. By including people with disabilities in user testing, AI designers can better understand the needs and challenges of this user group and create more inclusive and accessible AI systems.

Involving people with disabilities in the design process can help to ensure that AI systems are not just accessible, but also useful and valuable to this user group.

Universal design principles

AI systems that are made with universal design principles can be easily adapted to different users' needs and preferences. Universal design principles promote inclusivity and consider the needs of different people. For example, consider users with visual impairments.

An AI system that is designed with universal design principles would offer different options for visual displays, such as high-contrast mode or larger fonts. Another example is users with hearing impairments who may need captions or transcripts to understand audio content.

AI systems that are designed with universal design principles would offer different options for audio content, such as captions or transcripts. By applying universal design principles to AI systems, we can create systems that are more accessible and inclusive to all users.

Training developers and designers

Provide comprehensive training to developers and designers, covering accessibility and inclusivity best practices in depth. The training should include discussions on how to identify potential barriers to accessibility, as well as ways to mitigate them.

Furthermore, the training should emphasize the importance of designing for a diverse set of users, and provide guidance on how to conduct user research to understand the needs and preferences of different user groups.

By providing such training to developers and designers, they will be equipped with the knowledge and skills necessary to create truly inclusive AI systems that cater to the needs of a wide range of users.

7.6.3. Algorithmic Fairness and Bias Mitigation Techniques

Algorithmic fairness and bias mitigation techniques are essential for ensuring that AI systems make fair decisions and do not perpetuate existing biases. One of the most important reasons for this is that AI systems are being integrated into more and more aspects of our lives, from hiring decisions to credit scoring to healthcare. If these systems are not designed to be fair and unbiased, they can perpetuate and even exacerbate existing inequalities and injustices.

To address these concerns, a variety of methods are available. One approach is to use fairness metrics to evaluate an AI system's outputs and adjust them to ensure that they are fair and unbiased. Another approach is to use iterative algorithms, which adjust the system's outputs over time to reduce bias. Additionally, techniques such as counterfactual fairness and individual fairness can be used to ensure that the system is fair to all individuals and groups, regardless of their background or characteristics.

Overall, including algorithmic fairness and bias mitigation as a sub-topic is crucial for providing readers with an in-depth understanding of the importance of fairness in AI systems and the various methods available to ensure that these systems are fair and unbiased. By doing so, readers can gain a better understanding of the potential benefits and drawbacks of AI systems, and work towards creating a more just and equitable society.

Some key points to cover in this sub-topic include:

Fairness metrics

To obtain a more comprehensive understanding of the fairness of AI systems, it is important to introduce various fairness metrics. Here are some examples of such metrics:

- **Demographic Parity**: This metric measures the difference in the probability of a positive outcome between different demographic groups. If the difference is too large, then the system may be biased against certain groups.
- **Equalized Odds**: This metric ensures that the true positive rate and the false positive rate are equal across different demographic groups. If the rates are not equal, then the system may be biased against certain groups.
- **Calibration**: This metric ensures that the predicted probabilities of the system reflect the true probabilities of the outcomes. If the predicted probabilities are not calibrated, then the system may be biased against certain groups.

By using these fairness metrics, we can quantify the fairness of AI systems and identify potential biases. It is important to note that these metrics are not exhaustive and that other metrics may also be needed depending on the specific context of the AI system.

Pre-processing techniques

In order to ensure that the training data is as accurate and representative as possible, it is important to apply a variety of pre-processing techniques. One such technique is re-sampling, which involves adjusting the sample size of the data set to better reflect the overall population.

Another technique is re-weighting, which assigns different weights to different data points based on their importance or relevance. Data transformation is another important technique that can be used to standardize or normalize the data, making it more suitable for use with the AI model. By applying these and other pre-processing techniques, we can significantly reduce biases and improve the accuracy and effectiveness of our AI model.

In-processing techniques

There are a variety of in-processing techniques that can be used to ensure that fairness is incorporated directly into the AI model training process. For example, adversarial training involves training the model to recognize and mitigate the effects of potential biases in the data. Fairness constraints can also be used to ensure that the model is trained to produce results that are consistent with certain fairness criteria.

Fairness-aware learning can be used to incorporate fairness considerations into the objective function of the model, which can help to ensure that the model produces fair and equitable results. By exploring these different in-processing techniques, it is possible to develop AI models that are more fair, transparent, and accountable.

Post-processing techniques

When it comes to mitigating unfairness in AI models, post-processing can be a useful tool. In particular, threshold adjustment and equalized odds post-processing can help to adjust the AI model's outputs or decisions to improve fairness after training is complete.

Threshold adjustment involves changing the decision boundary of a model, which can help to reduce false positives or false negatives for specific groups. Meanwhile, equalized odds post-processing involves adjusting the model's output so that the probabilities of positive and negative outcomes are equal across different groups.

By utilizing these techniques, we can ensure that our AI models are not only accurate, but also fair and equitable for all individuals.

Continual monitoring and improvement

It is critical to stress the significance of continually monitoring artificial intelligence systems for fairness and continually refining them to resolve any biases or fairness concerns that emerge.

This ongoing process ensures that the AI system remains up-to-date with the latest standards and fairness guidelines, and that it continues to operate ethically and efficiently. It also helps to build trust in the system, as users are confident that it is being constantly reviewed and updated to ensure that it is fair and unbiased.

Continual monitoring and improvement can help to identify areas where the AI system can be further optimized or enhanced to provide even better outcomes for users. This could include new features or capabilities that improve the accuracy or speed of the system, or the incorporation of new data sources or algorithms to enhance its performance in specific areas.

Ultimately, the goal of continual monitoring and improvement is to ensure that the AI system is always operating at peak performance and delivering the best possible results for its users.

Chapter 7 Conclusion

In conclusion, Chapter 7 of this guide has focused on ensuring responsible AI usage, with a comprehensive exploration of the various ethical, security, privacy, and fairness concerns that arise when deploying AI systems, such as ChatGPT. As AI becomes increasingly integrated into our daily lives, it is essential to understand these aspects and work towards creating AI solutions that are both ethical and beneficial to all stakeholders.

We began this chapter by discussing the importance of mitigating biases in AI systems, covering the types of bias, techniques for detecting and reducing bias, and the significance of fairness-aware machine learning. We then explored privacy and security considerations, examining data privacy and anonymization techniques, secure deployment and data storage, and privacy-preserving machine learning. These discussions highlighted the importance of protecting user data and maintaining trust in AI systems.

Next, we delved into the ethical guidelines and best practices for AI development, focusing on principles for ethical AI development, industry standards, compliance, and the role of interdisciplinary collaboration. We emphasized the need for user consent and transparency in AI applications, discussing informed consent, communicating AI capabilities and limitations, and designing systems that respect user autonomy and agency.

AI governance and accountability were also addressed in this chapter, emphasizing the importance of establishing AI governance frameworks and monitoring AI systems to maintain accountability. This section underscored the need for organizations to have clear guidelines and oversight mechanisms in place to ensure that AI systems are deployed responsibly.

Lastly, we touched upon fairness, accessibility, and inclusivity in AI systems, examining the importance of serving diverse populations and promoting inclusive design and development. We also introduced algorithmic fairness and bias mitigation techniques, emphasizing the need for continual monitoring and improvement of AI systems.

In summary, responsible AI usage is crucial for creating AI systems that are not only powerful and useful but also ethical, fair, and transparent. By understanding and addressing the various concerns highlighted in this chapter, developers and organizations can contribute to a more responsible and inclusive AI ecosystem. As AI technology continues to evolve, it is imperative that we remain diligent in our pursuit of creating AI systems that align with our societal values and serve the best interests of all users.

Chapter 8 - Scaling and Deploying ChatGPT Solutions

In this chapter, we will explore the intricacies of scaling and deploying ChatGPT solutions effectively to meet the demands of modern web applications. By delving into the integration of ChatGPT into web applications, we will discover how to create an intuitive and seamless user experience. Additionally, we will focus on handling large-scale deployments, including the deployment of ChatGPT to multiple servers, so that the AI system can handle heavy traffic and remain highly available.

Monitoring and maintaining AI systems in production will also be discussed in detail, emphasizing the importance of a reliable and robust system. As AI-powered solutions continue to gain traction and become more prevalent, it is essential for developers and organizations to understand how to integrate these systems into their existing infrastructures while ensuring that they are both reliable and scalable.

8.1. Integration with Web Applications

When deploying ChatGPT solutions, one of the most common use cases is integrating the AI system with web applications to enhance user experience and provide intelligent functionalities. In this section, we will discuss various front-end and back-end integration techniques to help you incorporate ChatGPT into your web applications effectively.

One of the key benefits of integrating ChatGPT with a web app is its ability to provide personalized and dynamic responses to user queries. By analyzing user input and context, ChatGPT can generate specific and relevant responses that can help increase user engagement and satisfaction.

Moreover, ChatGPT can also be integrated with various other AI systems and services, such as voice assistants and chatbots, to provide a seamless and comprehensive user experience. This

can help reduce the time and effort required to interact with multiple systems and enhance overall productivity.

In terms of front-end integration, there are several techniques that can be used to incorporate ChatGPT into a web app, such as using chat widgets, popups, and custom UI components. On the other hand, back-end integration techniques include using APIs and webhooks to connect ChatGPT with the web app's backend architecture.

Overall, by effectively integrating ChatGPT into your web applications, you can provide users with a more personalized and efficient experience, while also enhancing your app's functionality and competitiveness in the market.

8.1.1. Front-end Frameworks and Libraries

To integrate ChatGPT with your web applications, you can leverage various front-end frameworks and libraries such as React, Angular, or Vue.js. These frameworks facilitate the creation of interactive user interfaces and allow you to easily incorporate ChatGPT into your application by making API calls to the backend.

You can customize ChatGPT's responses by modifying the backend code to suit the needs of your application. This can include creating new responses, modifying the tone of existing responses, or even adding new features to the ChatGPT model. Another approach to integrating ChatGPT into your application is to use pre-built chatbot platforms such as Dialogflow or Botpress.

These platforms provide a visual interface for creating chatbots without requiring extensive programming knowledge. However, they may not offer the same level of customization as integrating directly with a front-end framework. Ultimately, the approach you choose will depend on the specific needs of your application and the resources available to you.

Example code:

```
// Using axios library for making API requests
import axios from 'axios';

// Function to call ChatGPT API
async function getChatGPTResponse(prompt) {
  const response = await axios.post('https://api.openai.com/v1/engines/davinci-c
odex/completions', {
    prompt: prompt,
    max_tokens: 100,
    n: 1,
    stop: null,
    temperature: 1,
  });

  return response.data.choices[0].text;
}

// Call the function with a prompt
getChatGPTResponse('Translate the following English text to French: "{text}"').t
hen((response) => {
  console.log(response);
});
```

8.1.2. Back-end Integration Techniques

When integrating ChatGPT into your web applications, it is important to consider not only the front-end but also the backend. The backend plays a crucial role in handling API calls and data processing. In order to handle API calls, you can use backend technologies such as Node.js, Django, or Flask to create APIs that interact with ChatGPT.

Once the APIs are created, your application can send requests to the backend, which will then process the data and send it back to the front-end. This process can involve several steps such as authentication, data validation, and error handling.

Additionally, you may want to consider implementing caching strategies to optimize performance and reduce the load on your server. By taking these steps to optimize the backend,

you can ensure that your ChatGPT integration runs smoothly and efficiently, providing a seamless experience for your users.

Example code:

```javascript
// Using Node.js and Express for backend integration
const express = require('express');
const axios = require('axios');
const app = express();
const port = 3000;

app.get('/chatgpt', async (req, res) => {
  const prompt = req.query.prompt;

  try {
    const response = await axios.post('https://api.openai.com/v1/engines/davinci
-codex/completions', {
      prompt: prompt,
      max_tokens: 100,
      n: 1,
      stop: null,
      temperature: 1,
    });

    res.send(response.data.choices[0].text);
  } catch (error) {
    res.status(500).send('Error fetching ChatGPT response');
  }
});

app.listen(port, () => {
  console.log(`ChatGPT integration listening at http://localhost:${port}`);
});
```

There are several front-end and back-end integration techniques that you can utilize to effectively incorporate ChatGPT into your web applications, which will provide not only an enhanced user experience but also intelligent functionality. For example, you can explore the use of APIs to integrate ChatGPT's natural language processing capabilities with your website's front-end.

You can use webhooks to integrate ChatGPT with your website's back-end, allowing you to automate certain tasks and provide more personalized responses to users. Another technique that you can consider is implementing ChatGPT as a standalone application and then integrating it with your website through a third-party service.

This approach can give you more control over the user experience and allow you to customize ChatGPT to better fit your specific needs. By implementing these techniques, you can take full advantage of ChatGPT's capabilities and provide a more robust and engaging user experience for your website visitors.

8.1.3. Real-time Communication and ChatGPT

In some applications, it may be necessary to enable real-time communication between users and the ChatGPT system. This is especially important in applications where immediate response is required.

A common example of such an application would be customer support, where customers expect quick and accurate responses to their inquiries. To achieve real-time communication, one option is to use WebSockets, a communication protocol that enables full-duplex communication over a single connection.

WebSockets are particularly useful in situations where low latency is important, such as online gaming and real-time chat applications. With WebSockets, developers can create more responsive and interactive applications that provide a better user experience.

Example code:

1.   Install **socket.io** for real-time communication:

```
npm install socket.io
```

2.   Implement the server-side code with Node.js and Express:

```
const express = require('express');
const axios = require('axios');
const app = express();
const server = require('http').createServer(app);
const io = require('socket.io')(server);
const port = 3000;

io.on('connection', (socket) => {
  console.log('User connected');

  socket.on('chat message', async (msg) => {
    try {
      const response = await axios.post('https://api.openai.com/v1/engines/davin
ci-codex/completions', {
        prompt: msg,
        max_tokens: 100,
        n: 1,
        stop: null,
        temperature: 1,
      });

      io.emit('chat message', response.data.choices[0].text);
    } catch (error) {
      io.emit('chat message', 'Error fetching ChatGPT response');
    }
  });

  socket.on('disconnect', () => {
    console.log('User disconnected');
  });
});

server.listen(port, () => {
  console.log(`ChatGPT real-time communication listening at http://localhost:${p
ort}`);
});
```

3. Create a simple front-end using HTML, CSS, and JavaScript to interact with the WebSocket server:

```html
<!DOCTYPE html>
<html lang="en">
<head>
  <meta charset="UTF-8">
  <meta name="viewport" content="width=device-width, initial-scale=1.0">
  <title>ChatGPT Real-time Communication</title>
  <style>
    /* Add your CSS styles here */
  </style>
</head>
<body>
  <ul id="messages"></ul>
  <form id="form" action="">
    <input id="input" autocomplete="off" autofocus /><button>Send</button>
  </form>
  <script src="/socket.io/socket.io.js"></script>
  <script>
    const socket = io();
    const form = document.getElementById('form');
    const input = document.getElementById('input');
    const messages = document.getElementById('messages');

    form.addEventListener('submit', (e) => {
      e.preventDefault();
      if (input.value) {
        socket.emit('chat message', input.value);
        input.value = '';
      }
    });

    socket.on('chat message', (msg) => {
      const li = document.createElement('li');
      li.textContent = msg;
      messages.appendChild(li);
    });
  </script>
</body>
</html>
```

By integrating real-time communication using WebSockets, you can create a more interactive experience for users and enable seamless, instantaneous interaction with the ChatGPT system. This means that users can communicate with each other in real-time, allowing for a more natural and engaging conversation.

By enabling real-time communication, you can enable more sophisticated features in your application, such as live updates and notifications. This can help to increase engagement and keep users coming back to your application. Overall, integrating WebSockets into your ChatGPT system can help to create a more dynamic and engaging user experience, while also enabling new and innovative features.

8.1.4. Deployment and Hosting Solutions

When you are ready to make your ChatGPT-enabled web application accessible to the public, it is important to carefully consider your options for deployment and hosting. There are various platforms and services available that cater to different needs and budgets, and the right choice for your application will depend on a number of factors.

One key factor to consider is the expected amount of traffic your application will receive. If you anticipate heavy traffic, you will need a hosting solution that can handle a large volume of visitors without slowing down or crashing. Additionally, if you expect your application to grow over time, scalability will be an important consideration. You will want a hosting solution that can easily accommodate increases in traffic and usage as your application gains popularity.

Another important consideration is the desired performance of your application. You will want to choose a hosting solution that can deliver fast load times and responsive performance, as this will be critical to the user experience. There are a number of factors that can impact the performance of your application, including the type of server, the location of the server, and the amount of bandwidth available.

Ultimately, choosing the right deployment and hosting solutions is an important decision that can have a significant impact on the success of your web application. By carefully considering your options and weighing the various factors involved, you can make an informed choice that will help ensure the smooth and reliable operation of your application, both now and in the future.

Example code:

1. **Deploying the application using Heroku:**

a. Install Heroku CLI:

For macOS:

```
brew install heroku/brew/heroku
```

For Windows:

```
choco install heroku
```

b. Login to your Heroku account:

```
heroku login
```

c. Initialize a Git repository in your project directory:

```
git init
```

d. Add all files to the repository and create an initial commit:

```
git add .
git commit -m "Initial commit"
```

e. Create a new Heroku application:

```
heroku create
```

f. Push your code to Heroku:

```
git push heroku master
```

g. Open your application in a web browser:

```
heroku open
```

2. **Deploying the application using Vercel:**

a. Install Vercel CLI:

```
npm install —g vercel
```

b. Login to your Vercel account:

```
vercel login
```

c. Deploy your application:

```
vercel
```

d. Copy the provided URL to access your application in a web browser.

By choosing the right deployment and hosting solution, you can ensure that your ChatGPT-enabled web application is accessible, scalable, and performs well for your target audience. These platforms typically offer straightforward setup and deployment processes, allowing you to focus on developing and improving your application.

In addition, selecting the right hosting solution can also provide additional benefits such as improved security, better reliability, and faster load times. By ensuring your application is hosted on a reliable and secure platform, you can build trust with your audience and ensure that your application is always available and performing at its best.

Moreover, choosing a scalable hosting solution allows you to easily adapt to changes in traffic and demand. As your application grows and gains more users, a scalable hosting solution can ensure that your application continues to perform well and handle the increased traffic without any issues.

Furthermore, some hosting solutions offer additional tools and features that can help you optimize your application and improve its performance even further. These tools can include things like caching, content delivery networks, and load balancing, which can all help to improve load times and ensure that your application is always running smoothly.

In summary, selecting the right deployment and hosting solution is crucial for ensuring the success of your ChatGPT-enabled web application. By choosing a reliable, secure, and scalable hosting solution, you can ensure that your application is always accessible, performs well, and can easily adapt to changes in traffic and demand.

8.2. Building Chatbots and Virtual Assistants

In this section, we will discuss in detail how to utilize ChatGPT to create chatbots and virtual assistants that can be integrated into a wide range of messaging platforms and voice assistants. ChatGPT is a cutting-edge technology that has revolutionized the field of conversational AI, allowing developers to build highly sophisticated chatbots that can interact with users in natural language, understand their intents, and provide personalized responses based on their preferences and behavior.

One of the key benefits of using ChatGPT is its flexibility and scalability. With its modular architecture and powerful API, developers can easily customize and fine-tune their chatbots to meet the specific needs of their users and business. Moreover, ChatGPT supports a wide range of languages and dialects, making it an ideal choice for companies and organizations operating in global markets.

Another important feature of ChatGPT is its ability to learn from user interactions and improve its performance over time. By leveraging advanced machine learning algorithms and natural language processing techniques, ChatGPT can analyze user feedback, identify patterns and trends, and adapt its responses accordingly. This not only enhances the user experience but also helps businesses to gain valuable insights into customer behavior and preferences.

In addition to chatbots, ChatGPT can also be used to develop virtual assistants that can perform complex tasks such as scheduling appointments, setting reminders, and making reservations. With its voice recognition capabilities, ChatGPT enables users to interact with their virtual assistants in a natural and intuitive way, without the need for typing or clicking.

ChatGPT is an incredibly powerful tool that can help businesses and developers to create intelligent and engaging conversational agents that can enhance the user experience and drive business growth. Whether you are building a chatbot for customer support, lead generation, or e-commerce, ChatGPT has the features and capabilities to meet your needs.

8.2.1. Messenger Platforms and Integrations

Messenger platforms like Facebook Messenger, WhatsApp, Telegram, and Slack have become increasingly popular for building chatbots due to the widespread usage of these platforms and their ease of integration. Chatbots have proven to be an effective way of automating customer service, marketing, and other business operations. The use of chatbots has increased significantly in recent years, and it is expected that this trend will continue in the future.

In addition to APIs and SDKs, many messenger platforms also offer tools and services that can be used to enhance the functionality of chatbots. For example, Facebook Messenger offers a feature called "Quick Replies" that allows chatbots to present users with a set of predefined options to choose from. This can help to streamline the conversation and make it more efficient. Similarly, Telegram offers a feature called "Inline Bots" that allows chatbots to provide users with relevant information in response to their queries, without the need for the user to leave the chat interface.

Another advantage of using messenger platforms for building chatbots is the ability to leverage the existing user base of these platforms. This can help to increase the reach and visibility of chatbots, making them more effective in achieving their goals. Furthermore, messenger

platforms often have built-in features such as user authentication and payment processing, which can be used to enhance the functionality of chatbots and enable them to perform more complex tasks.

Messenger platforms provide a powerful and flexible platform for building chatbots. Their widespread usage, ease of integration, and built-in features make them an ideal choice for businesses of all sizes. With the continued growth of chatbot technology, it is clear that messenger platforms will play an increasingly important role in the future of customer service and business automation.

Example code:

Integrating ChatGPT with Facebook Messenger using Python and Flask:

a. Install the necessary libraries:

```
pip install Flask requests
```

b. Create a Flask app to handle incoming messages and respond using ChatGPT:

```python
import os
from flask import Flask, request
import requests

app = Flask(__name__)

ACCESS_TOKEN = 'your_facebook_page_access_token'
VERIFY_TOKEN = 'your_facebook_verification_token'
OPENAI_API_KEY = 'your_openai_api_key'

@app.route('/', methods=['GET', 'POST'])
def webhook():
    if request.method == 'GET':
        if request.args.get('hub.verify_token') == VERIFY_TOKEN:
            return request.args.get('hub.challenge')
        return 'Verification token mismatch', 403
    elif request.method == 'POST':
        data = request.get_json()
        if data['object'] == 'page':
            for entry in data['entry']:
                for messaging_event in entry['messaging']:
                    if 'message' in messaging_event:
                        sender_id = messaging_event['sender']['id']
                        message_text = messaging_event['message']['text']
                        response_text = get_chatgpt_response(message_text)
                        send_message(sender_id, response_text)
        return 'ok', 200

def send_message(recipient_id, message_text):
    params = {
        'access_token': ACCESS_TOKEN
    }
    headers = {
        'Content-Type': 'application/json'
    }
    data = {
        'recipient': {
            'id': recipient_id
        },
        'message': {
            'text': message_text
        }
    }
    requests.post('https://graph.facebook.com/v13.0/me/messages', params=params,
headers=headers, json=data)

def get_chatgpt_response(prompt):
    headers = {
        'Content-Type': 'application/json',
        'Authorization': f'Bearer {OPENAI_API_KEY}'
    }
    data = {
        'model': 'text-davinci-002',
        'prompt': prompt,
        'max_tokens': 50,
        'temperature': 0.5
    }
    response = requests.post('https://api.openai.com/v1/engines/davinci-codex/co
mpletions', headers=headers, json=data)
    return response.json()['choices'][0]['text'].strip()

if __name__ == '__main__':
    app.run(debug=True)
```

Replace **'your_facebook_page_access_token'**, **'your_facebook_verification_token'**, and **'your_openai_api_key'** with the respective access tokens.

8.2.2. Voice Assistants and Text-to-Speech Integration

Voice assistants like Amazon Alexa, Google Assistant, and Apple Siri offer APIs and SDKs that allow developers to create custom skills, actions, and applications.

These custom skills and actions can provide users with a wide variety of useful functionalities, ranging from simple tasks like setting reminders and alarms to more complex ones like ordering food or booking a ride.

By integrating ChatGPT with these voice assistants, developers can further enhance the user experience by enabling more interactive and engaging voice-based experiences. For instance, ChatGPT could be integrated with voice assistants to provide personalized recommendations based on user preferences, answer complex questions, or even provide emotional support.

This integration could also pave the way for new and innovative use cases, such as using ChatGPT as a language learning tool or a virtual assistant for people with disabilities.

Example code:

1. Install the required library:

```
pip install google-cloud-texttospeech
```

2. Create a service account in the Google Cloud Console and download the JSON key file.
3. Set the environment variable to the path of the JSON key file:

```
export GOOGLE_APPLICATION_CREDENTIALS="/path/to/your/keyfile.json"
```

4. Execute the following Python script:

```python
import openai
from google.cloud import texttospeech

openai.api_key = "your_openai_api_key"

# Function to generate ChatGPT response
def get_chatgpt_response(prompt):
    response = openai.Completion.create(
        engine="text-davinci-002",
        prompt=prompt,
        max_tokens=50,
        n=1,
        stop=None,
        temperature=0.7
    )
    return response.choices[0].text.strip()

# Function to convert text to speech using Google Text-to-Speech API
def text_to_speech(text, output_file):
    client = texttospeech.TextToSpeechClient()
    input_text = texttospeech.SynthesisInput(text=text)
    voice = texttospeech.VoiceSelectionParams(
        language_code="en-US", ssml_gender=texttospeech.SsmlVoiceGender.FEMALE
    )
    audio_config = texttospeech.AudioConfig(
        audio_encoding=texttospeech.AudioEncoding.MP3
    )

    response = client.synthesize_speech(
        input=input_text, voice=voice, audio_config=audio_config
    )

    with open(output_file, "wb") as out:
        out.write(response.audio_content)
        print(f"Audio content written to '{output_file}'")

# Example usage
prompt = "Tell me a fun fact about AI."
response = get_chatgpt_response(prompt)
print(response)
text_to_speech(response, "output.mp3")
```

Replace **'your_openai_api_key'** with your OpenAI API key. This example demonstrates how to generate a response from ChatGPT and convert it to speech using the Google Text-to-Speech API. The output audio file will be saved as "output.mp3" in the current working directory.

8.2.3. Multi-lingual Chatbots and Language Support

As more and more businesses and services expand their reach to cater to a global audience, it is becoming increasingly important to ensure that their chatbots and virtual assistants are capable of communicating with users in a variety of languages. Not only does this expand the potential user base, it also enhances the user experience by providing a more personalized level of service.

By taking advantage of the multi-lingual capabilities of ChatGPT, businesses and organizations can create chatbots that are able to understand and respond to users in different languages, making it easier for users to communicate and engage with the service or product being offered. This can ultimately lead to increased customer satisfaction and loyalty, and help businesses to stay ahead of the competition in an increasingly global marketplace.

Example code:

1. Creating a multi-lingual chatbot using ChatGPT:

```python
import openai

openai.api_key = "your_openai_api_key"

def get_chatgpt_response(prompt, language):
    if language not in ['en', 'fr', 'de', 'es', 'it', 'nl', 'pt']:
        raise ValueError("Unsupported language")

    model_map = {
        'en': 'text-davinci-002',
        'fr': 'text-davinci-002-fr',
        'de': 'text-davinci-002-de',
        'es': 'text-davinci-002-es',
        'it': 'text-davinci-002-it',
        'nl': 'text-davinci-002-nl',
        'pt': 'text-davinci-002-pt'
    }

    model = model_map[language]

    response = openai.Completion.create(
        engine=model,
        prompt=prompt,
        max_tokens=50,
        n=1,
        stop=None,
        temperature=0.7
    )

    return response.choices[0].text.strip()

# Example usage
prompt = "Quel temps fait-il aujourd'hui ?"  # French prompt
language = "fr"  # Language code for French
response = get_chatgpt_response(prompt, language)
print(response)
```

Replace **'your_openai_api_key'** with your OpenAI API key. This example demonstrates how to create a chatbot that can handle user input in different languages. The **get_chatgpt_response** function takes a prompt and a language code as input and returns a response in the specified language.

8.2.4. Sentiment Analysis and Emotion Recognition

Understanding the sentiment and emotions of users' input is an essential component of creating more engaging and personalized chatbot experiences. By incorporating sentiment analysis and emotion recognition techniques, your chatbot can better understand user emotions and respond accordingly, leading to improved user satisfaction and engagement.

For instance, by analyzing the sentiment of a user's input, a chatbot can determine if the user is happy, sad, frustrated, or angry. Based on this information, the chatbot can respond with an appropriate message that resonates with the user's emotional state, thereby creating a more personalized and engaging experience.

To integrate sentiment analysis with your ChatGPT-based chatbot, there are several third-party libraries available that you can use. For instance, you can use TextBlob or VADER sentiment analysis libraries, which are pre-trained and can analyze text for sentiment polarity. Additionally, these libraries can also provide other useful information, such as the subjectivity of the input text, which can also be used to improve the chatbot's responses.

Here's an example using TextBlob:

1. Install the TextBlob library:

```
pip install textblob
```

2. Analyze the sentiment of a user's input:

```python
from textblob import TextBlob

def analyze_sentiment(text):
    analysis = TextBlob(text)
    return analysis.sentiment.polarity

user_input = "I love the new features in your chatbot!"
sentiment_score = analyze_sentiment(user_input)

if sentiment_score > 0:
    response = "I'm glad you like the new features!"
elif sentiment_score == 0:
    response = "Thank you for your neutral feedback."
else:
    response = "I'm sorry to hear that. We'll work on improving it."

print(response)
```

This example demonstrates how to analyze user sentiment and generate a ChatGPT response based on the sentiment score. The response can then be used to guide the conversation and create more meaningful interactions.

8.3. Infrastructure and Cost Optimization

Deploying ChatGPT solutions at scale is a complex process that requires careful deliberation of infrastructure and cost optimization. The key to achieving success in this endeavor is to balance performance, cost, and efficiency. By doing so, we ensure that the user experience remains seamless and uninterrupted, even as the solution grows in scale and complexity.

To achieve this balance, there are various deployment options and strategies that you can consider. For instance, you can choose to deploy the solution on-premise or in the cloud. Each option has its pros and cons, and it's essential to carefully weigh them before making a decision.

In addition, you can also consider the use of containerization technology such as Docker, Kubernetes, or OpenShift. These technologies enable you to package the ChatGPT solution and its dependencies into a single container that can be easily deployed and managed.

You can optimize cost and infrastructure by leveraging cloud computing services such as Amazon Web Services (AWS), Google Cloud Platform (GCP), or Microsoft Azure. These services

provide a range of features and tools that enable you to manage and scale your ChatGPT solution cost-effectively.

Deploying ChatGPT solutions at scale requires a deep understanding of infrastructure and cost optimization. By carefully considering the available deployment options and strategies, you can ensure optimal performance, cost, and efficiency while providing a seamless user experience.

8.3.1. Cloud-based Deployment Options

Cloud-based deployment offers many advantages for deploying ChatGPT models. By using cloud providers such as AWS, Google Cloud Platform, or Microsoft Azure, you can take advantage of a wide range of resources, including pre-built AI services and APIs that can be easily integrated with your applications.

With the flexibility and scalability of cloud-based deployment, you can easily adjust the size of your infrastructure to meet the needs of your growing user base. Furthermore, the cloud allows for easy collaboration with teams located in different parts of the world, and provides a high level of security to protect your data and applications.

Cloud-based deployment is a reliable and efficient option for deploying ChatGPT models and other AI applications.

AWS:

To deploy a ChatGPT model on AWS, you have several tools available, including Amazon SageMaker and AWS Lambda. Amazon SageMaker is a machine learning platform that allows you to build, train, and deploy machine learning models at scale. You can use it to train your ChatGPT model and then deploy it to a SageMaker endpoint, where it can be accessed by your application.

AWS Lambda, on the other hand, is a serverless computing service that allows you to run your code without the need to provision or manage servers. You can use AWS Lambda to invoke your ChatGPT model on demand, without having to worry about managing infrastructure. With AWS Lambda, you can scale your application automatically based on demand, ensuring that you are always able to provide a fast and responsive service to your users.

AWS also provides a range of other services that can be used to support your ChatGPT application. For example, you can use Amazon S3 to store your model data, Amazon CloudWatch to monitor your application's performance, and Amazon API Gateway to manage

your API endpoints. By combining these services, you can build a powerful and scalable ChatGPT application that meets the needs of your users.

Google Cloud Platform:

Google Cloud is a cloud computing platform that offers a wide range of tools and services for businesses of all sizes. One of the key offerings of Google Cloud is AI Platform, which provides a suite of machine learning tools and services that can help businesses deploy and manage their machine learning models with ease. With AI Platform, businesses can access a range of features, such as data labeling, model training, and model deployment, all in one place.

In addition to AI Platform, Google Cloud also offers Google Cloud Functions, a serverless computing service that enables businesses to build and deploy ChatGPT models without having to manage their own infrastructure. This means that businesses can focus on developing and testing their models, while Google Cloud takes care of everything else, from scaling to security.

Microsoft Azure:

Azure Machine Learning is Microsoft's cloud-based service for building, training, and deploying machine learning models. This service is designed to help businesses of all sizes to build and deploy machine learning models faster and more effectively. With Azure Machine Learning, businesses can easily access a wide range of tools and resources that can help them to create and train powerful machine learning models.

One of the key benefits of Azure Functions is that it allows businesses to use serverless computing for their ChatGPT models. This means that businesses can run their ChatGPT models without worrying about infrastructure management. Azure Functions provides a cost-effective and flexible solution for businesses that want to use machine learning models without the need for complex infrastructure setup.

In addition to Azure Machine Learning and Azure Functions, Microsoft Azure offers a wide range of other cloud-based services that can help businesses to achieve their goals more effectively. These services include Azure Cognitive Services, Azure DevOps, and many others. With Microsoft Azure, businesses can access all the tools and resources they need to succeed in today's fast-paced and competitive marketplace.

8.3.2. Edge Computing and On-premises Solutions

When data privacy, security, and low-latency requirements are of utmost importance, deploying ChatGPT models using edge computing and on-premises solutions can be a suitable option.

Edge computing is a distributed computing paradigm that brings computation and data storage closer to the location where it is needed, thereby reducing the latency and bandwidth required.

On-premises solutions, on the other hand, are deployed within the organization's own infrastructure, providing greater control over the data and security. These solutions can also be customized to meet specific business needs, ensuring that the ChatGPT models are tailored to the organization's requirements. By utilizing edge computing and on-premises solutions, organizations can ensure that their ChatGPT models are secure and perform in real-time without compromising on data privacy.

Edge Computing:

Edge computing is an increasingly popular approach to deploying machine learning models. It involves deploying models on devices closer to the data source, such as IoT devices, smartphones, and edge servers. This approach can reduce latency and improve privacy by keeping data local. TensorFlow Lite and NVIDIA Jetson devices are two popular options for edge AI deployment.

One of the major benefits of edge computing is its ability to reduce latency. By processing data closer to the source, edge devices can provide faster responses than traditional cloud-based solutions. This can be particularly important in applications such as autonomous vehicles or industrial control systems, where rapid response times are critical.

Another benefit of edge computing is improved privacy. By keeping data local, edge devices can help ensure that sensitive information does not leave the device. This can be particularly important in applications such as healthcare, where patient data must be protected.

In addition to TensorFlow Lite and NVIDIA Jetson, there are a number of other tools and platforms available for edge AI deployment. These include Google Cloud IoT Edge, Microsoft Azure IoT Edge, and Amazon Web Services Greengrass, among others.

Overall, edge computing represents an exciting new approach to deploying machine learning models. With its ability to reduce latency and improve privacy, it is a promising technology that is likely to see continued growth in the coming years.

On-premises Solutions:

On-premises deployment is an option that provides greater control over data privacy and security by allowing you to deploy ChatGPT models on your own servers or data centers. This type of deployment is particularly useful for organizations that require strict control over their data, or for those that need to comply with regulatory requirements.

By using containerization technologies such as Docker or Kubernetes, you can manage your on-premises deployment more easily and efficiently. These technologies allow you to package ChatGPT models and their dependencies into self-contained units that can be easily moved between different environments. This means that you can deploy the same models across different servers or data centers, without having to worry about compatibility issues or other technical challenges.

To providing greater control over data privacy and security, on-premises deployment offers other benefits as well. For example, it can help to reduce latency and improve performance, since data does not need to be transmitted over the internet. This can be particularly important for applications that require real-time responses, such as chatbots or virtual assistants.

On-premises deployment is a powerful option that can help organizations to achieve their data privacy and security goals, while also providing flexibility, scalability, and performance. If you are considering deploying ChatGPT models, you should definitely consider on-premises deployment as an option.

Example using Docker:

1. Create a **Dockerfile**:

```
FROM python:3.8

WORKDIR /app

COPY requirements.txt .
RUN pip install -r requirements.txt

COPY . .

CMD ["python", "app.py"]
```

2. Build and run the Docker container:

```
docker build -t chatgpt-deployment .
docker run -p 5000:5000 chatgpt-deployment
```

This example demonstrates how to containerize a ChatGPT application using Docker, making it easier to deploy on-premises or in a cloud environment.

8.3.3. Monitoring and Autoscaling

Monitoring and autoscaling are crucial aspects of infrastructure and cost optimization in the context of ChatGPT solution. It is important to continuously monitor the system to ensure that it can handle the increasing demand from the users. To achieve this, you can use various monitoring tools such as Nagios, Zabbix, or Prometheus. These tools allow you to track system performance and detect anomalies that may lead to system failure or degradation in performance.

To monitoring, autoscaling is also a critical aspect to ensure that the resources allocated to the system can meet the fluctuating needs of the users. Autoscaling allows you to automatically adjust resources up or down based on the current demand. This can help you save costs by only using the resources you need, and also ensure that your system is always available and responsive to the users.

To implement autoscaling, you can use various tools such as AWS Auto Scaling, Google Cloud Autoscaler, or Kubernetes Horizontal Pod Autoscaler. These tools use metrics such as CPU utilization, memory usage, or network traffic to automatically adjust the resources allocated to the system.

Monitoring and autoscaling are essential aspects of infrastructure and cost optimization in the context of ChatGPT solution. By continuously monitoring the system and using autoscaling to adjust resources, you can ensure that your system is always available and responsive to the users, while also keeping your costs under control.

Monitoring:

Effective monitoring involves collecting and analyzing metrics from your deployed ChatGPT models, such as latency, throughput, and error rates. Monitoring tools offered by cloud providers can be leveraged to track and visualize these metrics in real-time.

To achieve effective monitoring, it is important to establish a monitoring plan that includes regular checks to ensure the metrics are up-to-date and accurate. This can be done by implementing automated checks and alerts that notify you of any fluctuations or anomalies in the metrics.

In addition, monitoring can also involve identifying and addressing potential issues before they become more serious problems. This can be done through proactive monitoring, which involves actively monitoring the system to identify any potential issues and taking steps to address them before they escalate.

Overall, effective monitoring is crucial to ensuring the performance and reliability of your ChatGPT models, and should be an integral part of any deployment strategy.

Examples of such tools include:

- AWS CloudWatch
- Google Cloud Monitoring
- Microsoft Azure Monitor

Example using AWS CloudWatch:

1. In your AWS Management Console, navigate to the CloudWatch service.
2. Create a new dashboard and select the desired metrics for monitoring, such as CPU usage, memory utilization, and request latency.
3. Configure alarms to be triggered when specific thresholds are reached, sending notifications to relevant team members.

Autoscaling:

Autoscaling is an incredibly useful feature that enables your ChatGPT deployment to automatically adjust the amount of resources it uses based on demand. This means that your system can automatically scale up or down in response to changes in traffic, ensuring that you always have enough resources to meet your needs.

When you use autoscaling, you benefit from optimal performance at all times, regardless of how much traffic your system is handling. This is because your system is constantly adjusting itself to meet your needs, ensuring that you always have the resources you need to keep your system running smoothly.

One of the best things about autoscaling is that it can be configured to meet your specific needs. Most cloud providers offer built-in autoscaling capabilities that can be customized to meet the unique needs of your ChatGPT deployment. This means that you can tailor your autoscaling settings to match your traffic patterns, ensuring that you always have the right amount of resources at the right time.

Autoscaling is an invaluable tool that can help you to minimize costs while maximizing performance. By ensuring that your system always has the resources it needs, you can focus on delivering great experiences to your users without worrying about infrastructure or costs.

Example using AWS Auto Scaling:

1. In your AWS Management Console, navigate to the EC2 service.
2. Under "Auto Scaling", create a new Launch Configuration, specifying the instance type, AMI, and other configurations for your ChatGPT deployment.
3. Create a new Auto Scaling Group, associating it with the Launch Configuration you created. Set up scaling policies based on metrics such as CPU usage or request count.

By implementing monitoring and autoscaling strategies, you can effectively manage your ChatGPT deployment's performance and costs while ensuring a seamless user experience.

Example:

It's important to note that most of the monitoring and autoscaling configurations are set up through the cloud provider's web console or CLI. However, we can provide an example using the AWS SDK for Python (Boto3) to interact with AWS CloudWatch and AWS Auto Scaling.

First, install the AWS SDK for Python (Boto3):

```
pip install boto3
```

Then, create a Python script with the following code to interact with AWS CloudWatch and AWS Auto Scaling:

```python
import boto3

# Initialize the CloudWatch and Auto Scaling clients
cloudwatch = boto3.client('cloudwatch')
autoscaling = boto3.client('autoscaling')

# Put a custom metric to CloudWatch
cloudwatch.put_metric_data(
    Namespace='MyAppNamespace',
    MetricData=[
        {
            'MetricName': 'MyCustomMetric',
            'Value': 42
        }
    ]
)

# Create an Auto Scaling launch configuration
autoscaling.create_launch_configuration(
    LaunchConfigurationName='MyChatGPTLaunchConfig',
    InstanceType='t2.small',
    ImageId='ami-xxxxxxxxxxxxxxxxx'
)

# Create an Auto Scaling group
autoscaling.create_auto_scaling_group(
    AutoScalingGroupName='MyChatGPTAutoScalingGroup',
    LaunchConfigurationName='MyChatGPTLaunchConfig',
    MinSize=1,
    MaxSize=5,
    DesiredCapacity=2,
    VPCZoneIdentifier='subnet-xxxxxxxxxxxxxxxxx'
)

# Create an Auto Scaling policy to scale out based on CPU usage
autoscaling.put_scaling_policy(
    AutoScalingGroupName='MyChatGPTAutoScalingGroup',
    PolicyName='MyChatGPTScaleOutPolicy',
    PolicyType='TargetTrackingScaling',
    TargetTrackingConfiguration={
        'PredefinedMetricSpecification': {
            'PredefinedMetricType': 'ASGAverageCPUUtilization'
        },
        'TargetValue': 50.0
    }
)
```

Please replace 'ami-xxxxxxxxxxxxxxxxx' with your desired Amazon Machine Image (AMI) ID and 'subnet-xxxxxxxxxxxxxxxxx' with your desired VPC subnet ID.

This example demonstrates how to use Boto3 to interact with AWS CloudWatch and AWS Auto Scaling. It puts a custom metric to CloudWatch, creates an Auto Scaling launch configuration, an Auto Scaling group, and a scaling policy that scales out based on CPU usage.

8.3.4. Serverless Architecture for ChatGPT Deployment

Serverless architecture is a modern approach that allows developers to focus solely on writing code without having to worry about managing and maintaining the underlying infrastructure. This approach significantly reduces the burden on developers, allowing them to concentrate on creating quality software applications that meet the needs of their clients.

Moreover, serverless platforms provide an efficient way to scale ChatGPT solutions to handle fluctuating workloads while optimizing costs. These platforms allow for automatic scaling, which means that resources are only provisioned when needed, and developers don't have to worry about managing servers or paying for idle resources.

Some of the most popular serverless platforms include AWS Lambda, Google Cloud Functions, and Azure Functions. While there are many other options available, these platforms are particularly well-suited for ChatGPT solutions.

Here, we'll dive deeper into the topic of serverless computing and explore how to deploy a ChatGPT application using a serverless platform. Specifically, we'll take AWS Lambda as an example and discuss the steps involved in setting up your application on this platform. By the end of this sub-topic, you'll have a solid understanding of how serverless platforms work and how they can benefit your ChatGPT solutions.

Code Example:

1. First, create a Python script named **lambda_function.py** with the following content:

```python
import json
import openai

def lambda_handler(event, context):
    # Replace "your-api-key" with your OpenAI API key
    openai.api_key = "your-api-key"

    prompt = event['prompt']
    response = openai.Completion.create(
        engine="text-davinci-002",
        prompt=prompt,
        max_tokens=50,
        n=1,
        stop=None,
        temperature=0.5,
    )

    return {
        'statusCode': 200,
        'body': json.dumps({'response': response.choices[0].text})
    }
```

2. Install the OpenAI Python library and package your Lambda function:

```
pip install openai -t .
zip -r chatgpt_lambda.zip .
```

3. Create an AWS Lambda function using the AWS Management Console or AWS CLI, and upload the **chatgpt_lambda.zip** package.
4. Configure the Lambda function's trigger, such as an API Gateway or a custom event source.
5. Test the Lambda function by invoking it with a sample event containing the **prompt** attribute.

By using a serverless architecture like AWS Lambda, you can deploy your ChatGPT application without provisioning or managing servers, enabling you to optimize costs and automatically scale your application in response to incoming requests.

8.4. Performance Monitoring and Analytics

Monitoring the performance of your ChatGPT application is crucial to ensure its effectiveness and user satisfaction. By evaluating user engagement, analyzing response quality, and continuously iterating on the model, you can improve the overall user experience.

One way to evaluate user engagement is to look at the frequency and duration of user interactions with the application. This can provide insight into which features are most frequently used and which ones may need improvement. Additionally, analyzing response quality can help identify areas where the application may be falling short in meeting user needs.

To continuously improve the performance of the application, it may be necessary to update the model periodically. This can involve incorporating new data, retraining the model, or even changing the underlying architecture. By taking a data-driven approach to model development, you can ensure that the application is always adapting to meet the changing needs of its users.

A robust monitoring and evaluation process is essential to ensuring the ongoing success of your ChatGPT application. By staying vigilant and making data-driven decisions, you can create an application that meets the needs of your users and delivers a high-quality experience.

8.4.1. Evaluating User Engagement

Measuring user engagement is an essential aspect of determining the success of your ChatGPT solution. It not only provides insights into how well your solution is performing, but it also helps you identify areas for improvement.

There are several metrics you can use to measure user engagement. For example, you can look at the number of active users, the frequency and length of conversations, and user retention rates. By analyzing these metrics, you can gain a deeper understanding of how users are interacting with your solution and identify any pain points that need to be addressed.

Understanding user behavior is critical to improving the overall user experience. By analyzing user engagement metrics, you can identify trends and patterns in user behavior, such as which features are most popular or which conversations tend to be the longest. Armed with this information, you can fine-tune your ChatGPT solution to better meet the needs and preferences of your users, ultimately leading to a more engaged and satisfied user base.

To track these metrics, you can integrate your application with analytics tools like Google Analytics, Mixpanel, or Amplitude. Here's a simple example of tracking events with Google Analytics:

1. Add the Google Analytics tracking code to your web application:

```
<!-- Global site tag (gtag.js) - Google Analytics -->
<script async src="https://www.googletagmanager.com/gtag/js?id=GA_MEASUREMENT_I
D"></script>
<script>
  window.dataLayer = window.dataLayer || [];
  function gtag(){dataLayer.push(arguments);}
  gtag('js', new Date());

  gtag('config', 'GA_MEASUREMENT_ID');
</script>
```

2. Track custom events in your JavaScript code:

```
function sendMessage() {
  // Your existing message sending logic

  // Track a custom event with Google Analytics
  gtag('event', 'message_sent', {
    'event_category': 'engagement',
    'event_label': 'ChatGPT',
  });
}
```

8.4.2. Analyzing and Improving Response Quality

To ensure that your ChatGPT application provides high-quality responses, it's essential to analyze its output and iterate on the model. One way to do this is to collect user feedback. By gathering feedback, you can better understand the strengths and weaknesses of your ChatGPT model. Additionally, you can use this feedback to fine-tune your ChatGPT model, making it more accurate and helpful for users.

Another way to improve your ChatGPT model is by adjusting its parameters. This involves tweaking various settings within the model to achieve better results. For example, you might adjust the learning rate, which controls how quickly the model adapts to new data. Alternatively, you could adjust the batch size, which determines how many examples the model processes at once.

Once you have made these adjustments, it's important to analyze the output of your ChatGPT model again. This will help you determine if the changes you made resulted in better responses. If not, you may need to iterate on the model further until you achieve the desired results.

For example, you can add a feedback form to your web application and store user feedback in a database for further analysis:

```html
<form id="feedback-form">
  <label for="feedback">Please rate the response quality:</label>
  <input type="range" id="feedback" name="feedback" min="1" max="5">
  <button type="submit">Submit Feedback</button>
</form>

<script>
document.getElementById("feedback-form").addEventListener("submit", (event) => {
  event.preventDefault();

  const feedback = document.getElementById("feedback").value;

  // Send the feedback to your server or a database for further analysis
  // ...

  // Track the feedback event with Google Analytics
  gtag('event', 'feedback', {
    'event_category': 'quality',
    'event_label': 'ChatGPT',
    'value': parseInt(feedback)
  });
});
</script>
```

By analyzing user engagement and response quality, you can identify areas for improvement and make data-driven decisions to optimize your ChatGPT solution. Regular monitoring and iteration ensure that your application continues to meet user expectations and provides a satisfactory experience.

8.4.3. A/B Testing and Experimentation

A/B testing and experimentation are incredibly valuable tools for optimizing your ChatGPT application. By systematically testing different aspects of your application, you can identify areas for improvement and make data-driven decisions that lead to better performance and user satisfaction.

One way to approach A/B testing is to experiment with different model parameters. For example, you might test different weights for different features in your model to see how each affects the performance of your application. Similarly, you could experiment with different prompt strategies to see which ones lead to more engaging conversations with users.

Another area to experiment with is the user interface of your application. Small changes to the layout, color scheme, or font can have a big impact on how users perceive your application and how likely they are to continue using it. By conducting A/B tests on different UI designs, you can identify the most effective layout for your application.

A/B testing and experimentation provide a powerful framework for optimizing your ChatGPT application. By using these tools to systematically test different aspects of your application, you can make data-driven decisions that lead to better performance and a more satisfying user experience.

Here's a simple example of setting up an A/B test with two different prompt strategies using JavaScript:

```javascript
// Function for sending a message to GPT-4 with different prompt strategies
async function sendMessageWithStrategy(strategy) {
  const inputMessage = document.getElementById("inputMessage").value;

  let prompt;
  if (strategy === "strategyA") {
    prompt = `User: ${inputMessage}\nAssistant:`;
  } else if (strategy === "strategyB") {
    prompt = `Conversation:\nUser: ${inputMessage}\nAssistant:`;
  }

  const response = await fetch('/generate_response', {
    method: 'POST',
    headers: {
      'Content-Type': 'application/json'
    },
    body: JSON.stringify({ prompt: prompt })
  });

  const data = await response.json();
  document.getElementById("response").innerHTML = data.generated_text;
}

// Randomly assign users to one of two strategies
const strategies = ["strategyA", "strategyB"];
const assignedStrategy = strategies[Math.floor(Math.random() * strategies.length)];

// Send the message with the assigned strategy
document.getElementById("sendButton").addEventListener("click", () => {
  sendMessageWithStrategy(assignedStrategy);
});
```

With this code, users are randomly assigned to one of two prompt strategies. You can then track user engagement and response quality for each group to determine which strategy leads to better outcomes.

Remember to use analytics tools to track the results of your A/B tests, such as Google Analytics, Mixpanel, or Amplitude, and analyze the results to make informed decisions on which changes to implement in your application.

8.4.4. Monitoring System Health and Performance

Regularly monitoring the health and performance of your ChatGPT application is crucial for maintaining a high-quality user experience. By using monitoring tools, you can ensure that your application is working as expected and that any issues are detected and resolved quickly. In addition to identifying bottlenecks, potential issues, and areas for optimization, monitoring can also provide valuable insights into user behavior and preferences.

With this information, you can make informed decisions about how to improve your application and deliver a better user experience. Furthermore, monitoring can help you stay ahead of the competition by keeping you up-to-date with the latest trends and developments in your industry.

All in all, investing time and resources into monitoring your ChatGPT application can pay off in the long run by improving user satisfaction, increasing revenue, and enhancing your overall reputation.

Example:

Here is a simple example of monitoring the response time of your ChatGPT API using Python and the **time** module:

```python
import requests
import json
import time

api_key = "your_api_key"
headers = {"Authorization": f"Bearer {api_key}"}
url = "https://api.openai.com/v1/engines/davinci-codex/completions"

def monitor_response_time(prompt):
    start_time = time.time()

    data = {
        "prompt": prompt,
        "max_tokens": 50
    }

    response = requests.post(url, headers=headers, json=data)
    response_time = time.time() - start_time
    return response_time

prompt = "Translate the following English text to French: 'Hello, how are you?'"
response_time = monitor_response_time(prompt)
print(f"Response time: {response_time} seconds")
```

This code measures the time taken to get a response from the ChatGPT API for a given prompt. You can use this information to monitor the performance of your application and make adjustments as needed.

In addition to response time, consider monitoring other metrics such as:

1. API error rates and types.
2. CPU and memory usage on your server.
3. Number of concurrent users or requests.

One way to ensure that your ChatGPT application is performing optimally is to use monitoring and logging tools like Amazon CloudWatch, Google Stackdriver, or Datadog. These tools can help you keep an eye on a variety of important metrics, such as response time and server load, and can alert you to potential issues before they become major problems.

You can use these tools to maintain the overall health of your application by identifying and addressing any performance bottlenecks or other issues that may arise. By taking advantage of these powerful monitoring and logging solutions, you can ensure that your ChatGPT application is running smoothly and delivering the best possible user experience.

8.5. Ensuring Reliability and High Availability

As your ChatGPT application continues to expand and gain more users, it becomes even more crucial to guarantee that it remains dependable and continuously available. To achieve this, the implementation of certain mechanisms is imperative. For instance, a load-balancing mechanism can be put in place to handle the increased traffic.

In addition, disaster recovery mechanisms can be implemented to ensure business continuity in the event of any potential failures. It is also essential to consider the use of redundant systems and failover mechanisms that can assure that the service stays up and running even during unforeseen outages. By having these measures in place, ChatGPT can maintain its reputation as a reliable and highly available application, ensuring that its users can access it anytime, anywhere.

8.5.1. Load Balancing and Traffic Management

Load balancing is an essential tool that helps to distribute traffic across multiple instances of your application, ensuring that no single instance becomes overwhelmed with requests. This, in turn, assists in maintaining optimal performance and ensuring that your application does not become a bottleneck.

There are several load balancing techniques and tools available which can be used to achieve this. These include cloud-based solutions from providers such as AWS, Google Cloud, and Azure, which have become popular in recent years due to their scalability, flexibility, and cost-effectiveness. By leveraging these tools, you can ensure that your application runs smoothly, even during periods of high traffic, and that your users have a seamless experience. Additionally, load balancing can help to improve the reliability and availability of your application by providing redundancy and failover capabilities.

This means that if one instance of your application fails, traffic is automatically redirected to another instance, ensuring that your application remains online and accessible to your users. Overall, load balancing is an essential component of modern application architecture that can help to improve performance, reliability, and scalability, making it a must-have for any organization that wants to stay competitive in today's fast-paced digital landscape.

Example using AWS Elastic Load Balancing (ELB):

1. Create an Amazon EC2 instance with your ChatGPT application deployed.
2. Configure the AWS ELB service to distribute incoming traffic across multiple instances of your application.
3. Set up health checks to monitor the status of your instances and automatically remove any unhealthy instances from the load balancer.

8.5.2. Backup and Disaster Recovery Strategies

Ensuring the continuity of your ChatGPT application is crucial in keeping your business running smoothly. In order to achieve this, having a solid backup and disaster recovery strategy in place is vital.

This not only entails regularly backing up your data and application configurations, but also testing these backups to ensure that they are functional. In addition, you must have a plan in place to quickly restore your application in the event of a disaster. This plan should include identifying the source of the problem, determining the extent of the damage, and determining the best course of action to get your application back online as quickly as possible.

Furthermore, it is essential to have a backup location or secondary data center to ensure that your data can be restored even if your primary data center is compromised. By taking these steps, you can be confident in the continuity of your ChatGPT application and ensure the longevity of your business.

Example using Amazon S3 for data backup:

```python
import boto3
import os

# Configure AWS credentials
aws_access_key_id = "your_access_key_id"
aws_secret_access_key = "your_secret_access_key"
aws_session_token = "your_session_token"

s3 = boto3.client("s3", aws_access_key_id=aws_access_key_id, aws_secret_access_k
ey=aws_secret_access_key, aws_session_token=aws_session_token)

# Upload a file to your S3 bucket
def upload_to_s3(file_path, bucket, s3_key):
    with open(file_path, "rb") as f:
        s3.upload_fileobj(f, bucket, s3_key)
    print(f"Uploaded {file_path} to s3://{bucket}/{s3_key}")

# Backup your chat logs
chat_logs_file_path = "chat_logs.json"
s3_bucket = "your_s3_bucket"
s3_key = "backups/chat_logs.json"

upload_to_s3(chat_logs_file_path, s3_bucket, s3_key)
```

This code example shows how to upload a file (e.g., chat logs) to an Amazon S3 bucket using the **boto3** library. You can schedule regular backups of your data and application configurations to minimize the risk of data loss.

For disaster recovery, consider using cloud-based services like AWS, Google Cloud, or Azure that offer built-in redundancy, automated backups, and recovery tools. Additionally, make sure to document your recovery plan and test it periodically to ensure that you can quickly restore your application when needed.

8.5.3. Auto-scaling and Resource Management

As the demand for your ChatGPT application fluctuates, it's crucial to have a system in place that can automatically scale resources to meet the changing needs. Auto-scaling helps you

maintain performance while minimizing costs by automatically adjusting the number of instances running based on predefined conditions, such as CPU usage or network traffic.

To elaborate, auto-scaling is a feature that allows your application to operate efficiently and effectively during periods of high traffic, ensuring that your customers have a seamless experience without any lag or downtime. This is especially important for businesses that experience sudden surges in website traffic, such as during a sale or promotion.

By automatically adjusting the number of instances running, auto-scaling ensures that your application can handle any sudden influx of traffic without crashing or slowing down. This means that your customers can continue to use your application without any interruption, increasing the likelihood that they will return in the future.

Auto-scaling can also save you money by automatically reducing the number of instances running during periods of low traffic. This means that you only pay for the resources that you need, helping you to reduce your overall costs and increase your profitability.

Overall, auto-scaling is an essential feature for any business that wants to provide a seamless experience for their customers while also reducing costs and increasing profitability.

Example using AWS Auto Scaling:

1. Create an Amazon EC2 instance with your ChatGPT application deployed.
2. Configure an AWS Auto Scaling group to manage your instances.
3. Define scaling policies to adjust the number of instances based on the desired conditions, such as average CPU utilization or network traffic.

```
# Example CloudFormation template to create an Auto Scaling group
Resources:
  ChatGPTAutoScalingGroup:
    Type: AWS::AutoScaling::AutoScalingGroup
    Properties:
      AvailabilityZones:
        - us-east-1a
        - us-east-1b
      LaunchConfigurationName: !Ref ChatGPTLaunchConfiguration
      MinSize: 2
      MaxSize: 10
      DesiredCapacity: 4
      MetricsCollection:
        - Granularity: '1Minute'

  ChatGPTLaunchConfiguration:
    Type: AWS::AutoScaling::LaunchConfiguration
    Properties:
      InstanceType: t2.micro
      ImageId: ami-0123456789abcdef0 # Replace with your ChatGPT application's A
mazon Machine Image (AMI) ID
      SecurityGroups:
        - !Ref ChatGPTSecurityGroup

  ChatGPTScalingPolicy:
    Type: AWS::AutoScaling::ScalingPolicy
    Properties:
      AutoScalingGroupName: !Ref ChatGPTAutoScalingGroup
      PolicyType: TargetTrackingScaling
      TargetTrackingConfiguration:
        TargetValue: 50
        PredefinedMetricSpecification:
          PredefinedMetricType: ASGAverageCPUUtilization
```

This example shows a CloudFormation template that creates an Auto Scaling group with a defined scaling policy to maintain an average CPU utilization of 50%. Adjust the parameters as needed for your specific use case. With auto-scaling and efficient resource management, you can optimize performance and cost as your ChatGPT application scales.

8.5.4. Monitoring and Alerting

Monitoring the performance and health of your ChatGPT application is crucial to ensure reliability and high availability. Therefore, you must implement monitoring and alerting systems to proactively detect and respond to issues that may affect your application's performance, user experience, or availability.

One way to do this is by using performance metrics such as response time, throughput, and error rate. By monitoring these metrics, you can identify potential performance issues before they become critical and take corrective action.

Another approach is to implement health checks that periodically verify the availability and functionality of your application's components. These checks can be as simple as pinging your application's endpoints or as complex as running automated tests.

Additionally, you can use logs and traces to gain insight into your application's behavior and diagnose issues that may not be immediately visible through performance metrics or health checks. By analyzing your application's logs and traces, you can identify patterns and trends that may help you improve your application's performance and reliability.

To sum up, monitoring and alerting are critical components of any ChatGPT application. By implementing these systems and using various techniques such as performance metrics, health checks, and logs, you can proactively detect and respond to issues, ensure high availability, and provide a better user experience.

Example using Amazon CloudWatch:

1. Configure Amazon CloudWatch to monitor your ChatGPT application's metrics, such as CPU usage, memory consumption, latency, and error rates.
2. Create custom CloudWatch dashboards to visualize the collected metrics.
3. Set up CloudWatch alarms to trigger notifications or automated actions based on predefined thresholds.

```yaml
# Example CloudFormation template to create a CloudWatch alarm
Resources:
  ChatGPTCpuUtilizationAlarm:
    Type: AWS::CloudWatch::Alarm
    Properties:
      AlarmName: ChatGPT-CPU-Utilization
      AlarmDescription: "Trigger an alarm if the average CPU utilization exceeds
80% for 5 minutes"
      Namespace: AWS/EC2
      MetricName: CPUUtilization
      Dimensions:
        - Name: AutoScalingGroupName
          Value: !Ref ChatGPTAutoScalingGroup
      Statistic: Average
      Period: 300
      EvaluationPeriods: 1
      Threshold: 80
      ComparisonOperator: GreaterThanThreshold
      AlarmActions:
        - !Ref ChatGPTAlarmTopic

  ChatGPTAlarmTopic:
    Type: AWS::SNS::Topic
    Properties:
      DisplayName: ChatGPT-Alarm-Notification
      Subscription:
        - Protocol: email
          Endpoint: you@example.com # Replace with your email address
```

This example shows a CloudFormation template that creates a CloudWatch alarm to monitor the average CPU utilization of your ChatGPT application, triggering a notification via email if the utilization exceeds 80% for 5 minutes. You can customize the metrics, thresholds, and notification channels to suit your needs. By implementing monitoring and alerting systems, you can quickly identify and resolve issues, ensuring your ChatGPT application remains reliable and highly available.

Chapter 8 Conclusion

In conclusion, Chapter 8 discussed the various aspects of scaling and deploying ChatGPT solutions, ensuring that they are reliable, performant, and cost-effective. As AI applications become more sophisticated and widely adopted, it is crucial to address the practical aspects of deploying these solutions in real-world environments.

We began by exploring how ChatGPT can be integrated with web applications, focusing on front-end frameworks and libraries, back-end integration techniques, and APIs. We then moved on to building chatbots and virtual assistants, discussing various messenger platforms and integrations, voice assistants and text-to-speech integration, and support for multi-lingual chatbots.

Next, we addressed infrastructure and cost optimization by examining cloud-based deployment options, edge computing, on-premises solutions, and efficient model deployment strategies. It is essential to choose the appropriate infrastructure and deployment strategy to ensure that ChatGPT solutions are both cost-effective and performant.

Furthermore, we discussed the importance of performance monitoring and analytics. By evaluating user engagement and analyzing response quality, developers can fine-tune ChatGPT applications, ensuring that they meet users' needs and expectations. This continuous improvement process is essential for maintaining a high-quality user experience.

Lastly, we explored the critical aspects of ensuring reliability and high availability of ChatGPT solutions. By implementing load balancing and traffic management, backup and disaster recovery strategies, and monitoring and alerting systems, developers can create highly available applications that can scale to accommodate growing user demand and remain operational in the face of unexpected challenges.

In summary, this chapter provided a comprehensive overview of the practical aspects of scaling and deploying ChatGPT solutions. By leveraging the techniques and best practices discussed in this chapter, developers can build robust, scalable, and cost-effective AI applications that can serve a wide range of use cases and industries.

Chapter 9 - Staying Up-to-Date with ChatGPT Developments

In this chapter, we will discuss the importance of staying informed about the latest developments in the rapidly evolving field of AI, particularly as it pertains to ChatGPT and related technologies. As AI continues to advance, it is crucial for developers, researchers, and users to keep abreast of new research, tools, and best practices to ensure that they are leveraging the full potential of ChatGPT and contributing to the broader AI community.

One of the most important reasons for staying informed about the latest developments in AI is the potential for ChatGPT to be used in a variety of fields. For instance, in the medical field, ChatGPT can be used to assist doctors and nurses in diagnosing and treating patients. In the education field, ChatGPT can be used to help students learn more effectively and efficiently. In the business world, ChatGPT can be used to improve customer service, automate repetitive tasks, and even develop new products and services.

Moreover, staying informed about the latest AI developments is not only important for leveraging the full potential of ChatGPT, but also for contributing to the broader AI community. By staying up-to-date with the latest research, tools, and best practices, developers, researchers, and users can help advance the field of AI as a whole. This can lead to new breakthroughs, better tools and methodologies, and ultimately, greater benefits for society as a whole.

9.1. OpenAI Community and Resources

One of the best ways to stay up-to-date with ChatGPT developments is to engage with the OpenAI community and utilize the wealth of resources they provide. By being an active member of the OpenAI community, you can stay informed about the latest advancements in machine learning, artificial intelligence, and natural language processing. OpenAI's community includes researchers, engineers, and AI enthusiasts who contribute to the development of cutting-edge AI models, such as GPT-4, and share their findings, tools, and techniques with the broader AI

community. This not only allows you to stay up-to-date with the latest developments but also to learn about the process of developing advanced AI models and the challenges that come with it.

In addition to the OpenAI community, there are various other resources provided by the broader AI community that can help you stay informed about the latest advancements in ChatGPT. These resources include AI conferences, research papers, and online forums. Attending conferences and reading research papers can provide you with valuable insights into the latest advancements in AI, while online forums can allow you to connect with other AI enthusiasts and exchange ideas and knowledge.

By utilizing these resources, you can not only stay informed about the latest advancements in ChatGPT but also deepen your knowledge and understanding of AI as a whole. This can help you develop new ideas and techniques for building advanced AI models and contribute to the growth of the AI community as a whole.

9.1.1. OpenAI Website and Blog

The OpenAI organization is a leading contributor to the field of artificial intelligence, constantly publishing research on the latest AI models, techniques, and applications. The organization has a website, https://www.openai.com, where users can access all the latest information about OpenAI's research, products, and tools. Additionally, OpenAI maintains a blog, https://www.openai.com/blog, which features articles and research papers covering a wide range of topics related to artificial intelligence.

One of the most popular topics covered on the OpenAI blog is ChatGPT, an innovative application of artificial intelligence that has revolutionized the way we interact with computers. ChatGPT is constantly being updated and improved, with new advancements being made every day. By regularly following the OpenAI blog, you can stay up to date on all the latest developments in ChatGPT and other AI applications.

To its research and development efforts, OpenAI is also committed to promoting the ethical and responsible use of AI technology. Through its various initiatives and collaborations with other organizations, OpenAI is working to ensure that AI is used in a way that benefits society as a whole. By supporting OpenAI and staying informed about its activities, you can help shape the future of AI and ensure that it is used in a responsible and ethical manner.

9.1.2. GitHub Repositories

OpenAI is a company that specializes in artificial intelligence and machine learning. In order to share their work with the public, they maintain several GitHub repositories that contain code, pre-trained models, and other resources. One of their most popular repositories is the official ChatGPT repository (**https://github.com/openai/ChatGPT**), which houses the latest versions of the ChatGPT code, pre-trained models, and documentation.

By following the repository, you can stay up-to-date with the latest developments in the field of artificial intelligence. The updates, bug fixes, and new features that are implemented in the repository can be a valuable resource for researchers and developers who are working on similar projects. Additionally, contributing to the development of the project can be a great way to gain experience and build your portfolio.

Overall, OpenAI's GitHub repositories are a valuable resource for anyone interested in artificial intelligence and machine learning. They provide access to cutting-edge technology and the latest research in the field, and offer opportunities for collaboration and learning. So if you're looking to stay informed and get involved in the exciting world of AI, be sure to check out OpenAI's GitHub repositories today!

9.1.3. Research Papers and Publications

OpenAI has a rich history of conducting and publishing research on a wide range of AI topics. One such topic is language models, where they have made significant contributions through the creation of GPT-4. Their research papers are not only informative but also a valuable resource that can help one gain a deeper understanding of the underlying technologies used in AI.

The papers are written in a language that is accessible to both experts and non-experts alike, making it easy to follow. Readers can also stay informed about the latest advancements in AI research by regularly checking out OpenAI's website. Besides the website, these research papers can also be found in academic journals and conferences. In summary, OpenAI's research papers offer a wealth of knowledge and can provide readers with valuable insights into the world of AI research.

9.1.4. Online Forums and Social Media

Participating in online forums and following relevant social media accounts can help you stay connected with the AI community and learn about new developments in ChatGPT. Some popular forums include the OpenAI Community (**https://community.openai.com**), the Machine Learning subreddit (**https://www.reddit.com/r/MachineLearning**), and the AI Stack

Exchange (**https://ai.stackexchange.com**). Additionally, following OpenAI's official Twitter account (**https://twitter.com/OpenAI**) and other AI-related accounts can help you stay informed about the latest news and research in the field.

9.1.5. Workshops, Conferences, and Meetups

Attending AI workshops, conferences, and meetups can provide valuable opportunities to learn about the latest advancements in ChatGPT and other AI technologies. These events often feature presentations and discussions by leading researchers and practitioners in the field, allowing you to gain insights into new research and applications, as well as network with other AI enthusiasts. Some notable AI conferences include NeurIPS, ICML, and ACL, among others. You can also look for local AI meetups and workshops in your area to connect with like-minded individuals and share your experiences with ChatGPT.

In addition to the resources mentioned above, there are several other ways to stay informed about the latest developments in ChatGPT and related AI technologies. One way is to actively participate in online forums and communities dedicated to AI, where you can interact with other professionals and enthusiasts and exchange ideas and knowledge. You can also follow AI blogs and news websites to get regular updates on the latest research, tools, and best practices in the field.

Another way to expand your knowledge and skills in ChatGPT and AI is to take online courses and tutorials. Many online learning platforms offer courses on a wide range of AI topics, including natural language processing, machine learning, and deep learning. By taking these courses, you can gain a deeper understanding of the underlying principles and techniques of ChatGPT and other AI technologies, and learn how to apply them to your own projects and applications.

Finally, consider joining AI-focused professional organizations and associations, which can provide access to exclusive resources, events, and networking opportunities. These organizations often have local chapters and special interest groups, which can help you connect with other professionals in your area and stay up-to-date on the latest trends and developments in ChatGPT and AI.

By engaging with the OpenAI community and leveraging these resources, you can stay informed about the latest advancements in ChatGPT and related AI technologies. This will enable you to make the most of ChatGPT in your applications and contribute to the broader AI community.

In summary, staying informed about ChatGPT developments is essential for developers, researchers, and users to ensure that they are leveraging the full potential of ChatGPT and contributing to the AI community. By engaging with the OpenAI community, utilizing the wealth

of resources available, and participating in events and online discussions, you can remain at the forefront of AI advancements and ensure that you are making the most of ChatGPT in your applications.

9.2. AI Research and Improvements

The field of artificial intelligence, particularly natural language processing, is advancing at a breakneck pace. This rapid evolution of technology has led to a significant increase in the number of applications of AI, and ChatGPT is one such application that is poised to revolutionize the way we interact with machines. In order to keep up with the latest advancements in AI, it is essential to stay up to date with the latest research and developments in this field.

There are various ways to stay informed about the ongoing developments in AI research. One way is to attend conferences and seminars related to AI and natural language processing. These events provide an opportunity to engage with experts in the field and learn about the latest research and developments.

Another way to stay informed is to read academic journals and publications related to AI. These publications provide in-depth analysis and discussion of the latest research and advancements in the field. There are many online resources available that provide regular updates on the latest developments in AI, including blogs, podcasts, and newsletters.

It is also important to stay connected with the broader AI community. Social media platforms such as Twitter and LinkedIn offer opportunities to connect with other researchers and practitioners in the field, and to share knowledge and insights.

Staying informed about the ongoing developments in AI research is essential for anyone interested in the field of natural language processing. By attending conferences and seminars, reading academic publications, and staying connected with the broader AI community, it is possible to stay up to date with the latest advancements in this rapidly evolving field.

9.2.1. Academic Journals and Conferences

One of the most effective ways to stay informed about the latest AI research is by following academic journals and conferences. These publications and events often feature cutting-edge research, including new techniques, algorithms, and applications relevant to ChatGPT.

In addition to academic journals and conferences, there are other resources that can help you stay up-to-date on AI research. Online forums, such as Reddit's AI subreddit and the AI section of Stack Exchange, can be great places to discuss the latest developments and ask questions.

Following blogs and social media accounts of prominent AI researchers and research institutions can also provide valuable insights into the latest trends and breakthroughs in the field.

Furthermore, attending AI-related events and meetups can be an excellent way to network with other professionals in the field and learn about the latest research and trends. Many cities have local AI meetups and groups that hold regular events and talks.

While following academic journals and conferences is a great way to stay informed about AI research, there are many other resources available to help you stay on top of the latest developments. By taking advantage of these resources, you can stay ahead of the curve and make sure that your knowledge and skills in the field of AI are always up-to-date.

Some notable conferences and journals in the field of AI and NLP include:

- Association for Computational Linguistics (ACL)
- Conference on Neural Information Processing Systems (NeurIPS)
- International Conference on Learning Representations (ICLR)
- Conference on Empirical Methods in Natural Language Processing (EMNLP)

By regularly attending conferences and reading articles from these sources, you can stay up-to-date with the most recent advancements in AI research.

9.2.2. Preprint Servers and Repositories

Preprint servers and repositories such as arXiv and OpenReview are excellent resources for finding the latest AI research papers before they are published in journals or presented at conferences.

By following the relevant categories on these platforms, you can access new research findings and methodologies as they emerge. This can be especially beneficial for researchers who want to stay up-to-date with the most recent advancements in the field. You can also use these resources to discover emerging trends and topics, helping you to identify potential areas for future research or collaboration.

Preprint servers and repositories provide a platform for researchers to share their work with a wider audience, facilitating the dissemination of knowledge and potentially leading to new collaborations and insights. By leveraging these resources effectively, researchers can stay on the cutting edge of AI research and contribute to the ongoing development of the field.

9.2.3. Online AI Communities and Blogs

Various online AI communities and blogs provide valuable insights, discussions, and summaries of the latest research. These platforms can be accessed from various devices like smartphones, laptops, and tablets, making it easy to stay up-to-date on the latest trends and advances in the field.

By engaging with other professionals on these platforms, individuals can gain a deeper understanding of complex concepts and get feedback on their own insights and ideas. Moreover, these platforms can also serve as a source of inspiration for those who are just starting out in the field, as they offer a vast repository of knowledge and expertise that can be tapped into at any time.

Examples of such resources include:

- The Gradient: An online publication that covers the latest AI research, news, and opinions.
- AI Alignment: A blog focused on AI safety, ethics, and alignment.
- Distill: An online journal that provides clear and interactive explanations of machine learning concepts.

9.2.4. Follow Researchers and Organizations on Social Media

One effective way to stay informed about the latest developments in the field of AI and ChatGPT is to actively follow prominent AI researchers, organizations, and research labs on social media platforms such as Twitter and LinkedIn. In doing so, you can gain access to a wealth of information that is constantly updated and readily available at your fingertips.

Not only can you stay up-to-date on new research and projects, but following these individuals and organizations can also help you gain insights into the inner workings of the AI community itself. By observing the discussions and debates that take place online, you can gain a deeper understanding of the current challenges facing the field and the potential directions it may take in the future.

Moreover, following prominent AI researchers, organizations, and research labs on social media platforms can also help you identify opportunities for collaboration and networking. It can be a great way to connect with like-minded individuals who share your passion for AI and ChatGPT, and potentially even form partnerships to work on exciting new projects together.

In short, actively following individuals and organizations involved in AI and ChatGPT on social media platforms is an excellent way to stay informed, gain insights, and identify opportunities for collaboration and networking.

In conclusion, staying up-to-date with AI research and improvements is crucial for developers, researchers, and users working with ChatGPT. By following academic journals, conferences, preprint servers, online communities, blogs, and social media, you can ensure that you are well-informed about the latest advancements in the field and can effectively incorporate new findings and techniques into your ChatGPT applications.

9.3. Industry Trends and Future Directions

It is important to keep abreast of the latest developments and future directions in the field of artificial intelligence and natural language processing to ensure that your ChatGPT applications continue to be effective and relevant. In this section, we will explore some of the key trends and potential future developments in the AI industry that may have a significant impact on ChatGPT and its applications.

One of the most significant trends in the field of AI is the increasing use of machine learning algorithms to analyze and interpret large amounts of data. This has led to the development of more advanced natural language processing (NLP) techniques that can be used to analyze and understand human language more accurately. As a result, ChatGPT applications are becoming more sophisticated and capable of handling more complex queries.

Another important trend in the AI industry is the increasing focus on explainable AI. This refers to the ability of AI systems to explain their decision-making processes and provide clear explanations for their actions. This is particularly important for ChatGPT applications, which need to be able to explain their responses to users in order to build trust and credibility.

Looking to the future, there are a number of potential developments that could have a significant impact on ChatGPT and its applications. One of the most exciting of these is the development of quantum computing, which has the potential to greatly enhance the speed and accuracy of AI systems. Additionally, the development of advanced neural networks and deep learning techniques is likely to continue, further enhancing the capabilities of ChatGPT applications and other AI systems.

9.3.1. Improved Pretraining and Fine-tuning Techniques

As AI research continues to evolve, it is highly anticipated that we will witness significant advancements in pretraining and fine-tuning techniques for language models such as ChatGPT.

With these advancements, we can expect to see a variety of benefits including more efficient training processes, enhanced generalization capabilities, and improved performance across a range of tasks.

Staying up-to-date with the latest research in this field can help ensure that your ChatGPT applications are making use of the most advanced training techniques available, ultimately resulting in more effective and impactful results.

9.3.2. More Efficient and Environmentally Friendly Models

There is an increasing worry among researchers and environmentalists alike about the environmental impact and resource consumption of large-scale language models. The energy consumption and carbon footprint of these models are significant, and there is a pressing need to address these issues.

To this end, researchers are working on developing models that are more efficient and sustainable. This involves exploring new approaches to the architecture and design of language models, as well as investigating alternative sources of energy and materials. By reducing energy requirements and carbon emissions, these efforts may lead to the development of more environmentally friendly language models.

In turn, this may make ChatGPT applications more sustainable in the long run, providing a more reliable and ethical option for businesses and individuals alike.

9.3.3. Enhanced Multimodal Integration

Multimodal integration, the process of combining information from multiple modalities such as text, images, and audio, is an exciting area of research in the field of artificial intelligence. This approach holds great promise for the development of language models like ChatGPT, which could potentially revolutionize the way we interact with technology.

By integrating information from multiple modalities, AI systems can gain a more comprehensive understanding of the world around them, allowing them to better interpret and generate content. For example, multimodal models could be used to create more engaging and interactive applications, such as virtual assistants that can understand and respond to voice commands, or educational tools that incorporate text, images, and audio to help students learn more effectively.

Despite the potential benefits of multimodal integration, there are still many challenges that must be overcome. For example, developing effective algorithms for combining information

from different modalities is a complex task that requires expertise in multiple disciplines. Additionally, there are still many unanswered questions about how humans integrate information from different modalities, which makes it difficult to design AI systems that can truly mimic human intelligence.

Despite these challenges, research in multimodal integration is moving forward at a rapid pace, and it is likely that we will see many exciting developments in this area in the coming years. As AI systems become more sophisticated and capable of integrating information from multiple modalities, we may see entirely new types of applications that we can't even imagine yet.

9.3.4. AI Safety and Ethics

As AI systems become more advanced and pervasive, it is imperative that we prioritize safety and ethical considerations. One way to do this is through increased research on AI safety, including its implications on society and potential unintended consequences.

We must work to mitigate any biases that may be present in the development process, as this could have serious implications on how the technology is implemented and received. Furthermore, it is important to emphasize responsible usage of AI, particularly in regards to user privacy and consent.

By fostering an environment of responsible and thoughtful development, we can ensure that ChatGPT applications are not only effective but also respectful of users and their needs.

9.3.5. AI Explainability and Interpretability

Understanding the reasoning behind AI-generated outputs and being able to explain their behavior is essential for building trust in AI systems. While AI has enabled us to make significant progress in various fields, people are often wary of the decisions made by AI models.

This is where research in AI explainability and interpretability comes into play. By developing techniques that enable users to better understand the decisions made by AI models like ChatGPT, we can build a more trustworthy and transparent AI system.

Moreover, this research can also help improve the performance of AI models and ensure that they are accountable to users. By following these developments, you can ensure your ChatGPT applications are transparent, reliable, and accountable to users.

In conclusion, keeping track of industry trends and future directions in AI and natural language processing is essential for staying competitive and ensuring the success of your ChatGPT

applications. By monitoring advancements in pretraining and fine-tuning techniques, model efficiency, multimodal integration, AI safety and ethics, and AI explainability, you can stay at the forefront of AI development and create more effective, reliable, and user-friendly ChatGPT applications.

Chapter 9 Conclusion

In conclusion, staying up-to-date with the latest developments in the ChatGPT and AI research field is critical for ensuring the success and relevance of your applications. This chapter has provided an overview of several key areas to watch, including OpenAI community resources, research advancements, and industry trends that may shape the future of ChatGPT and its applications.

We discussed the importance of engaging with the OpenAI community and leveraging available resources such as research papers, blog posts, and forums to stay informed about the latest findings and best practices in AI research. By doing so, you can ensure that you remain at the cutting edge of AI developments, which will have a direct impact on the effectiveness and capabilities of your ChatGPT applications.

We also highlighted the significance of monitoring advancements in AI research, especially in areas such as pretraining and fine-tuning techniques, model efficiency, multimodal integration, AI safety and ethics, and AI explainability. By keeping track of these developments, you can adapt your ChatGPT applications to take advantage of new techniques and technologies, ensuring that your applications remain relevant and competitive.

Finally, we discussed some of the key industry trends and future directions in AI and natural language processing that may influence ChatGPT and its applications. By staying informed about these trends, you can anticipate shifts in the AI landscape and proactively update your ChatGPT applications to stay ahead of the curve.

In summary, maintaining a deep understanding of the AI research landscape and staying informed about the latest developments in ChatGPT technology is essential for building successful and effective applications. By staying engaged with the OpenAI community, monitoring AI research advancements, and keeping an eye on industry trends, you can ensure that your ChatGPT applications continue to deliver value and remain at the forefront of AI-driven innovation.

Chapter 10 - Conclusion, summary and keep Learning

In this final chapter, we will provide a more in-depth analysis of ChatGPT and its applications. We will start by summarizing the key takeaways, insights, and best practices that we have covered throughout this guide, but we will also expand on these topics by examining more advanced techniques and strategies. By exploring these advanced techniques, you will be better equipped to leverage ChatGPT effectively in various applications, ensuring that you are making the most of its capabilities.

One important technique that we will cover is the use of transfer learning, which allows ChatGPT to learn from a diverse range of data sources and apply this knowledge to new applications. We will also explore the use of pre-training and fine-tuning, which can further enhance ChatGPT's performance and accuracy.

Another area that we will delve into is the ethical considerations surrounding the use of ChatGPT. As with any AI technology, it is crucial to be aware of potential biases and ensure that ChatGPT is being used in an ethical and responsible manner.

Overall, this chapter aims to provide a more comprehensive understanding of ChatGPT and its potential applications. By expanding on the key takeaways and exploring more advanced techniques, you will be better equipped to leverage this powerful tool in various contexts.

10.1. Key Takeaways

Throughout this guide, we have extensively explored several important aspects of working with ChatGPT. We have covered the fundamental building blocks of ChatGPT's underlying architecture, including its neural network-based models, training mechanisms, and natural language processing capabilities.

We have also discussed the practical applications of ChatGPT in various domains, such as customer service, content generation, and language translation. In addition, we have examined various deployment strategies for ChatGPT, ranging from cloud-based solutions to on-premise installations, and have provided recommendations for selecting the optimal approach based on specific use cases.

Overall, this guide offers a comprehensive overview of working with ChatGPT, providing readers with the knowledge and insights necessary to effectively leverage this powerful tool in their own projects and applications.

Below are some of the key takeaways from our exploration:

1. ChatGPT is built on the powerful GPT architecture and benefits from its strengths in natural language understanding and generation, making it suitable for a wide range of applications, from chatbots to content generation and more.
2. Fine-tuning is essential for adapting the pre-trained ChatGPT model to specific tasks and domains, ensuring that the model can deliver high-quality and relevant responses.
3. Effective model evaluation and testing are crucial for determining the performance of your ChatGPT applications, and using a combination of quantitative and qualitative evaluation techniques can help you identify areas for improvement.
4. Customizing tokenizers and vocabulary, as well as employing advanced fine-tuning techniques such as curriculum learning and few-shot learning, can further enhance the performance of your ChatGPT applications.
5. Adapting ChatGPT for specific industries requires understanding the unique challenges and requirements of each domain, from healthcare and legal compliance to gaming and interactive storytelling.
6. Ensuring responsible AI usage is critical when working with ChatGPT, which includes mitigating biases, addressing privacy and security concerns, adhering to ethical guidelines, obtaining user consent, and establishing AI governance and accountability frameworks.
7. Scaling and deploying ChatGPT solutions involve integrating with web applications, building chatbots and virtual assistants, optimizing infrastructure and costs, monitoring performance and analytics, and ensuring reliability and high availability.
8. Staying up-to-date with ChatGPT developments and AI research is essential for maintaining the effectiveness of your applications and remaining at the forefront of AI-driven innovation.

By keeping these key takeaways in mind, you will be well-prepared to tackle the challenges of building and deploying effective ChatGPT applications across a wide range of domains and use cases. It is important to note that building and deploying these applications requires significant

technical expertise and an in-depth understanding of the underlying technologies and methodologies.

It is crucial to stay up-to-date with the latest trends and developments in the field in order to ensure that your applications remain competitive and effective. This can involve attending industry conferences, participating in online communities, and engaging with thought leaders in the space.

Finally, it is important to remember that effective ChatGPT applications are not just about the technology - they also require a deep understanding of human behavior, language, and communication. By combining technical expertise with a human-centered approach, you can create truly effective and impactful applications that meet the needs of users across a wide range of domains and use cases.

10.2. Expanding Your ChatGPT Knowledge

Building on the key takeaways from this guide, it's important to continue expanding your knowledge about ChatGPT and related AI technologies. By staying informed about the latest advancements, best practices, and emerging tools, you can better adapt to the fast-paced evolution of AI and ensure that your applications remain effective and competitive.

One way to expand your knowledge is by attending industry conferences and events. These gatherings are a great opportunity to learn from experts in the field, network with other professionals, and stay up-to-date on the latest trends and developments.

Another method for expanding your knowledge is through self-study. There are numerous online courses, tutorials, and resources available that can help you deepen your understanding of AI and ChatGPT specifically. Additionally, reading books and articles written by thought leaders in the industry can provide valuable insights and perspectives.

It's also important to collaborate with other professionals who are working with AI and ChatGPT. By sharing ideas, experiences, and best practices, you can gain a broader understanding of the technology and its potential applications.

It's important to experiment with AI tools and technologies yourself. By testing out different tools and approaches, you can gain hands-on experience and a deeper understanding of how ChatGPT and other AI technologies work. This can help you identify new opportunities and strategies for using AI to improve your business or projects.

Here are some suggestions for further expanding your ChatGPT knowledge:

1. **Cuantum Technologies Books:** At Cuantum, we constantly strive to stay up-to-date with the most recent advancements in the field of programming, AI, and other new technologies. By keeping abreast of the latest developments, we are better equipped to provide our clients with the cutting-edge solutions that they require.

   In order to ensure that we stay ahead of the curve, we have built a comprehensive library of books that cover a broad range of topics related to these fields. These books are designed to be easy to read and understand, even for those who are new to the subject matter.

   By visiting https://books.cuantum.tech, you can gain access to our complete library of books. Whether you are a seasoned professional or a newcomer to the world of programming and AI, you are sure to find something of interest in our collection. So why not take a look today and see what you can discover?

2. **Follow AI research publications:** In order to keep up-to-date with the latest developments in AI, it is essential to follow the progress of the top research conferences, journals, and websites. You can do this by keeping an eye on reputable sources such as NeurIPS, ICLR, ACL, and arXiv.org. These sources will provide you with invaluable insights into the latest research in NLP, GPT, and other AI-related fields. Staying up-to-date with the latest research is crucial for any AI professional, as it helps you to identify new trends and technologies, and to stay ahead of the curve. By following these sources, you can ensure that you are always at the forefront of the latest developments in the field of AI.

3. **Engage with online communities**: One great way to get involved in the world of AI and ChatGPT is to participate in online forums, discussion boards, and social media groups. There are many platforms available for this, such as Reddit, Stack Overflow, and GitHub. By actively engaging with these communities, you can share ideas, learn from others, and stay up-to-date with the latest trends in the field. You may even have the opportunity to collaborate with other professionals or showcase your own work. Ultimately, being an active member of online communities can help you build a stronger network and deepen your knowledge and skills in AI and ChatGPT.

4. **Explore OpenAI's resources**: In order to keep up with the latest developments in ChatGPT and other AI technologies, we suggest that you take advantage of OpenAI's many resources. OpenAI regularly publishes research papers, blog posts, and updates on its website, and also offers a newsletter that you can subscribe to in order to stay on top of the latest news and trends. By staying informed about the latest research and trends in AI, you can gain a deeper understanding of the field and improve your own knowledge and skills.

5. **Attend AI conferences and workshops**: In order to stay up-to-date with the latest trends and advancements in the field of AI, it is highly recommended to attend AI

conferences, workshops, and meetups. These events offer a great opportunity to learn from experts and thought leaders in the industry, as well as to share your own knowledge and experiences with others who are passionate about AI. Whether you choose to attend these events in person or virtually, you can be sure to gain invaluable insights and make important connections that can help you advance your ChatGPT applications and take your career to the next level.

6. **Take online courses, attend webinars, and join online communities**: Expand your AI and ChatGPT knowledge by enrolling in online courses or attending webinars. These are great ways to learn about the latest advancements in the field and to connect with other professionals in the industry. Many universities and organizations offer AI-related courses, and platforms like Coursera, edX, and Udacity provide a wide range of learning opportunities. Additionally, joining online communities like Reddit and LinkedIn can be a valuable resource for staying up-to-date on the latest trends and for networking with other professionals. You can also participate in online forums and groups to ask questions, share your own knowledge, and learn from others.

7. **Experiment with open-source AI tools and libraries**: Hands-on experience is invaluable for deepening your understanding of ChatGPT and related technologies. One possible way to gain such experience is by exploring open-source AI tools and libraries, such as Hugging Face's Transformers, TensorFlow, and PyTorch, and working on personal projects to build your skills and knowledge.

For instance, you could try using Hugging Face's Transformers to fine-tune a pre-trained model on a specific task, such as sentiment analysis or question answering. This would give you a chance to see how the model behaves in practice and to experiment with different hyperparameters and training settings.

Alternatively, you could use TensorFlow or PyTorch to implement a custom deep learning model from scratch and train it on a relevant dataset. This would require a deeper understanding of the underlying concepts and techniques, as well as some programming skills. However, it would also allow you to tailor the model to your specific needs and to explore different architectures and algorithms.

In addition, you could contribute to existing open-source projects by fixing bugs, adding features, or improving documentation. This would give you exposure to real-world software development practices and collaboration workflows, as well as a chance to get feedback from other developers and users.

Overall, experimenting with open-source AI tools and libraries is a great way to learn more about ChatGPT and related technologies, and to develop your skills and expertise in this exciting field.

By actively engaging in these activities and resources, such as attending ChatGPT conferences and workshops, participating in online forums and discussions, and reading relevant articles and books, you can continue to expand your ChatGPT knowledge and stay ahead of the curve in the rapidly evolving world of AI.

This will not only benefit you personally, but also enable you to create more effective, innovative, and responsible AI applications for your projects and organizations. By being well-versed in the latest developments and best practices in the field, you can maximize the potential benefits of ChatGPT and contribute to the advancement of the AI industry as a whole.

10.3. Pursuing Further Opportunities in AI

As the field of AI continues to grow and evolve at an unprecedented pace, the demand for professionals and enthusiasts with a deeper understanding of AI has also increased significantly. With the rapid advancements in technology, it's essential for individuals to stay informed and proactive in learning about new developments, tools, and techniques to remain competitive in this ever-changing landscape.

One way to stay up-to-date with the latest trends and advancements in AI is by attending conferences, workshops, and seminars. These events provide a platform for individuals to network with like-minded professionals, engage in discussions and debates on the latest trends, and learn about the latest tools and techniques from industry experts.

Another way to enhance one's knowledge and skills in AI is by enrolling in online courses and degree programs. Several universities and online learning platforms offer comprehensive courses and degree programs in AI, ranging from introductory courses to advanced degree programs. These courses provide individuals with the opportunity to gain a deeper understanding of AI concepts and applications, and equip them with the necessary skills to pursue a career in this field.

In addition to attending conferences and enrolling in courses, individuals can also stay informed about the latest developments in AI by reading research papers and articles published in leading academic and industry publications. This not only enhances one's knowledge but also provides insights into the latest trends and applications of AI.

Overall, with the exponential growth of AI, staying informed and proactive in learning about the latest developments, tools, and techniques is essential for professionals and enthusiasts to remain competitive and pursue new opportunities in this exciting field.

Here are some suggestions for pursuing further opportunities in AI:

1. **Collaborate on open-source projects**: Contributing to open-source AI projects can be a great way to gain practical experience and build a strong portfolio. By joining or contributing to such projects, you can learn from others and improve your skills while also making valuable contributions to the community. Collaborating with other developers on open-source projects can help you build your professional network and establish connections that may lead to future opportunities. Platforms like GitHub and GitLab host numerous open-source AI projects that you can explore and engage with. So why not take advantage of this opportunity to enhance your skills and make a positive impact on the world of AI?

2. **Start your own AI project**: Identifying a problem or opportunity where AI can make a difference is the first step in starting your own AI project. You can then brainstorm and research different approaches and techniques to address the problem or opportunity. Developing an AI project can be a great way to refine your skills, experiment with new ideas, and demonstrate your expertise to potential employers or clients. Working on your own project allows you to gain experience in managing and executing a project from start to finish, which can be valuable in any field. Remember, starting small and building up your project over time can be a great way to ensure success and avoid feeling overwhelmed. So go ahead, take the leap and start your own AI project today!

3. **Join AI competitions and hackathons**: Participating in AI competitions is a great way to test your skills and learn from others. In addition to the opportunity to win prizes, these events provide a platform for networking and showcasing your abilities to a wider audience. You can participate in popular contests such as Kaggle, as well as other hackathons that focus on AI-related projects. These events are a great way to meet like-minded individuals, collaborate with others in the field, and gain valuable experience. By participating in these competitions, you can also stay up to date with the latest trends and technologies in the field of AI, which will help you to further develop your skills and knowledge.

4. **Network with AI professionals**: To further expand your reach and connect with more AI professionals, consider attending industry events such as conferences and seminars. You can also join online communities and forums dedicated to AI where you can participate in discussions and share ideas. Consider reaching out to professionals in your field through LinkedIn and Twitter to establish new connections and exchange information. By building a strong network and engaging with others in the field, you can stay up-to-date on the latest industry trends and gain valuable insights that can help you advance your career.

5. **Consider advanced education**: There are many benefits to pursuing advanced degrees or certifications in AI, machine learning, or related fields. Not only can it deepen your knowledge and credibility, but it can also open up new career opportunities and increase your earning potential.

   Many universities and institutions offer specialized programs that can help you gain a strong foundation and develop expertise in specific areas. By enrolling in these

programs, you'll have the chance to learn from experienced professionals and collaborate with like-minded individuals. Additionally, you may have the opportunity to participate in research projects or internships, which can provide valuable hands-on experience.

Overall, pursuing advanced education in AI and related fields can be a great way to stay current with the latest trends and advancements in the industry, as well as set yourself apart from other professionals in the field.

6. **Explore AI job opportunities**: As AI becomes more ubiquitous in various industries, the demand for professionals with AI expertise continues to increase. This means that there are now more job opportunities in the field of AI than ever before. Some of the most in-demand roles include AI researcher, data scientist, machine learning engineer, and AI product manager.

    To take advantage of this growing trend, it's important to have a solid understanding of the skills and qualifications that are necessary for each of these roles. For instance, AI researchers typically need to have a strong background in mathematics and computer science, while data scientists should have expertise in statistics and data analysis.

    In addition to having the right skills and qualifications, it's also important to have a strong online presence that showcases your work and highlights your achievements. This can include building a strong portfolio of AI-related projects, contributing to open source projects, and participating in online communities and forums related to AI.

    Once you have these key ingredients in place, it's time to start exploring job opportunities that align with your interests and skills. This may involve researching companies that are working on AI-related projects, attending job fairs and industry conferences, and networking with other professionals in the field.

    By taking these steps, you can position yourself as a strong candidate for AI job opportunities and increase your chances of landing the role that's right for you.

7. **Stay informed about AI policies and regulations**: In order to develop AI in a responsible manner, it is important to stay up-to-date with the latest policies, regulations, and ethical guidelines related to AI. By doing so, you can ensure that your work adheres to industry standards and best practices, and you can help to mitigate the potential risks associated with AI. Additionally, staying informed about AI-related policies can help you navigate the complex landscape of AI applications, which can be especially challenging given the rapid pace of technological advancement in this field.

Whether you are working on developing AI algorithms, designing AI systems, or implementing AI solutions in your organization, staying informed about AI policies and regulations is essential for success.

By taking advantage of these opportunities, you can not only advance your career, but also acquire new skills and knowledge that will make you a valuable asset to any organization. Furthermore, staying proactive in your AI education can help you stay up-to-date with the latest developments and trends in the field.

This will enable you to create innovative AI solutions that can address some of the most pressing challenges facing society today, such as climate change, healthcare, and transportation. Additionally, your contributions to the broader AI community can help foster collaboration and knowledge-sharing among professionals, leading to even more breakthroughs and advancements in the field.

As AI continues to reshape industries and societies, the potential for growth and impact in this field is virtually limitless, and by continuously expanding your expertise and network, you can position yourself at the forefront of this exciting and rapidly evolving field.

Chapter 10 Conclusion

In conclusion, this book has provided an extensive overview of ChatGPT, its applications, and the various considerations to keep in mind when using and deploying this powerful AI technology. As we've discussed throughout the chapters, ChatGPT has the potential to revolutionize various industries, from healthcare and finance to education and entertainment. By understanding the underlying principles, techniques, and best practices, you are now well-equipped to leverage ChatGPT in your own projects and create innovative, impactful solutions.

The key takeaways from this book include understanding the foundations of GPT-based models, learning how to fine-tune and adapt ChatGPT for specific tasks and industries, ensuring responsible AI usage, and scaling and deploying ChatGPT solutions effectively. Furthermore, we have covered essential topics such as mitigating biases, maintaining privacy and security, promoting ethical AI development, and ensuring fairness and inclusivity.

As the field of AI continues to grow and evolve, it is crucial to stay up-to-date with new developments, tools, and techniques. This book has provided you with the knowledge and resources to further your ChatGPT expertise, but it is essential to remain proactive in learning and exploring new opportunities in AI. By engaging with the AI community, participating in

competitions and hackathons, pursuing advanced education, and networking with other professionals, you can continue to grow your skills and contribute to the field's progress.

Finally, it is important to remember that as AI practitioners, we have a responsibility to ensure that AI technologies like ChatGPT are developed and deployed ethically, transparently, and inclusively. By adhering to ethical guidelines, considering the implications of our work, and striving for fairness and accessibility, we can ensure that AI technologies serve diverse populations and contribute positively to the well-being of individuals and societies alike.

In closing, we hope this book has provided you with the knowledge and inspiration to harness the power of ChatGPT and embark on your own AI journey. The future of AI is full of opportunities, challenges, and innovations, and your skills and expertise will play a crucial role in shaping this rapidly evolving landscape.

Once again, we at Cuantum Technologies would like to thank you for choosing this book as your guide to ChatGPT. It has been a pleasure to support you on this exciting journey, and we hope that the knowledge and insights shared have been invaluable in your pursuit of AI excellence.

As you continue to explore the world of AI, we encourage you to stay connected with us and explore our other offerings at **https://books.cuantum.tech**. Our ever-growing library of titles covers a wide range of AI topics and technologies, designed to empower you to stay at the forefront of this rapidly evolving field.

We look forward to accompanying you on your future AI adventures and being a part of your ongoing learning journey. Remember, the world of AI is vast and full of potential, and we are here to support you every step of the way. So, until we meet again in the pages of our next book or through our online resources, we wish you the best of luck in all your AI endeavors. See you soon!

Best regards, The Cuantum Technologies Team.

Where to continue?

If you've completed this book, and are hungry for more programming knowledge, we'd like to recommend some other books from our software company that you might find useful. These books cover a wide range of topics and are designed to help you continue to expand your programming skills.

1. "**Master Web Development with Django**" - This book is a comprehensive guide to building web applications using Django, one of the most popular Python web frameworks. It covers everything from setting up your development environment to deploying your application to a production server.
2. "**Mastering React**" - React is a popular JavaScript library for building user interfaces. This book will help you master the core concepts of React and show you how to build powerful, dynamic web applications.
3. "**Data Analysis with Python**" - Python is a powerful language for data analysis, and this book will help you unlock its full potential. It covers topics such as data cleaning, data manipulation, and data visualization, and provides you with practical exercises to help you apply what you've learned.
4. "**Machine Learning with Python**" - Machine learning is one of the most exciting fields in computer science, and this book will help you get started with building your own machine learning models using Python. It covers topics such as linear regression, logistic regression, and decision trees.
5. "**Mastering ChatGPT and Prompt Engineering**" - In this book, we will take you on a comprehensive journey through the world of prompt engineering, covering everything from the fundamentals of AI language models to advanced strategies and real-world applications.

All of these books are designed to help you continue to expand your programming skills and deepen your understanding of the Python language. We believe that programming is a skill that can be learned and developed over time, and we are committed to providing resources to help you achieve your goals.

We'd also like to take this opportunity to thank you for choosing our software company as your guide in your programming journey. We hope that you have found this book of Python for beginners to be a valuable resource, and we look forward to continuing to provide you with high-quality programming resources in the future. If you have any feedback or suggestions for future books or resources, please don't hesitate to get in touch with us. We'd love to hear from you!

Know more about us

At Cuantum Technologies, we specialize in building web applications that deliver creative experiences and solve real-world problems. Our developers have expertise in a wide range of programming languages and frameworks, including Python, Django, React, Three,js, and Vue.js, among others. We are constantly exploring new technologies and techniques to stay at the forefront of the industry, and we pride ourselves on our ability to create solutions that meet our clients' needs.

If you are interested in learning more about our Cuantum Technologies and the services that we offer, please visit our website at books.cuantum.tech. We would be happy to answer any questions that you may have and to discuss how we can help you with your software development needs.

www.cuantum.tech

Made in the USA
Middletown, DE
11 October 2023

CLAIM YOUR
FREE MONTH

As part of our reward program for our readers, we want to give you a **full free month** of...

www.cuantum.ai

THE PROCESS IS SIMPLE

1 Go to Amazon and leave us your amazing book review

2 Send us your name and date of review to books@cuantum.tech

3 Join **cuantum.ai** and we will activate the Creator Plan for you, free of charge.

What is CuantumAI?

All-in-one AI powered content generator and money factory

A complete Eco-system

AI Powerded Chatbot Mentors - Templates - Documents - Images - Audio/Text Transcriptions - And more...

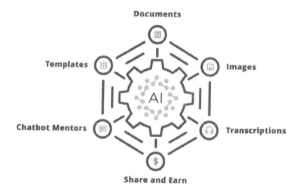

Get all your AI needs in one place to boost productivity, advance your career, or start an AI-powered business.

Do the research - Write the content - Generate the Image - Publish - Earn Money

CLAIM IT TODAY! LIMITED AVAILABILITY